POSTCARDS

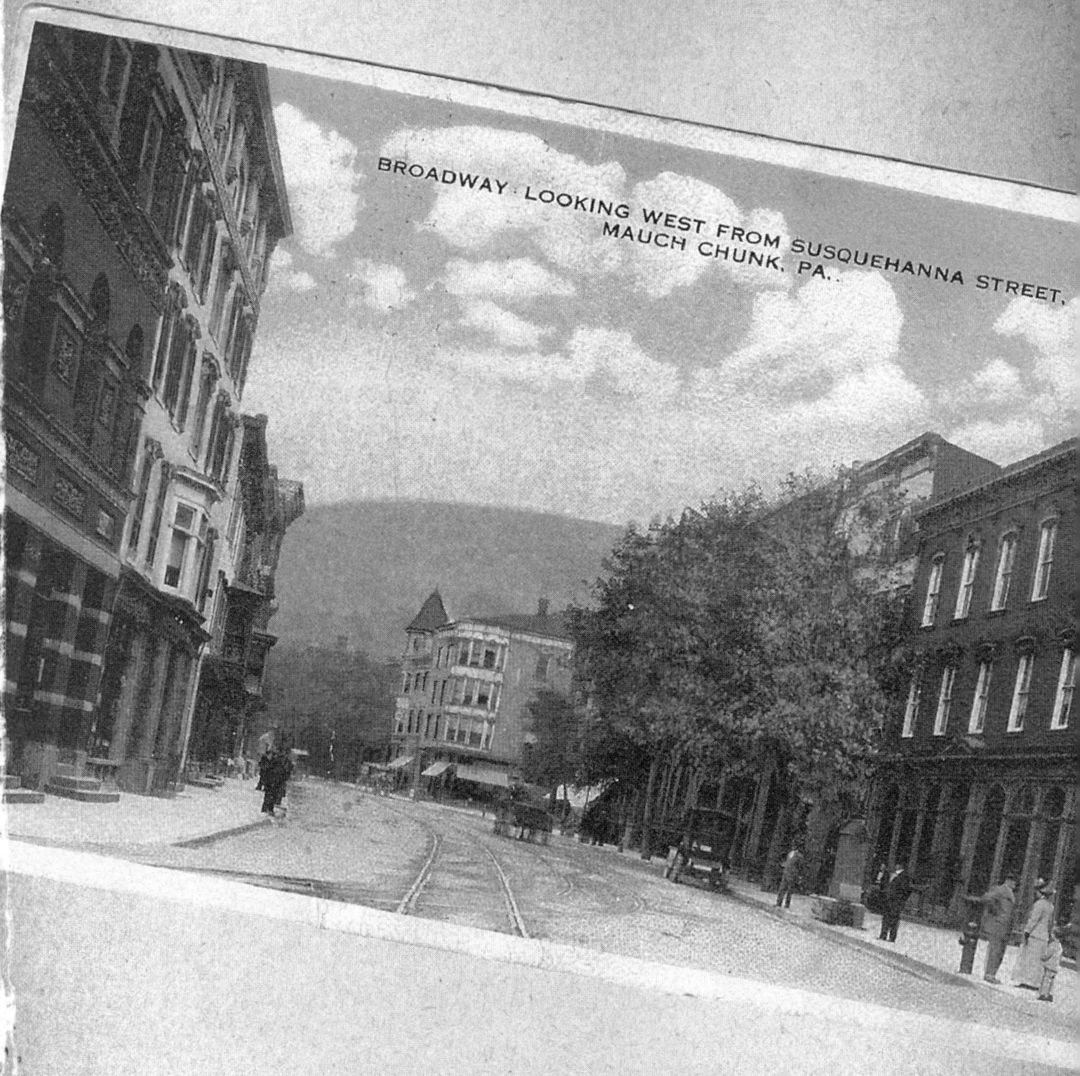
BROADWAY LOOKING WEST FROM SUSQUEHANNA STREET,
MAUCH CHUNK, PA.

Postcard 1 (top):

XMAS—SNOW SCENES SERIES

U.S. POSTAGE
ONE CENT

5 PM
1910
PA.

Dear Amity,

I thought I
would tell you mama
is sick she had an abcess
on her left side & it has
broke she isn't at all
well one will & I would have
tried to come up for Xmas
I hope you are all in the best
of health. Goodbye
from Aunt Kate.
Give love to all.

1606 Junction St.
South Williamsport
Pa.

Postcard 2 (bottom):

POST CARD

THIS SPACE FOR WRITING   THIS SIDE IS FOR THE ADDRESS

UNITED STATES POSTAGE

HARRISONBURG
OCT 12
5 30 AM
1931
VA.

Dear Aunt Emma:
We are down here
over the week-end with
friends — It is lovely here.
You would like it very
much. George & I will be
to see you soon.

Love
Ruth & George.

Mrs Emma Fritz
Arden
Delaware

Pub. by Asheville Post Card Co., Asheville, N. C.

IN THE HEART OF THE BLUE RIDGE

POSTCARDS

TRUE STORIES THAT NEVER HAPPENED

JASON RODRIGUEZ
Editor

JAMES POWELL
Assistant Editor

JASON HANLEY
Additional Letters

VILLARD ⓥ NEW YORK

A Villard Books Trade Paperback Original

Copyright © 2007 by Eximious Press, LLC
"The History of a Marriage," copyright © 2007 by Harvey Pekar, LLC, and Matt Kindt
"Best Side Out," text copyright © 2007 by Antony Johnston

Published in the United States by Villard Books, an imprint of The Random House Publishing Group, a division of Random House, Inc., New York.

VILLARD and "V" CIRCLED Design are registered trademarks of Random House, Inc.

ISBN 978-0-345-49850-2

Printed in the United States of America

www.villard.com

9 8 7 6 5 4 3 2 1

Book design by Matt Kindt

Graphic
Novel
F

CONTENTS

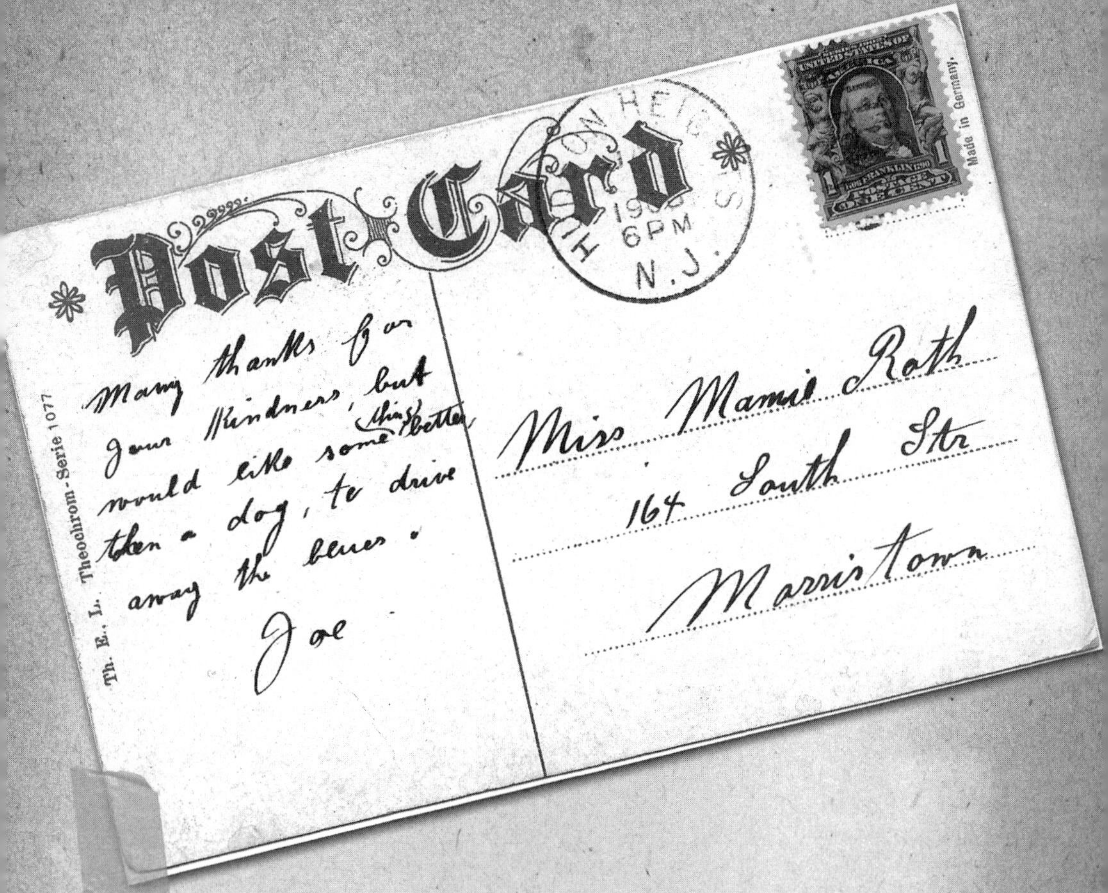
Post Card
ON HEIG
190
6PM
N.J.
UNITED STATES OF AMERICA
POSTAGE
FRANKLIN
ONE CENT
Made in Germany.
Th. E. L. Theochrom-Serie 1077
Many thanks for
your kindness, but
would like something better
then a dog, to drive
away the blues.
Joe
Miss Mamie Roth
164 South Str
Morristown

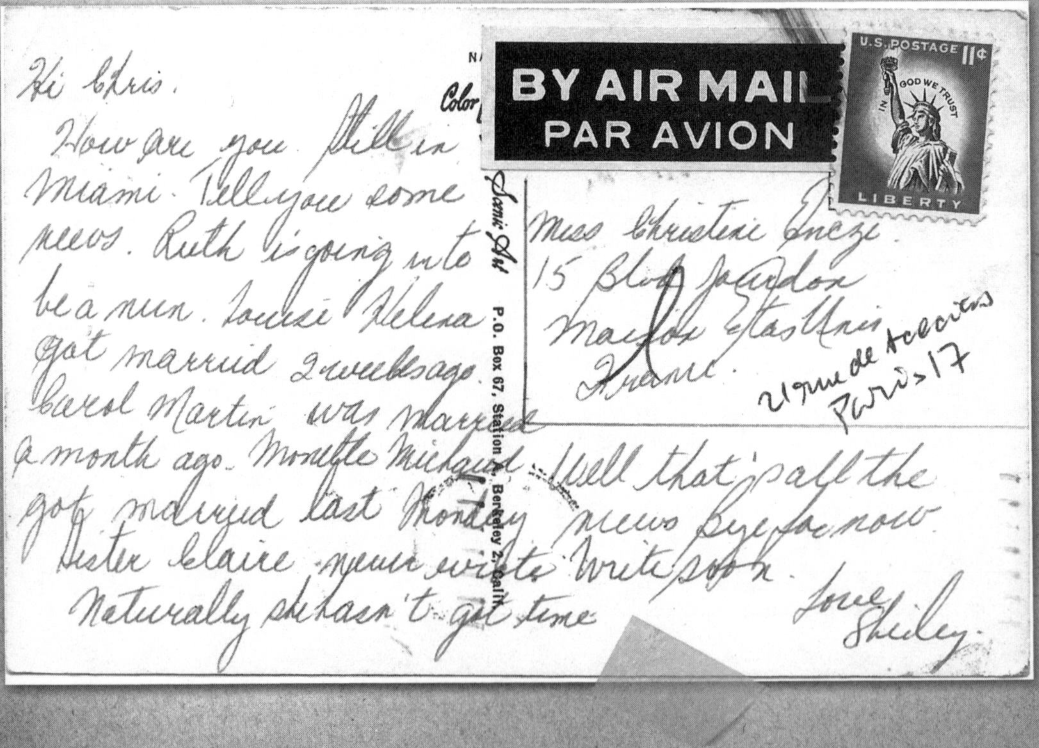
Hi Chris.
How are you Still in
Miami. Tell you some
news. Ruth is going into
be a nun. Louise Helena
got married 2 weeks ago
Carol Martin was married
a month ago. Monette Michaud
got married last Monday
Sister Claire never writes
Naturally she hasn't got time
BY AIR MAIL
PAR AVION
U.S. POSTAGE 11¢
IN GOD WE TRUST
LIBERTY
Color
Samis Art
P.O. Box 67, Station A, Berkeley 2, Calif.
Miss Christine Enczi
15 Blvd Jourdan
Maison Etats Unis
France
Paris 17
Well that's all the
news bye for now
Write soon
Love
Shirley

Introduction

My fascination with postcards is fairly recent. It was January 2006 — I was in Hershey, Pennsylvania, pampering my girlfriend, Robin, on her birthday with two nights of chocolate and relaxation at the Hotel Hershey spa.

On our second day, Robin tells me she wants to go antique shopping. This is not my idea of a good time. I want a hot-stone massage and a steak dinner — chocolate martinis and peanuts by the fireplace while a jazz quartet occasionally deviates from swinging music and pushes the well-to-do folks' sensibilities with some improvisational jamming. It's her birthday, however, so I keep my mouth shut and we step into an antique mall a couple of miles from the hotel.

My lack of verbal protests doesn't mean I'm the most supportive boyfriend in the world. I walk two steps behind her, sighing heavily every time she pauses to browse a cabinet filled with various knickknacks she has no intention of buying.

About ten minutes in, Robin starts rifling through a shoebox filled with postcards. There must be several hundred cards in there and I'm having none of it — I let the mother of all sighs escape my mouth and receive a very nasty look in return.

"You know," she tells me as she walks away from the shoebox, "some of those postcards were mailed."

Robin knows me well — she knows I'm the type of guy who likes to find stories in people's residuals. I'll create stories based on writings I've seen on bathroom walls or in the margins of used books. I've always found that people's true personalities come out when they don't think they're being analyzed. A simple song lyric scratched into a library table can give more insight into how someone is feeling than an hour-long conversation.

I do exactly what Robin expects me to do — I start digging through the box of postcards. The first postcard I pull out is a godsend. It was sent from Private Earl Pace to his mother in 1942, the day before Earl's brother, Lehr, was to be shipped out to fight in the war. In the card, Earl is telling his mother he'll likely be going soon, too, and he'll write her when he gets back.

Earl Pace went to fight in Eastern Europe. He left his family and his girlfriend behind. He was in the trenches, got injured several times, and fell for a nurse during a hospital visit. His father found out about his cheating ways, purchased an engagement ring, and gave it to Earl's girlfriend back home. Took a picture of the girlfriend with the ring and sent it to Earl, told him that he was an engaged man now and he'd better start acting like it. Earl then finished his tour, earned several medals, came home, and married his fiancée. They had five kids together. Earl opened a local bar and lived out the remainder of his too-short life as a neighborhood hero.

That's not Earl's story — that's my grandfather's story. Maybe Earl died in training the day after his postcard was mailed. Maybe he went MIA and spent the rest of his life roaming Europe without an identity. Maybe he came home disabled, found out his girl had fallen for someone else, and had to put his life back together.

The only thing we know for sure is that Earl Pace was supposed to go fight in World War II. There's a good chance that, with the exception of things like birth and death certificates, this may be our only insight into Earl Pace's life. And it was on sale at an antique mall in Hershey, Pennsylvania, for fifty cents.

I stayed hunched over that box of postcards for hours, and the idea for this anthology began taking shape in my mind. Not long after, I was assembling some of comics greatest creators to look at these old postcards and complete their stories. What they created were stories about our own lives. Our romances and our regrets, our mistakes and our dreams.

True stories that never happened.

POSTCARDS

Post card. Postkarte. Carte postale
Dopisnice. Correspondenzkarte. Levelező-L
Cartolina postale. Weltpostverein. Briefkaart.
Union postale universelle. Unione postale universe
Всемірный почтовый союзъ. Россія. Открытое письмо
Karta korespondencyjna. Korespondencní lístek.
Cartão postal. Brefkort. Brevkort. Tarjeta postal.

This is one of a set of
four that I am going
to send you. Please
don't slap my mug.
I would tell her
name, but I don't
now it myself.

Miss Bessie Burdick
Wayland, N. g
Care of E. E. Malabar

Th. E. L, Serie 992

ELEPHANT HOTEL, MARGATE CITY, AN OLD LAND MARK, ATLANTIC CITY, N. J.

© ATLANTIC PHOTO SERVICE

There was a postcard in my collection that I wanted to be the inspiration behind the lead story. The front was a nighttime scene of the boardwalk in Atlantic City before the casinos moved in. When I saw it, I thought of my friend Chris Stevens. He occasionally tells me stories handed down from his family about a more innocent Atlantic City, an Atlantic City that most people aren't familiar with. One that exists as a memory and is documented by old postcards like the one I found. I asked if he could come up with a story using just the front, one that explores what the image on a postcard means to someone. He loved the idea, but he had a different Atlantic City monument in mind that would require a different postcard. The story was beautiful, moving, and deeply personal. It prompted me to go out and buy the postcard to match it. Gia-Bao brought the vision to life and the book had its lead story, one that shows the profound connection that a postcard can cause.

blue
Story by Chris Stevens
Illustrated by Gia-Bao Tran
EXIT
HONK!
HOLLAND TUNNEL
New Jersey Turnpike
SOUTH
95
SOUTH
NEXT RIGHT
9
Everyone has landmarks of their youth. Places they'll never forget.
Asbury Park 33
Atlantic City 102
Wildwood 147
Places that remain mysterious however old you are and despite how much you know better.
I have many, places built eternally in the architecture of memory...
Their foundations set as deeply in the stardust of an eight-year-old's dreams as they were in concrete and receipts and souvenirs.

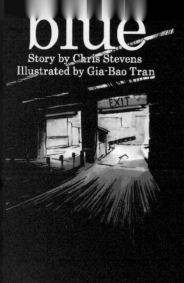

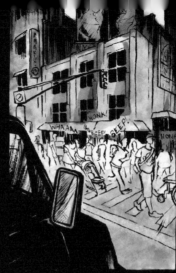

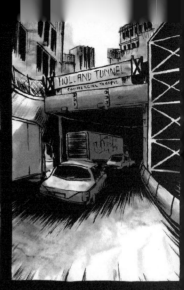

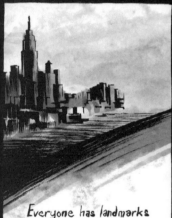

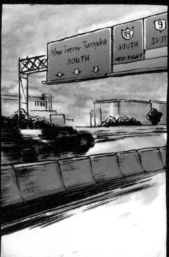

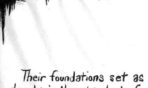

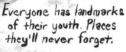

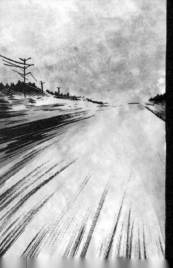

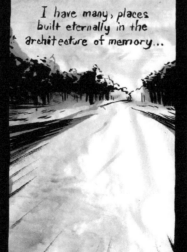

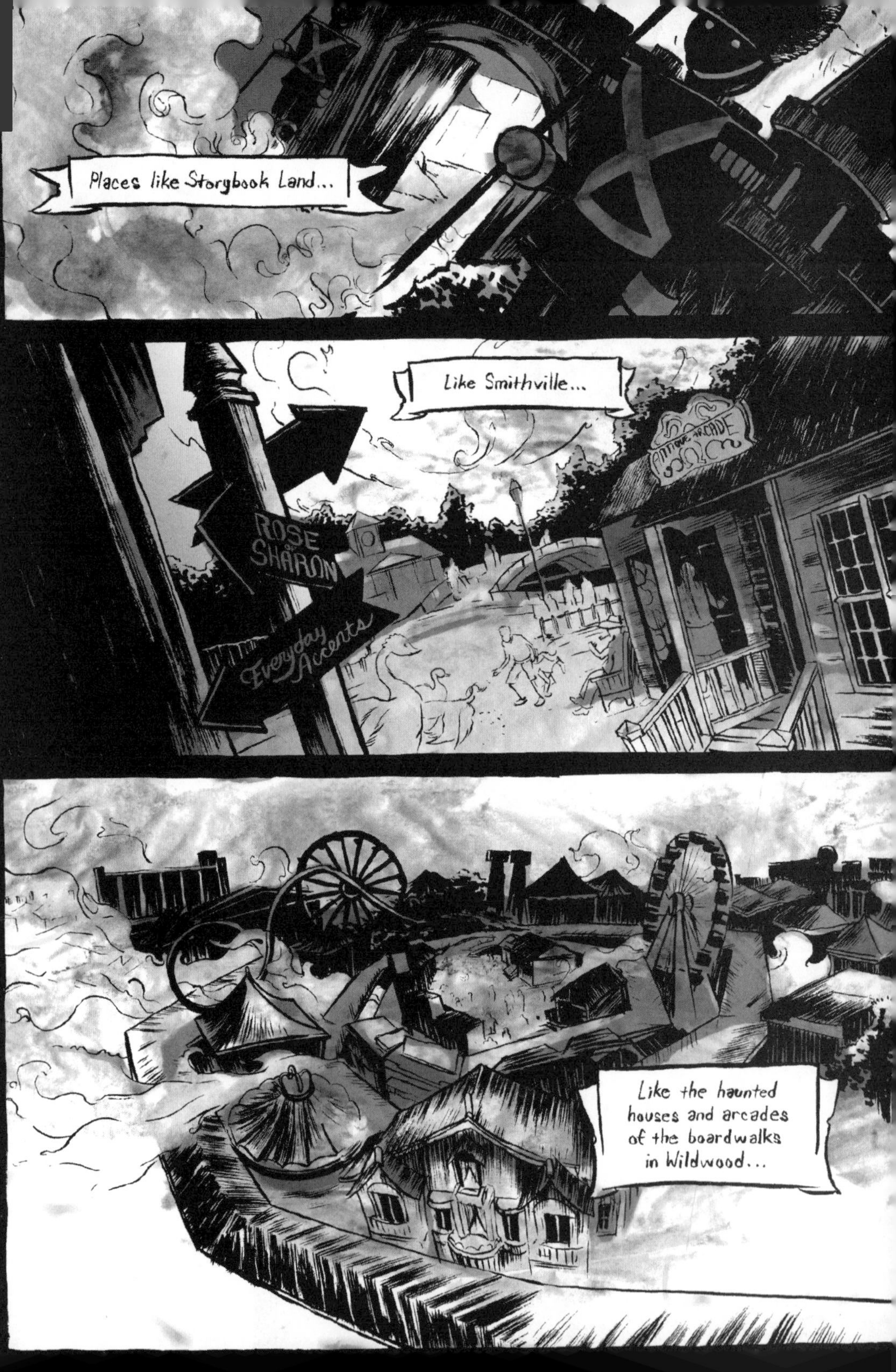
Places like Storybook Land...
Like Smithville...
ANTIQUE ARCADE
ROSE OF SHARON
Everyday Accents
Like the haunted houses and arcades of the boardwalks in Wildwood...

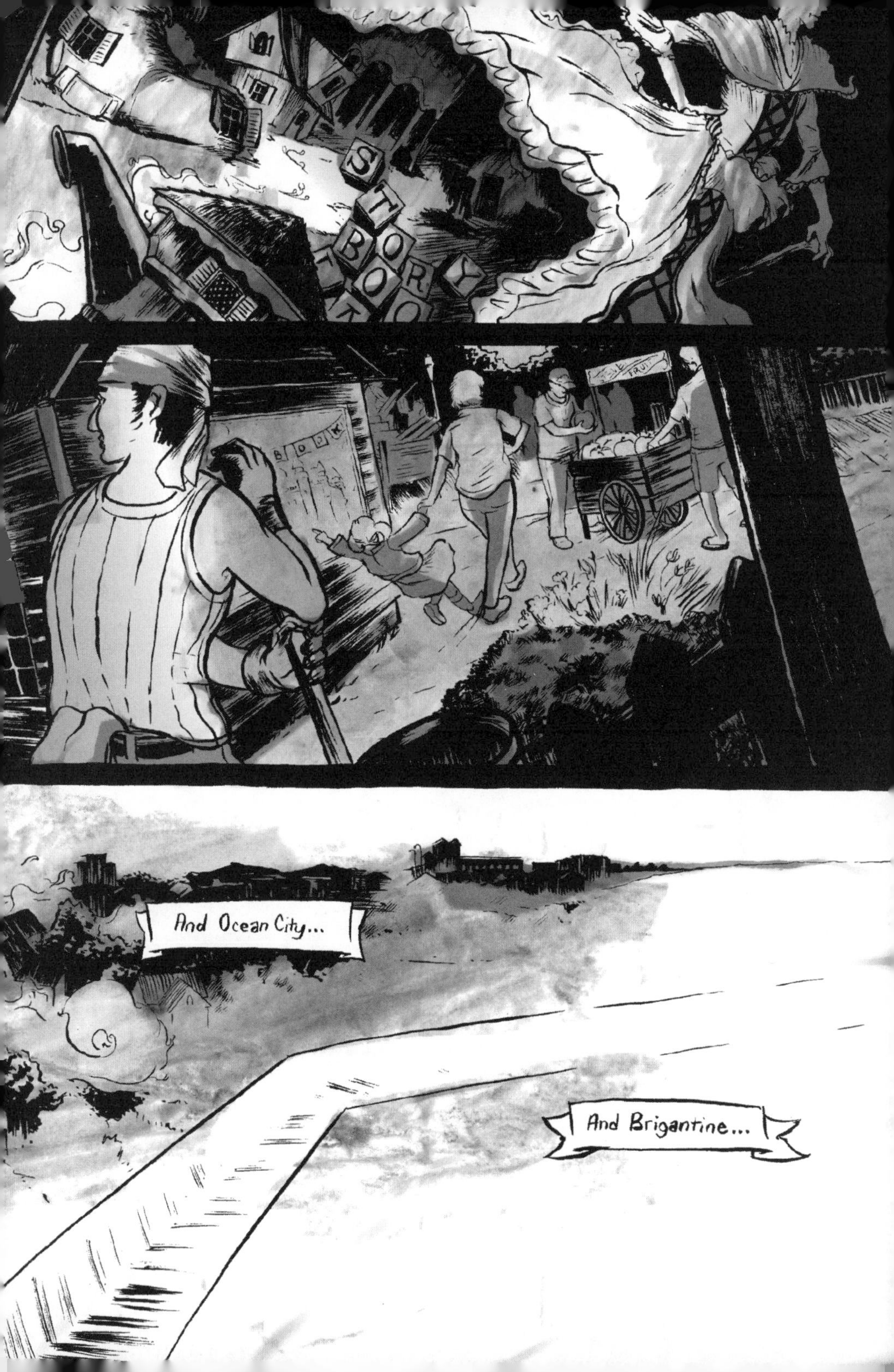
STORY
And Ocean City...
And Brigantine...

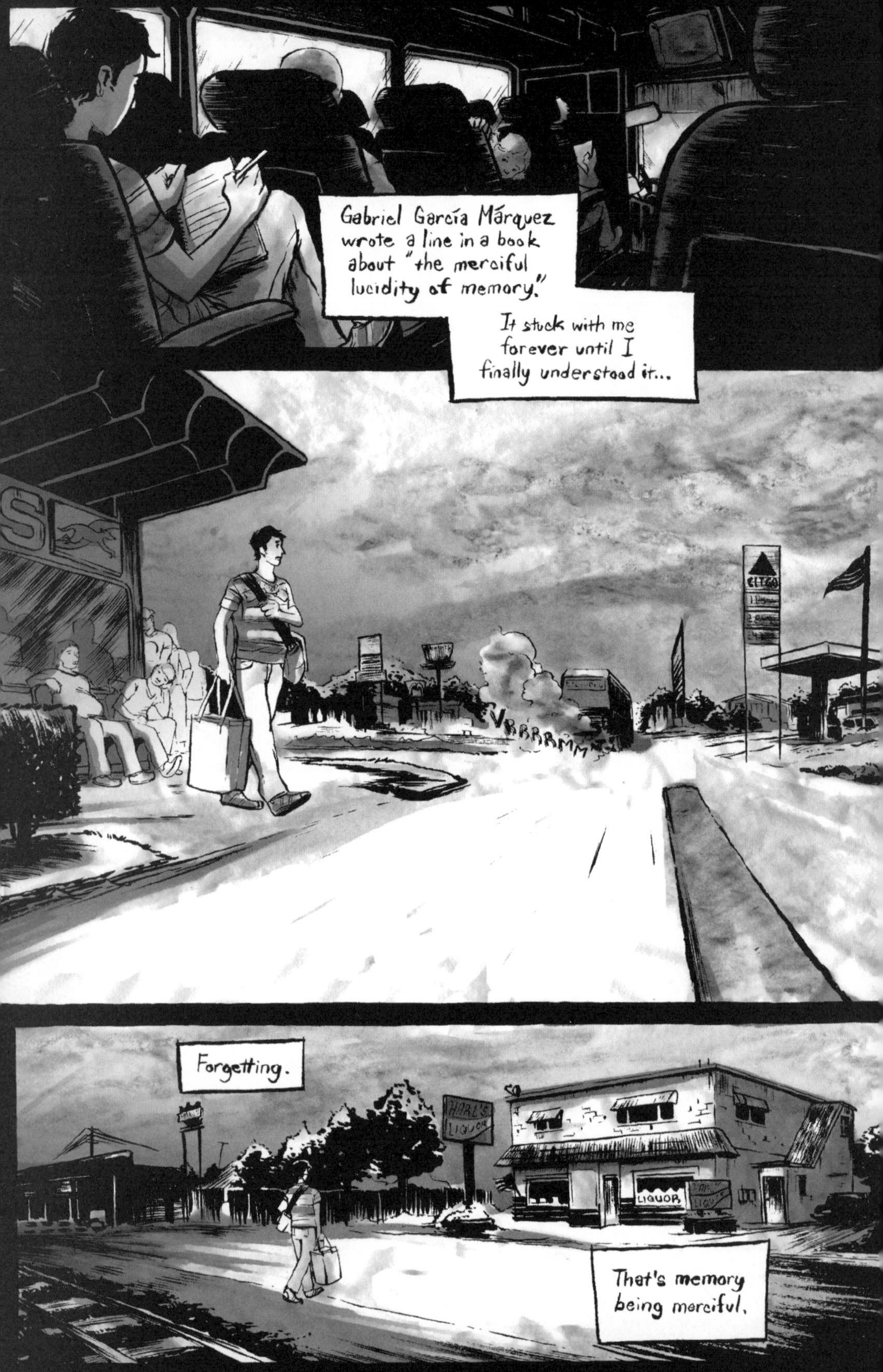
Gabriel García Márquez wrote a line in a book about "the merciful lucidity of memory."
It stuck with me forever until I finally understood it...
CITGO
VRRRRMMM
Forgetting.
LIQUOR
That's memory being merciful.

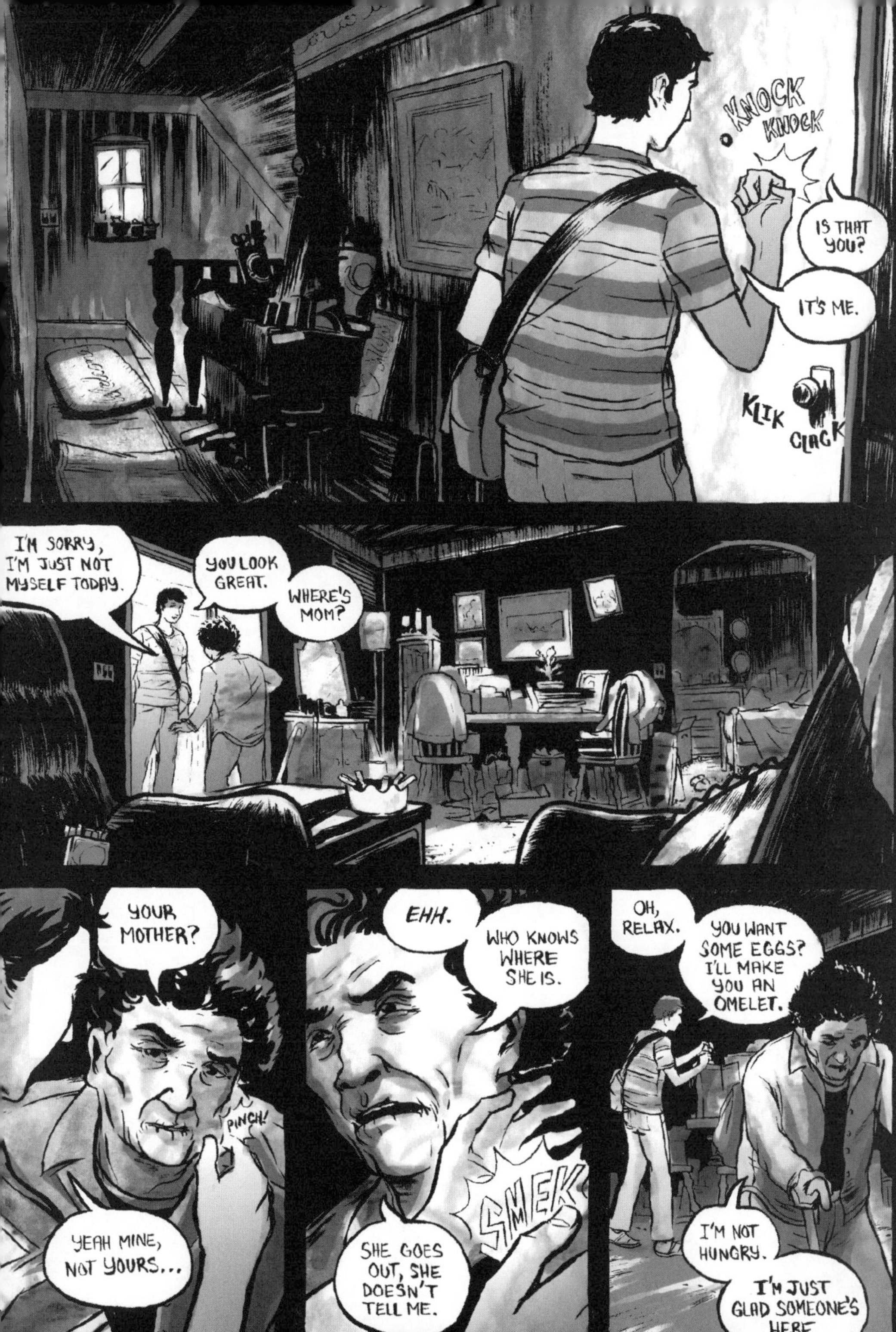
KNOCK KNOCK
IS THAT YOU?
IT'S ME.
KLIK CLACK
I'M SORRY, I'M JUST NOT MYSELF TODAY.
YOU LOOK GREAT.
WHERE'S MOM?
YOUR MOTHER?
PINCH!
YEAH MINE, NOT YOURS...
EHH.
WHO KNOWS WHERE SHE IS.
SMEK
SHE GOES OUT, SHE DOESN'T TELL ME.
OH, RELAX.
YOU WANT SOME EGGS? I'LL MAKE YOU AN OMELET.
I'M NOT HUNGRY.
I'M JUST GLAD SOMEONE'S HERE.

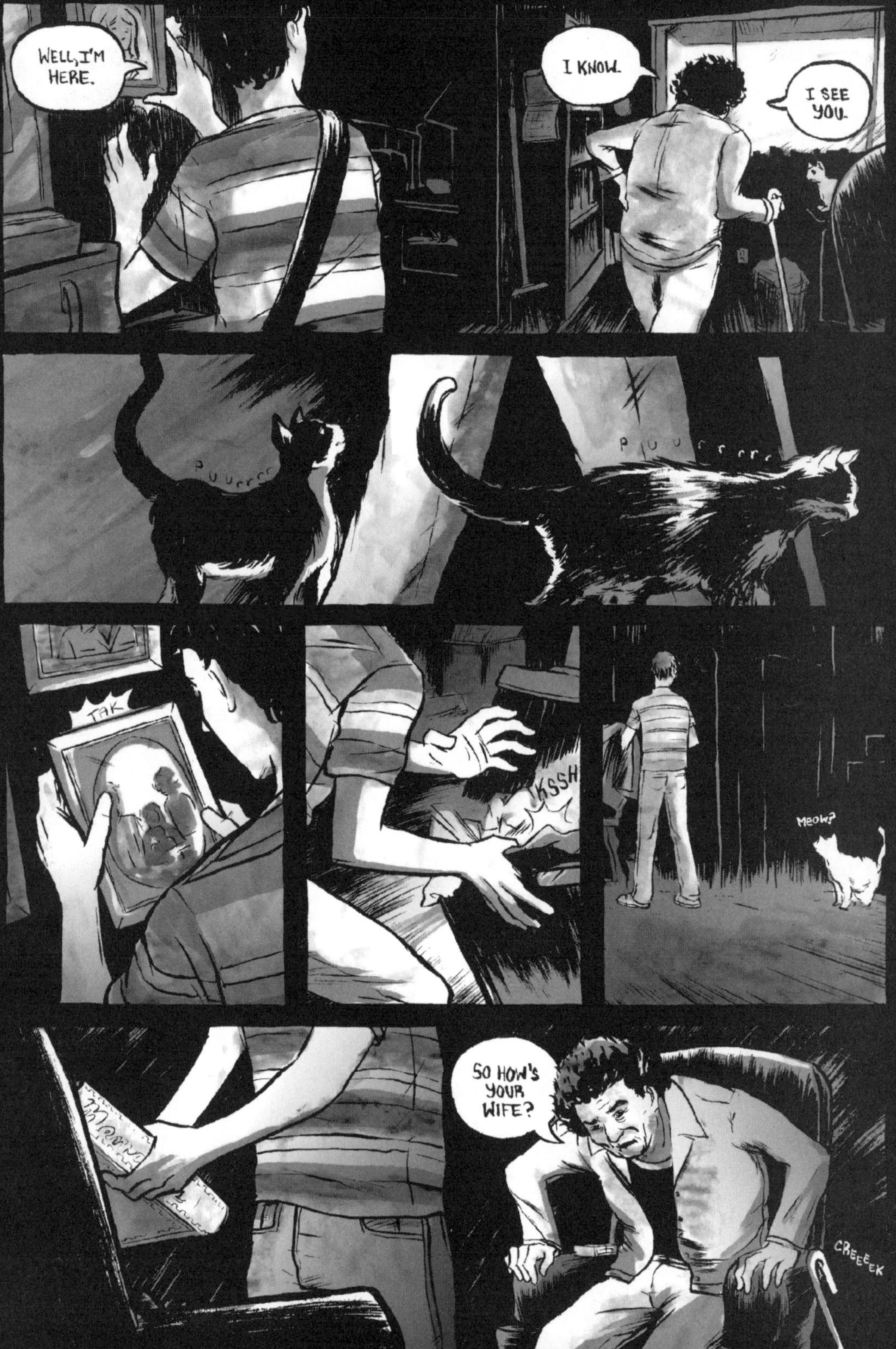
WELL, I'M HERE.
I KNOW.
I SEE YOU.
PUUrrrr
PUUrrrr
TAK
KSSH
MEOW?
SO HOW'S YOUR WIFE?
CREEEEK

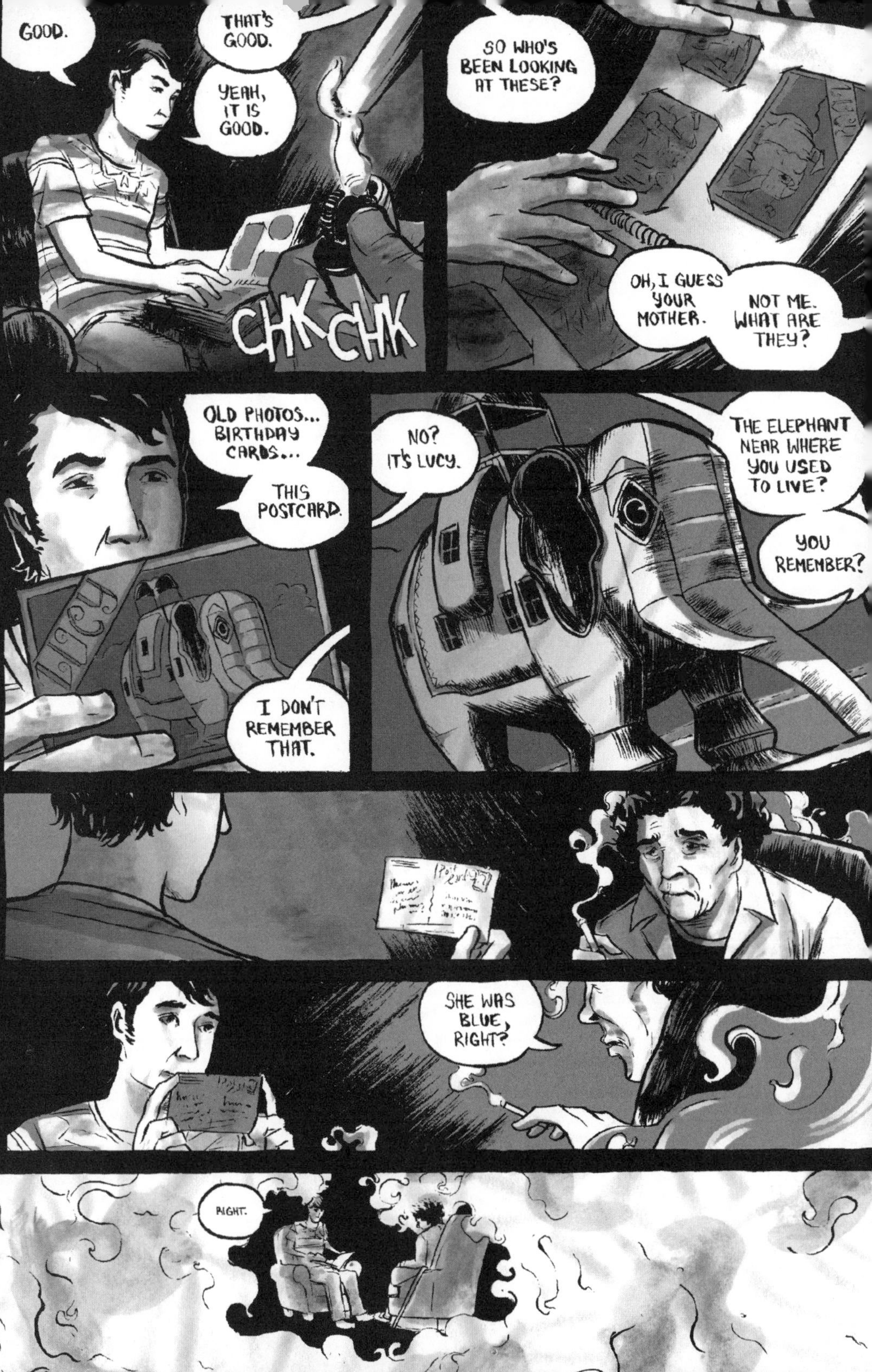
GOOD.
THAT'S GOOD.
YEAH, IT IS GOOD.
CHK CHK
SO WHO'S BEEN LOOKING AT THESE?
OH, I GUESS YOUR MOTHER.
NOT ME. WHAT ARE THEY?
OLD PHOTOS... BIRTHDAY CARDS...
THIS POSTCARD.
I DON'T REMEMBER THAT.
NO? IT'S LUCY.
THE ELEPHANT NEAR WHERE YOU USED TO LIVE?
YOU REMEMBER?
SHE WAS BLUE, RIGHT?
RIGHT.

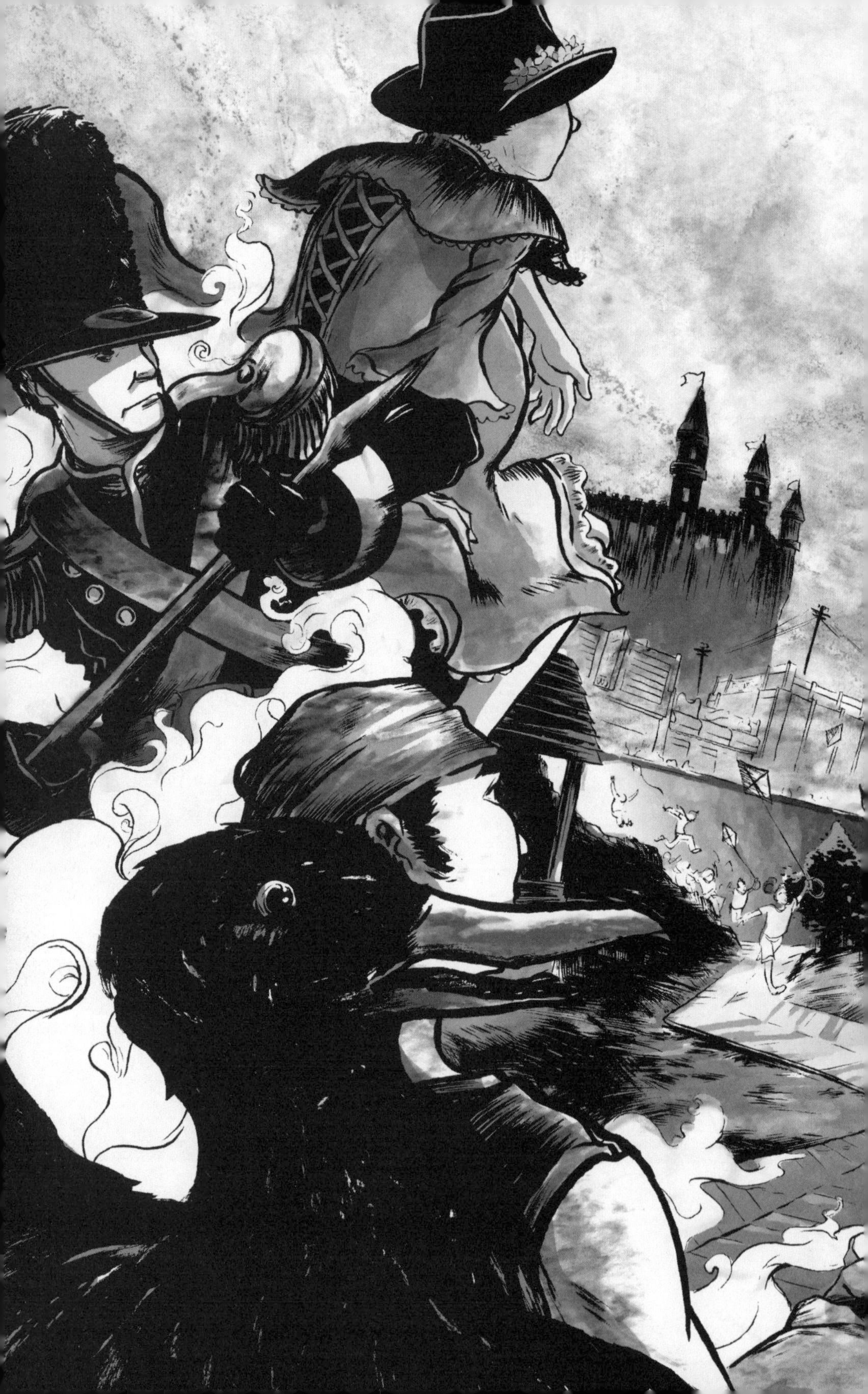

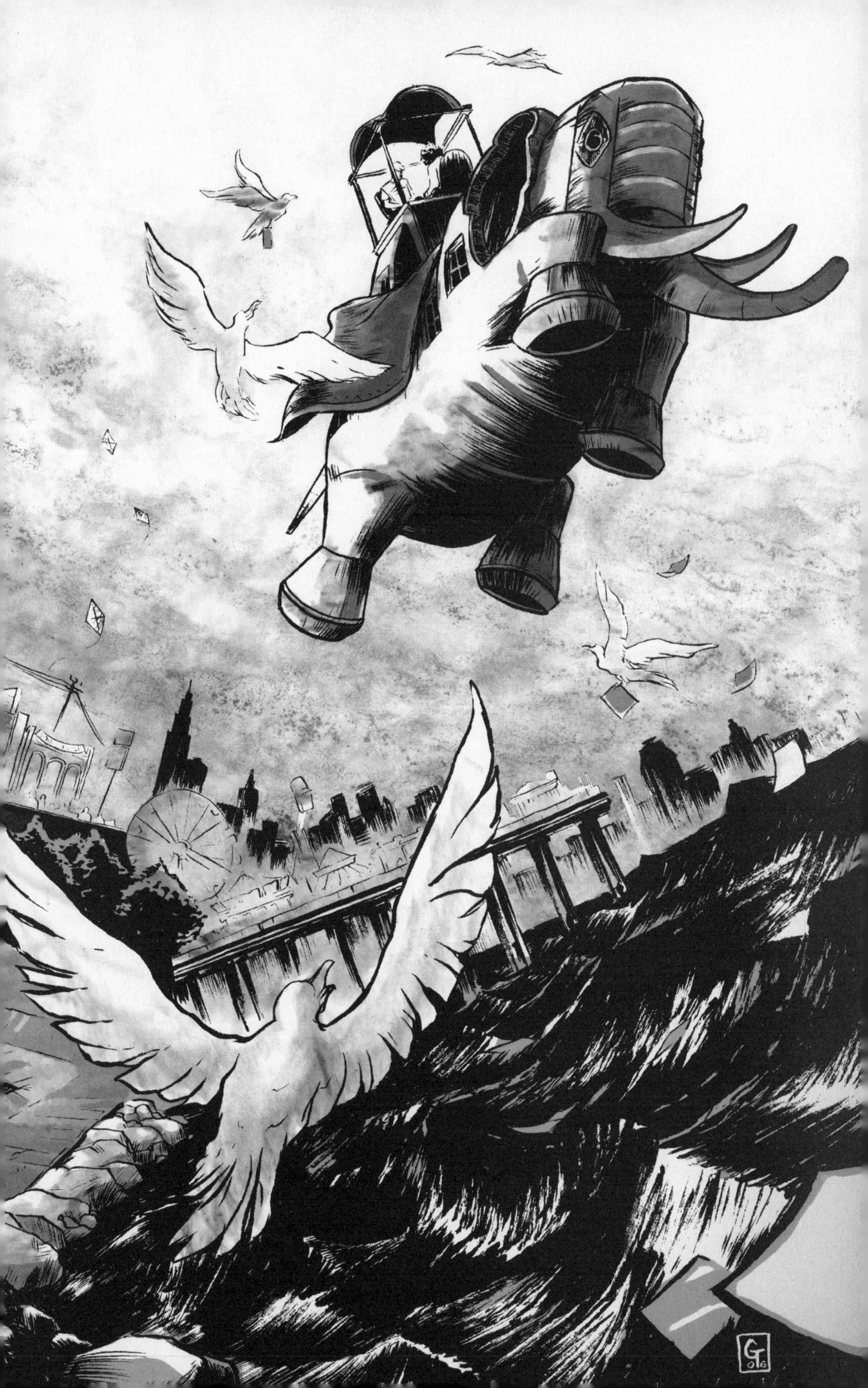

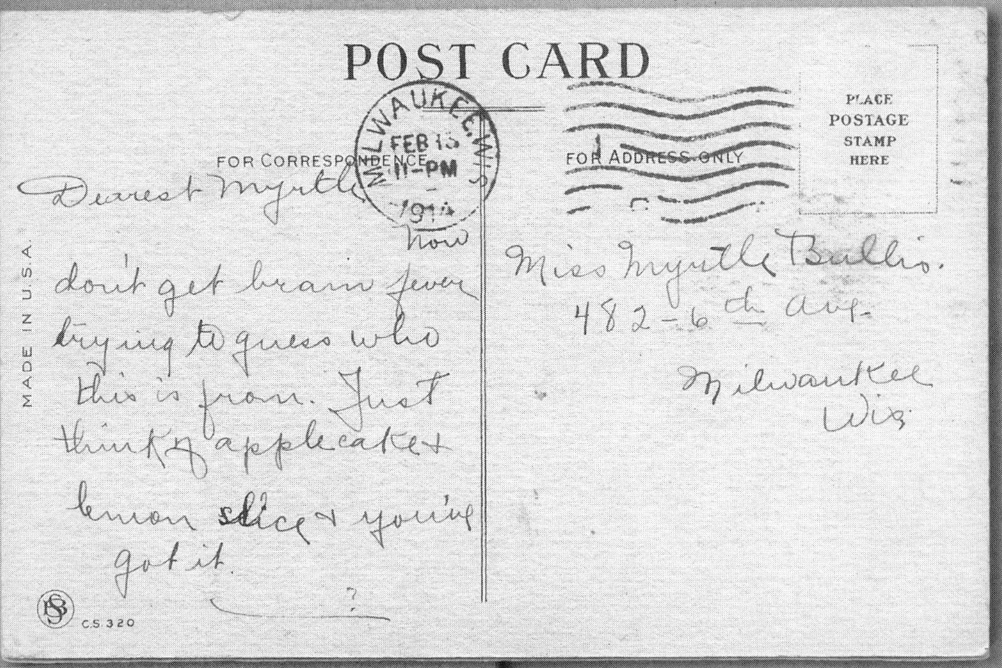
POST CARD
FOR CORRESPONDENCE
FOR ADDRESS ONLY
PLACE POSTAGE STAMP HERE
MILWAUKEE, WIS.
FEB 15
11-PM
MADE IN U.S.A.
Dearest Myrtle
Now don't get brain fever trying to guess who this is from. Just think of apple cake & lemon slice & you've got it.
?
Miss Myrtle Bullis.
482-6th Ave.
Milwaukee
Wis.
C.S. 320

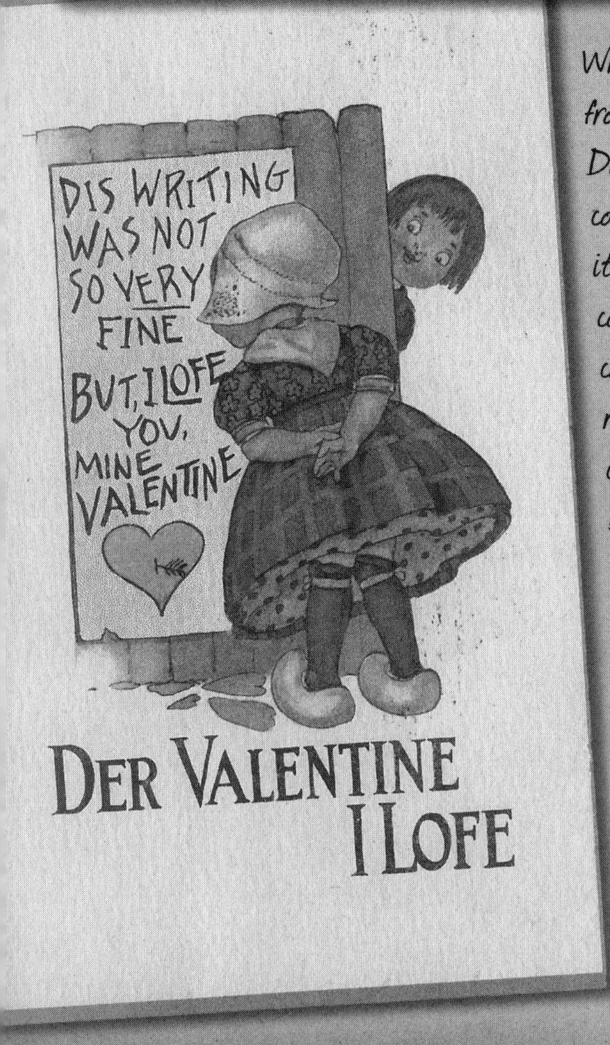
DIS WRITING WAS NOT SO VERY FINE
BUT, I LOFE YOU, MINE VALENTINE
DER VALENTINE I LOFE

When I first saw this postcard, sent from a secret admirer on Valentine's Day, I knew Tom would be the comics creator perfectly suited to tell its story. His Eisner nominated comic book is a retelling of his own chance meeting and subsequent romance, after all. Tom's story captures the spirit of this book and builds off of "Blue" by exploring the lasting significance of the back of a postcard. It is relatable and moving; it shows us the impact a single sentence can have—how a postcard can define an entire life.

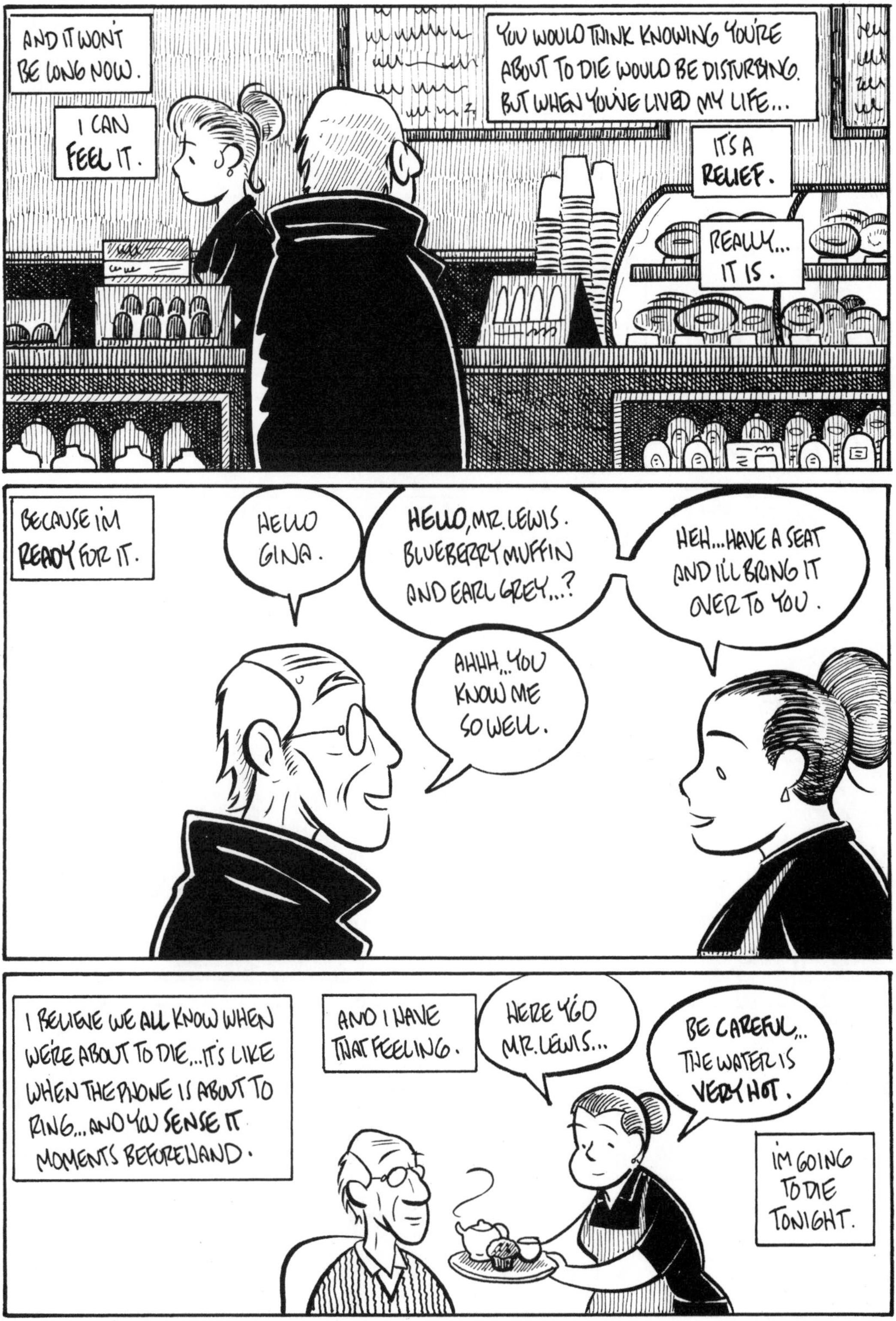
AND IT WON'T BE LONG NOW.
I CAN FEEL IT.
YOU WOULD THINK KNOWING YOU'RE ABOUT TO DIE WOULD BE DISTURBING. BUT WHEN YOU'VE LIVED MY LIFE...
IT'S A RELIEF.
REALLY... IT IS.
BECAUSE I'M READY FOR IT.
HELLO GINA.
HELLO, MR. LEWIS. BLUEBERRY MUFFIN AND EARL GREY...?
HEH... HAVE A SEAT AND I'LL BRING IT OVER TO YOU.
AHHH... YOU KNOW ME SO WELL.
I BELIEVE WE ALL KNOW WHEN WE'RE ABOUT TO DIE... IT'S LIKE WHEN THE PHONE IS ABOUT TO RING... AND YOU SENSE IT MOMENTS BEFOREHAND.
AND I HAVE THAT FEELING.
HERE Y'GO MR. LEWIS...
BE CAREFUL... THE WATER IS VERY HOT.
I'M GOING TO DIE TONIGHT.

YES...IM SURE THAT SOUNDS **MACABRE**... TO EMBRACE DEATH LIKE CHRISTMAS...

BUT MY RELATIVES ARE GONE...AS ARE MY GOOD FRIENDS...AS IS MY SWEET MYRTLE... ALL OF THEM...GONE.

YOU NEVER WANT TO BE THE LAST ONE IN THE BAR...ITS **PATHETIC**. BUT THAT'S HOW LIFE IS FOR ME. IM MORE ALONE **ALIVE** THAN **DEAD**.

I LOOK AROUND THE ROOM AND...MY GOD...EVERYONE IS SO VERY...**YOUNG**.

I DON'T ENVY THAT YOUTH.

THERE ARE SO MANY **CHALLENGES** THAT LAY AHEAD FOR THESE PEOPLE.

YOU REACH AN **APEX** IN LIFE... A CAREER...FAMILY...FRIENDS. AND THEN, SLOWLY, ONE BY ONE, YOU WATCH IT ALL SLIP AWAY.

UNTIL ALL ARE GONE.

AND IT'S ONLY YOU.

...

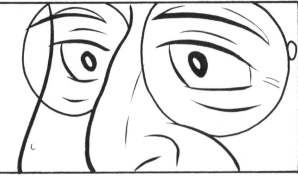

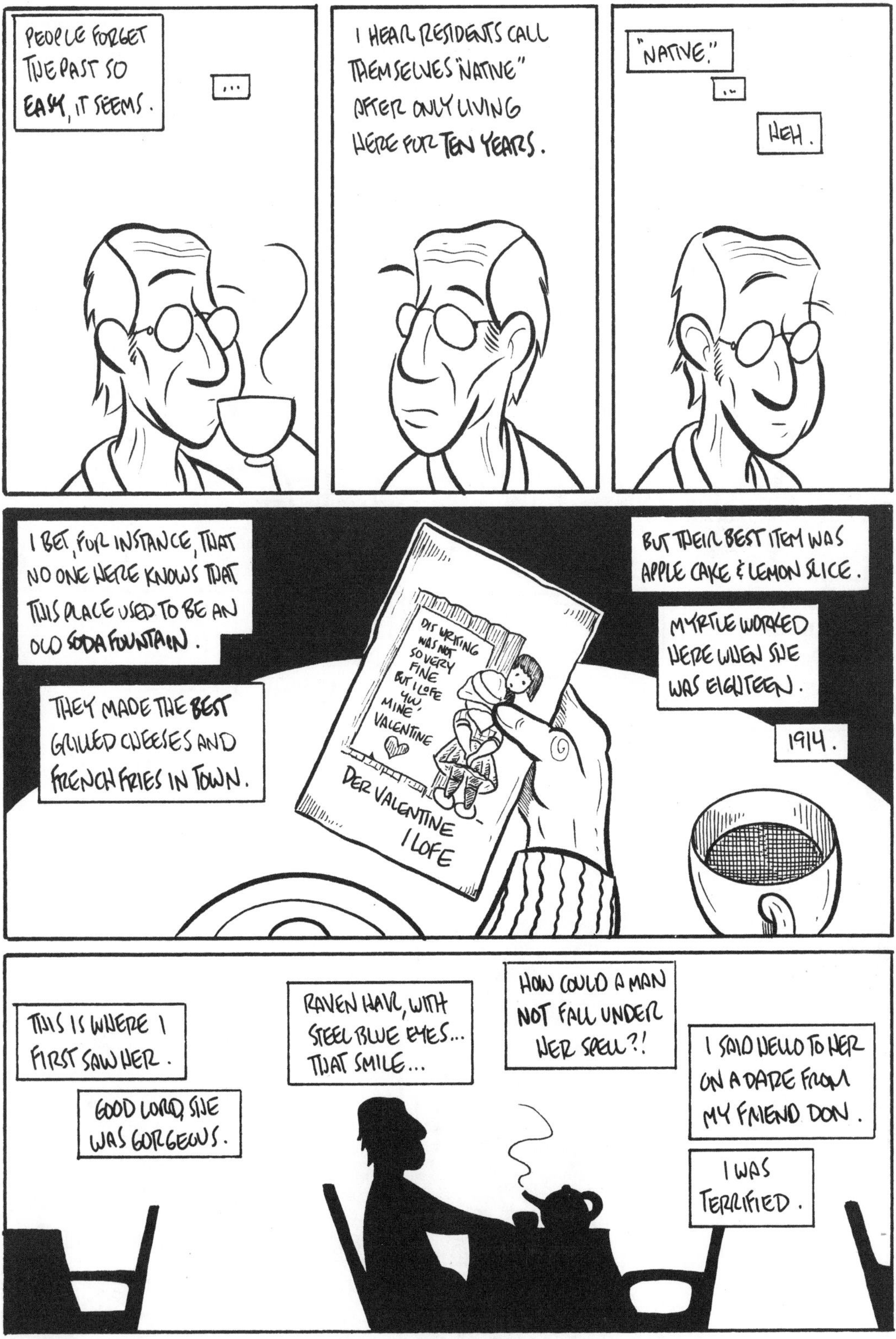
PEOPLE FORGET THE PAST SO EASY, IT SEEMS.
...
I HEAR RESIDENTS CALL THEMSELVES "NATIVE" AFTER ONLY LIVING HERE FOR TEN YEARS.
"NATIVE."
..
HEH.
I BET, FOR INSTANCE, THAT NO ONE HERE KNOWS THAT THIS PLACE USED TO BE AN OLD SODA FOUNTAIN.
THEY MADE THE BEST GRILLED CHEESES AND FRENCH FRIES IN TOWN.
DIS WRITING WAS NOT SO VERY FINE BUT I LOFE YW, MINE VALENTINE
DER VALENTINE I LOFE
BUT THEIR BEST ITEM WAS APPLE CAKE & LEMON SLICE.
MYRTLE WORKED HERE WHEN SHE WAS EIGHTEEN.
1914.
THIS IS WHERE I FIRST SAW HER.
GOOD LORD, SHE WAS GORGEOUS.
RAVEN HAIR, WITH STEEL BLUE EYES... THAT SMILE...
HOW COULD A MAN NOT FALL UNDER HER SPELL?!
I SAID HELLO TO HER ON A DARE FROM MY FRIEND DON.
I WAS TERRIFIED.

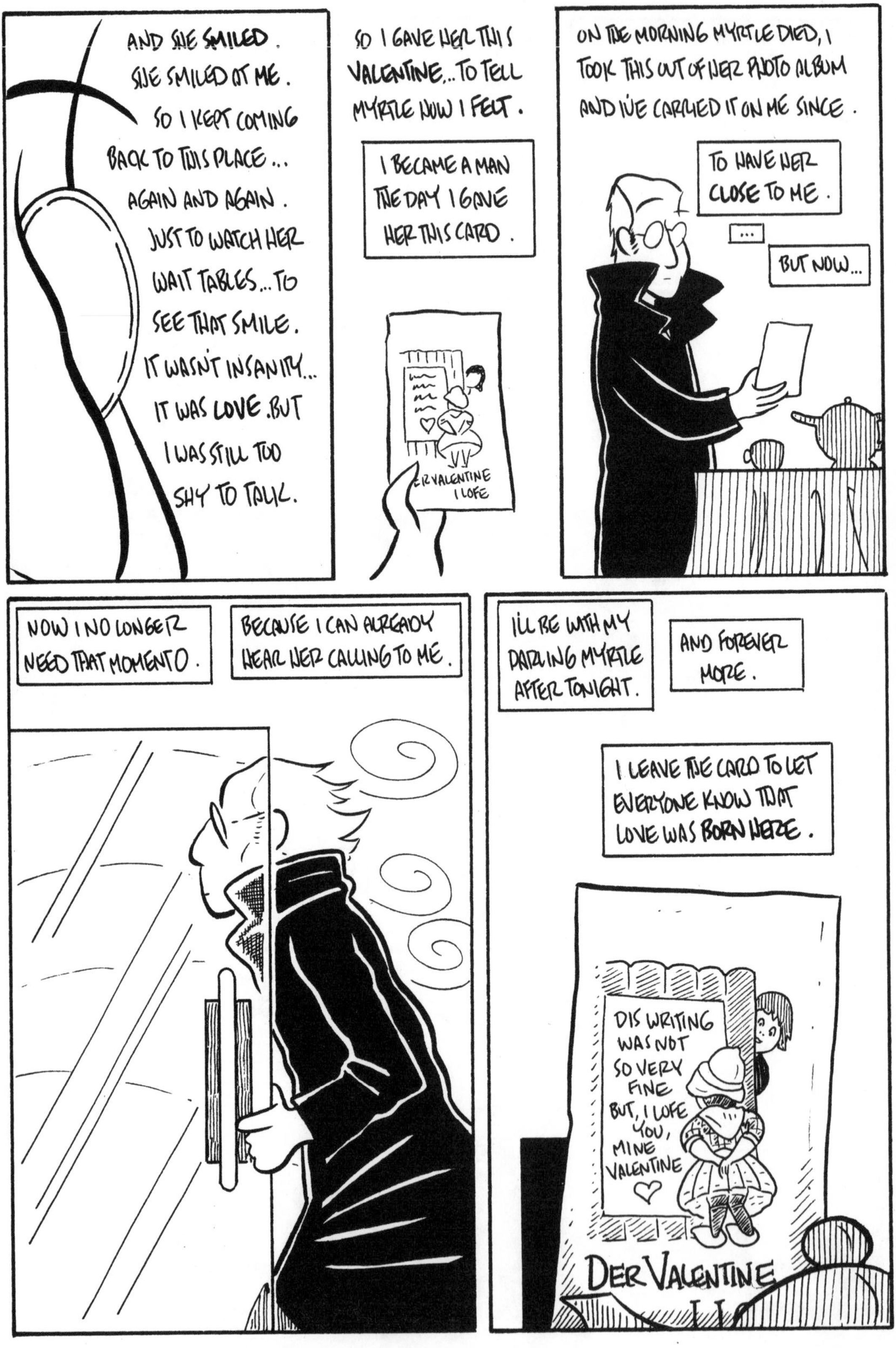
AND SHE SMILED. SHE SMILED AT ME. SO I KEPT COMING BACK TO THIS PLACE... AGAIN AND AGAIN. JUST TO WATCH HER WAIT TABLES... TO SEE THAT SMILE. IT WASN'T INSANITY... IT WAS LOVE. BUT I WAS STILL TOO SHY TO TALK.
SO I GAVE HER THIS VALENTINE... TO TELL MYRTLE HOW I FELT.
I BECAME A MAN THE DAY I GAVE HER THIS CARD.
ER VALENTINE
I LOFE
ON THE MORNING MYRTLE DIED, I TOOK THIS OUT OF HER PHOTO ALBUM AND I'VE CARRIED IT ON ME SINCE.
TO HAVE HER CLOSE TO ME.
...
BUT NOW...
NOW I NO LONGER NEED THAT MOMENTO.
BECAUSE I CAN ALREADY HEAR HER CALLING TO ME.
I'LL BE WITH MY DARLING MYRTLE AFTER TONIGHT.
AND FOREVER MORE.
I LEAVE THE CARD TO LET EVERYONE KNOW THAT LOVE WAS BORN HERE.
DIS WRITING WAS NOT SO VERY FINE BUT, I LOFE YOU, MINE VALENTINE
DER VALENTINE

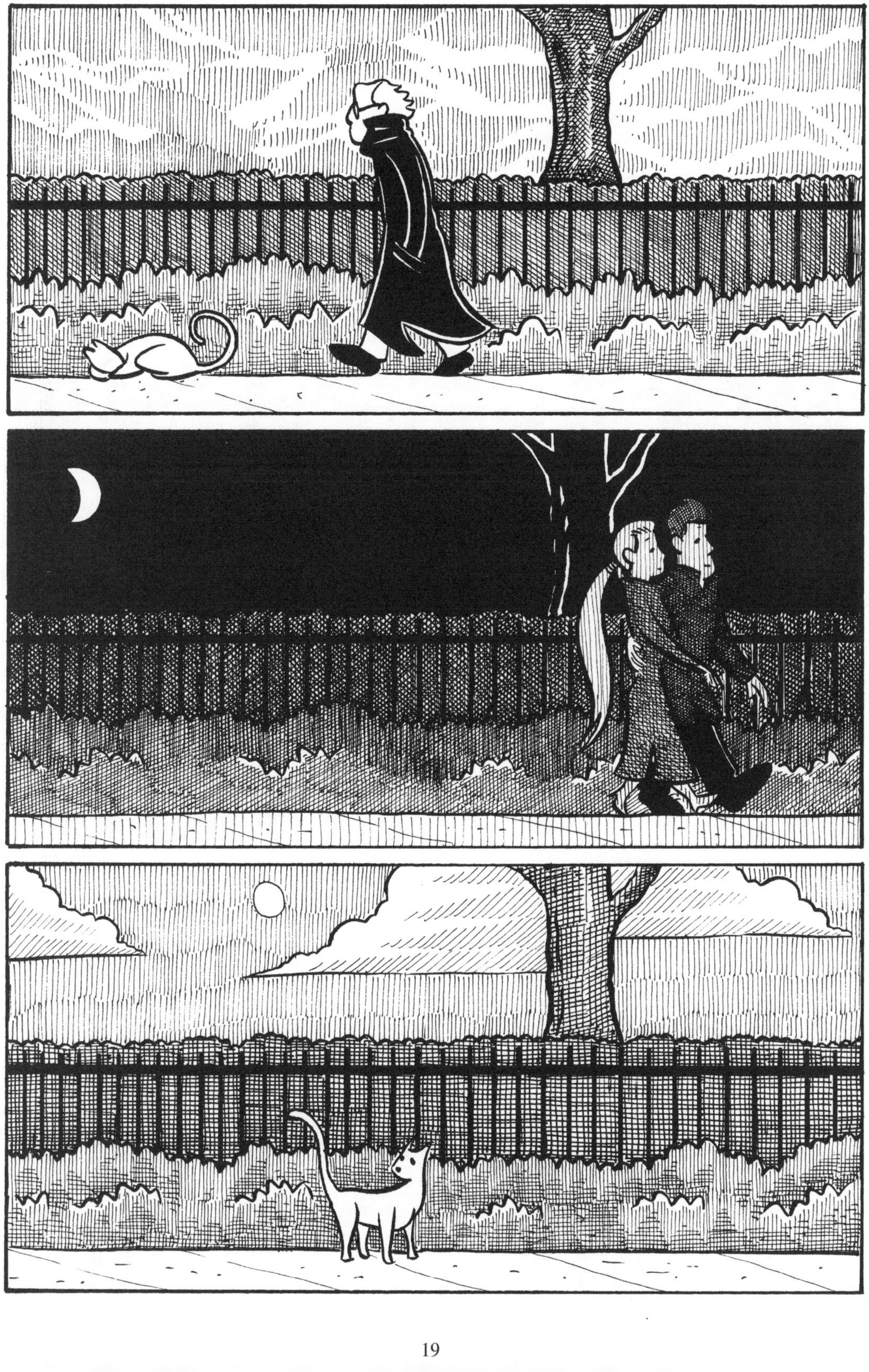

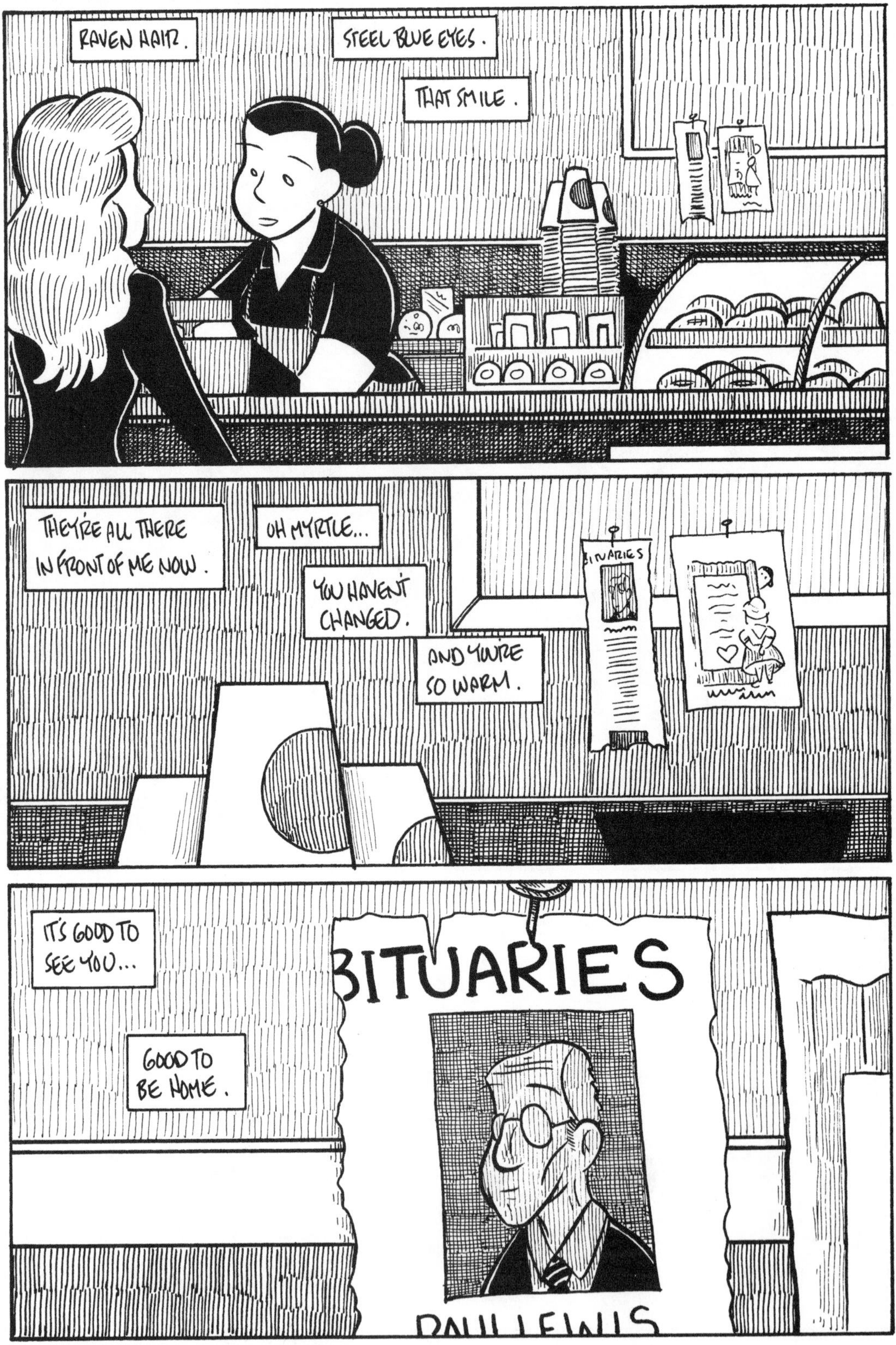
RAVEN HAIR.
STEEL BLUE EYES.
THAT SMILE.
THEY'RE ALL THERE IN FRONT OF ME NOW.
OH MYRTLE...
YOU HAVEN'T CHANGED.
AND YOU'RE SO WARM.
IT'S GOOD TO SEE YOU...
GOOD TO BE HOME.
BITUARIES

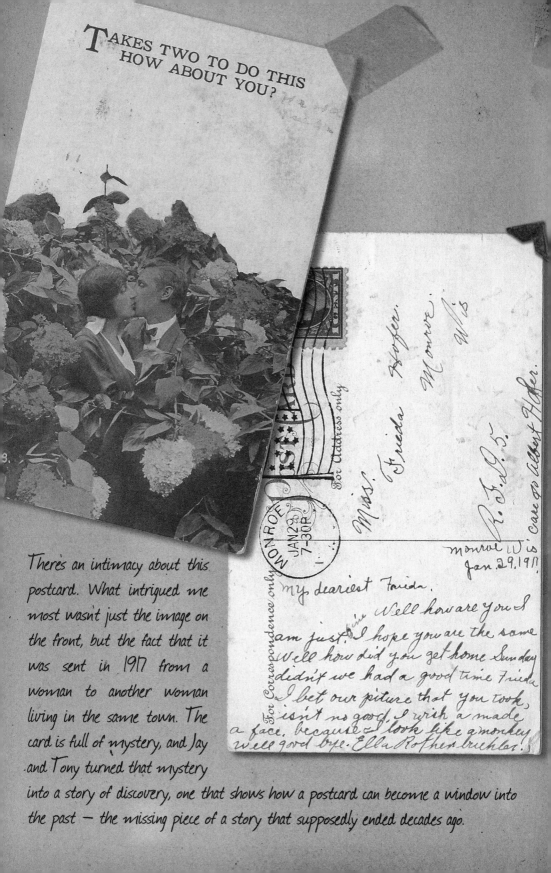

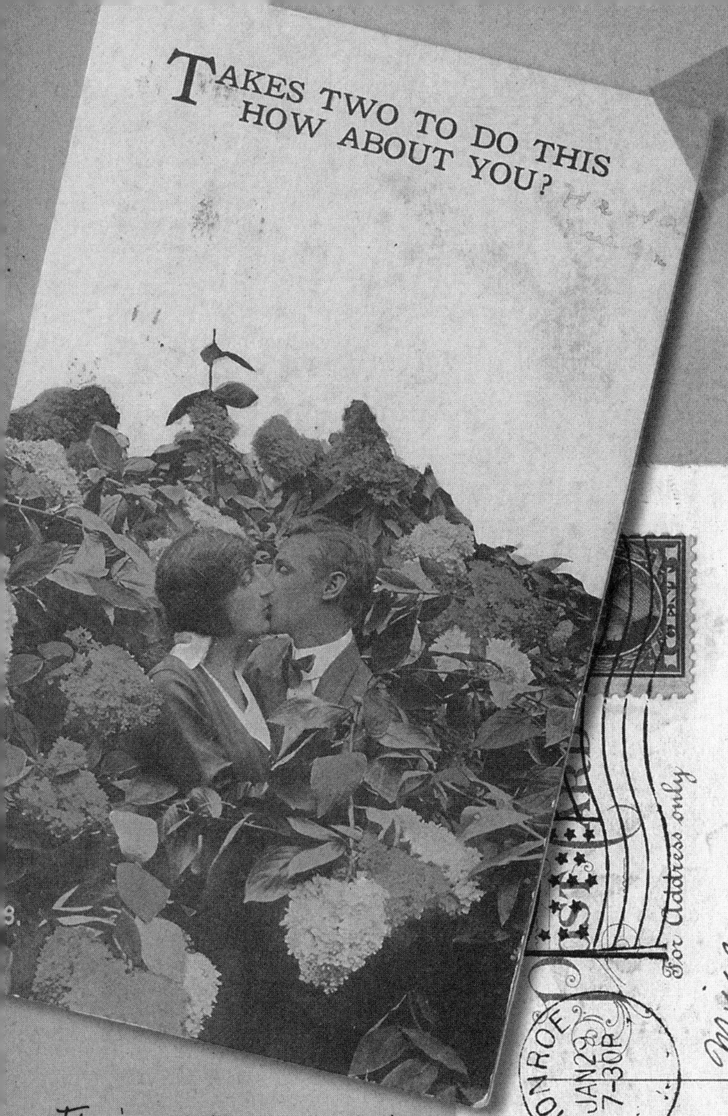
TAKES TWO TO DO THIS
HOW ABOUT YOU?

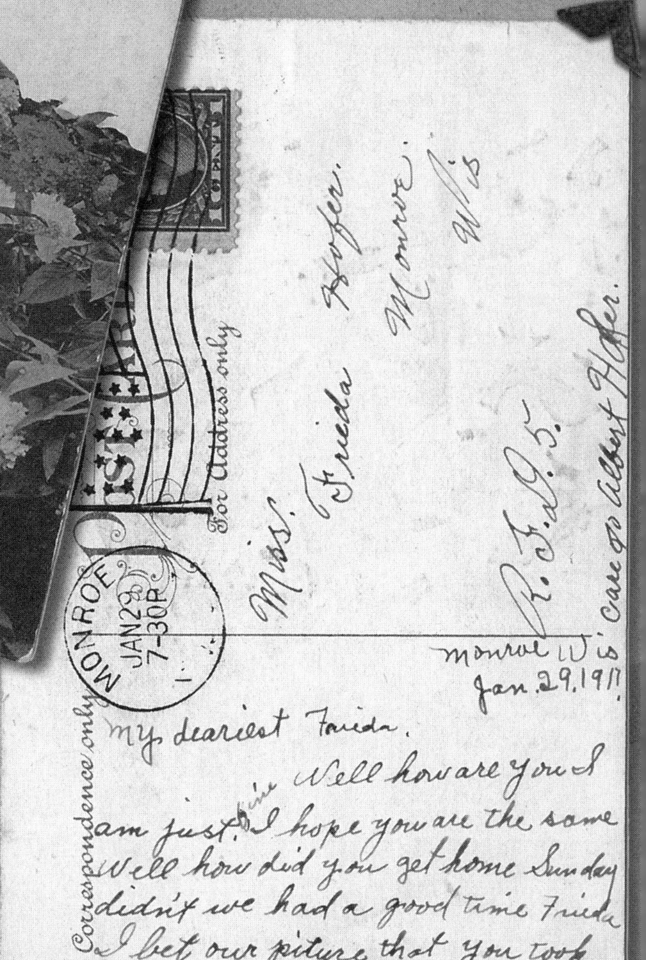
For Address only
For Correspondence only
MONROE JAN 29 7-30P
Miss. Frieda Hofer.
Monroe. Wis
R.F.D. 5.
care of Albert Hofer.
Monroe Wis
Jan. 29. 1917
My dearest Frieda.
Well how are you I
am just fine I hope you are the same
Well how did you get home Sunday
didn't we had a good time Frieda
I bet our piture that you took,
isn't no good, I wish a made
a face. because I look like a monkey
well good bye. Ella Rothenbuehler.

There's an intimacy about this postcard. What intrigued me most wasn't just the image on the front, but the fact that it was sent in 1917 from a woman to another woman living in the same town. The card is full of mystery, and Jay and Tony turned that mystery into a story of discovery, one that shows how a postcard can become a window into the past — the missing piece of a story that supposedly ended decades ago.

Meet Me Tonight in Dreamland...

STORY BY JAY BUSBEE ILLUSTRATED BY TONY FLEECS

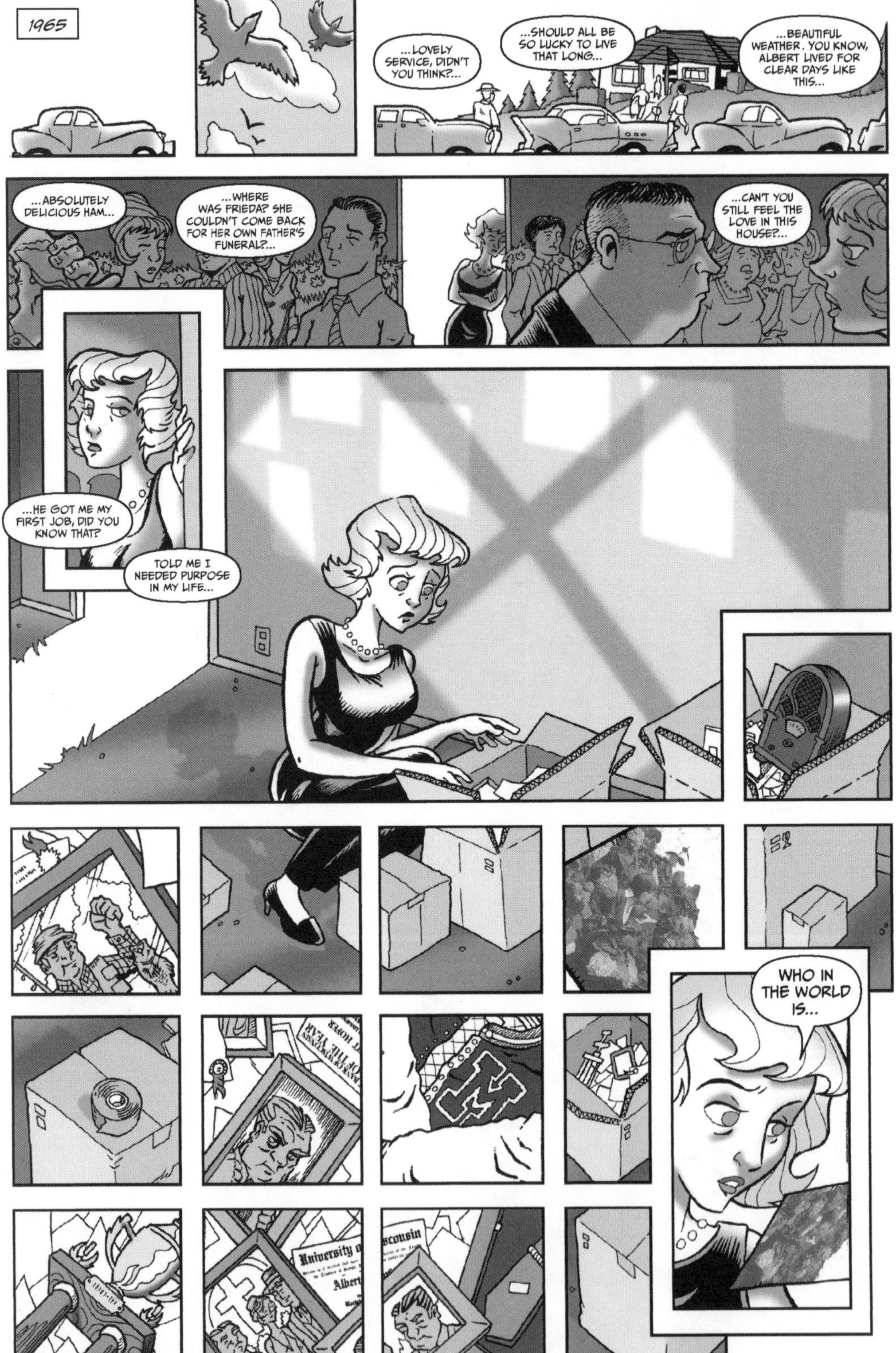
1965
...LOVELY SERVICE, DIDN'T YOU THINK?...
...SHOULD ALL BE SO LUCKY TO LIVE THAT LONG...
...BEAUTIFUL WEATHER. YOU KNOW, ALBERT LIVED FOR CLEAR DAYS LIKE THIS...
...ABSOLUTELY DELICIOUS HAM...
...WHERE WAS FRIEDA? SHE COULDN'T COME BACK FOR HER OWN FATHER'S FUNERAL?...
...CAN'T YOU STILL FEEL THE LOVE IN THIS HOUSE?...
...HE GOT ME MY FIRST JOB, DID YOU KNOW THAT?
TOLD ME I NEEDED PURPOSE IN MY LIFE...
WHO IN THE WORLD IS...

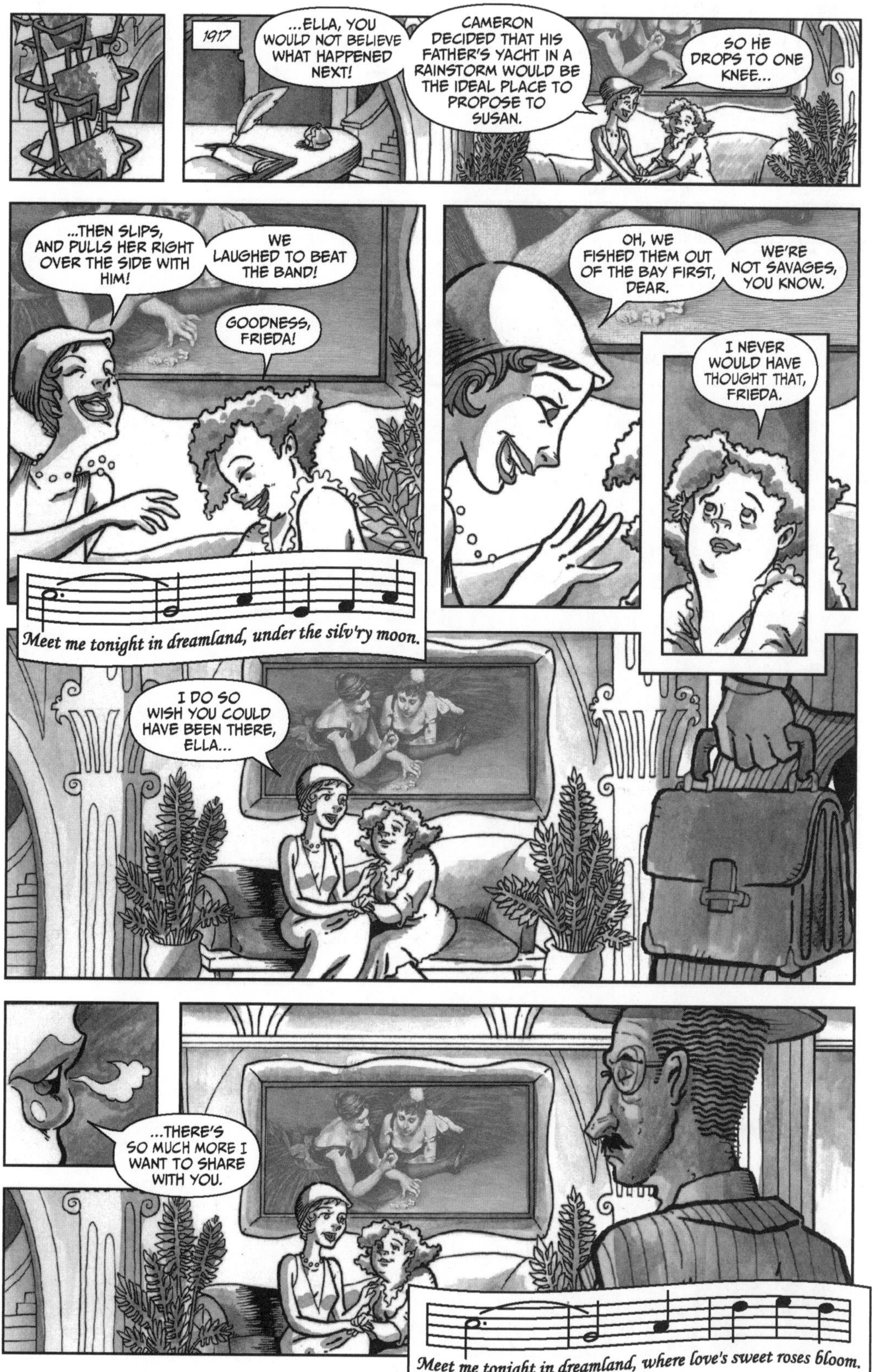
1917
...ELLA, YOU WOULD NOT BELIEVE WHAT HAPPENED NEXT!
CAMERON DECIDED THAT HIS FATHER'S YACHT IN A RAINSTORM WOULD BE THE IDEAL PLACE TO PROPOSE TO SUSAN.
SO HE DROPS TO ONE KNEE...
...THEN SLIPS, AND PULLS HER RIGHT OVER THE SIDE WITH HIM!
WE LAUGHED TO BEAT THE BAND!
GOODNESS, FRIEDA!
OH, WE FISHED THEM OUT OF THE BAY FIRST, DEAR.
WE'RE NOT SAVAGES, YOU KNOW.
I NEVER WOULD HAVE THOUGHT THAT, FRIEDA.
Meet me tonight in dreamland, under the silv'ry moon.
I DO SO WISH YOU COULD HAVE BEEN THERE, ELLA...
...THERE'S SO MUCH MORE I WANT TO SHARE WITH YOU.
Meet me tonight in dreamland, where love's sweet roses bloom.

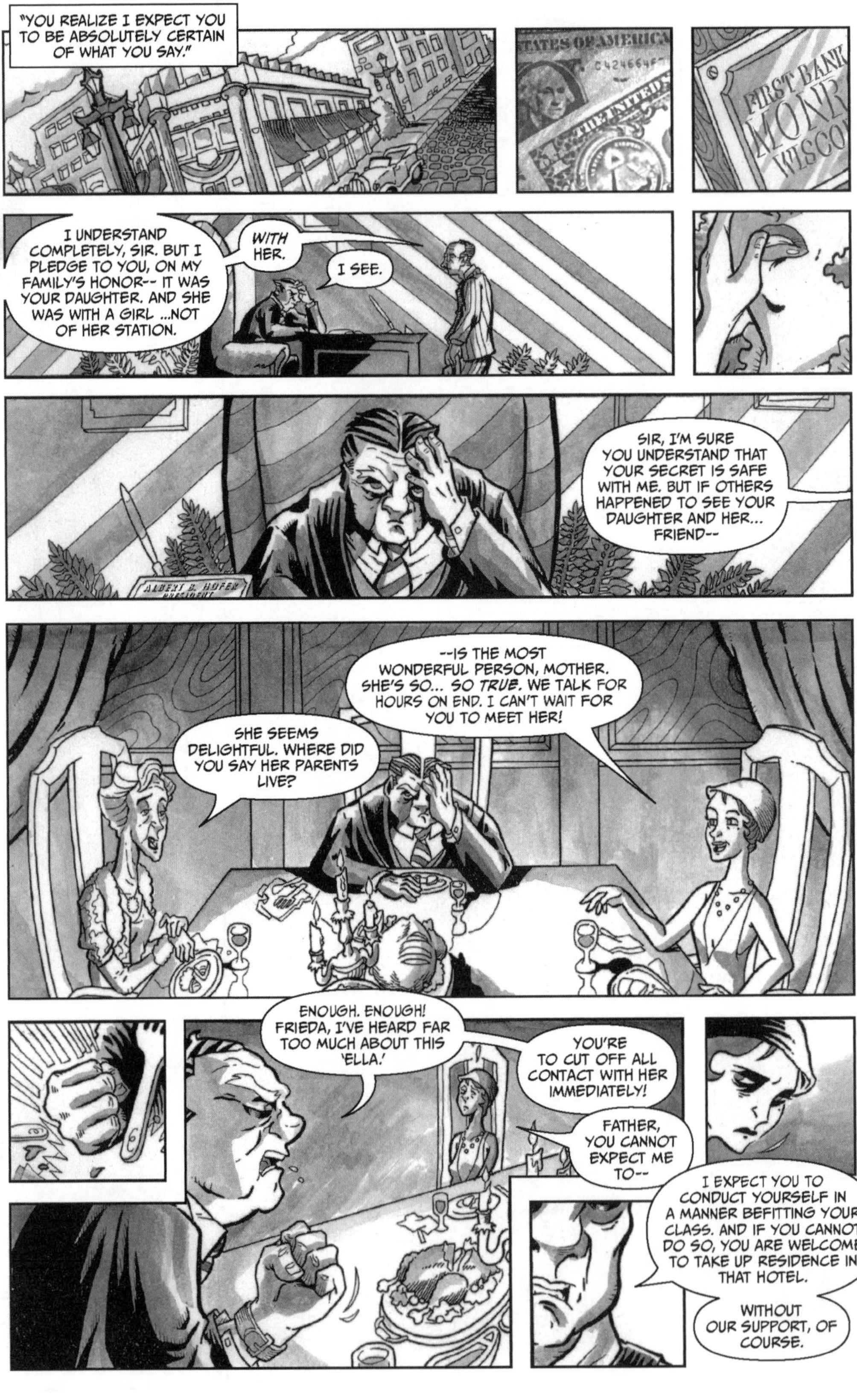
"YOU REALIZE I EXPECT YOU TO BE ABSOLUTELY CERTAIN OF WHAT YOU SAY."
FIRST BANK
I UNDERSTAND COMPLETELY, SIR. BUT I PLEDGE TO YOU, ON MY FAMILY'S HONOR-- IT WAS YOUR DAUGHTER. AND SHE WAS WITH A GIRL ...NOT OF HER STATION.
WITH HER.
I SEE.
SIR, I'M SURE YOU UNDERSTAND THAT YOUR SECRET IS SAFE WITH ME. BUT IF OTHERS HAPPENED TO SEE YOUR DAUGHTER AND HER... FRIEND--
--IS THE MOST WONDERFUL PERSON, MOTHER. SHE'S SO... SO *TRUE*. WE TALK FOR HOURS ON END. I CAN'T WAIT FOR YOU TO MEET HER!
SHE SEEMS DELIGHTFUL. WHERE DID YOU SAY HER PARENTS LIVE?
ENOUGH. ENOUGH! FRIEDA, I'VE HEARD FAR TOO MUCH ABOUT THIS 'ELLA.'
YOU'RE TO CUT OFF ALL CONTACT WITH HER IMMEDIATELY!
FATHER, YOU CANNOT EXPECT ME TO--
I EXPECT YOU TO CONDUCT YOURSELF IN A MANNER BEFITTING YOUR CLASS. AND IF YOU CANNOT DO SO, YOU ARE WELCOME TO TAKE UP RESIDENCE IN THAT HOTEL.
WITHOUT OUR SUPPORT, OF COURSE.

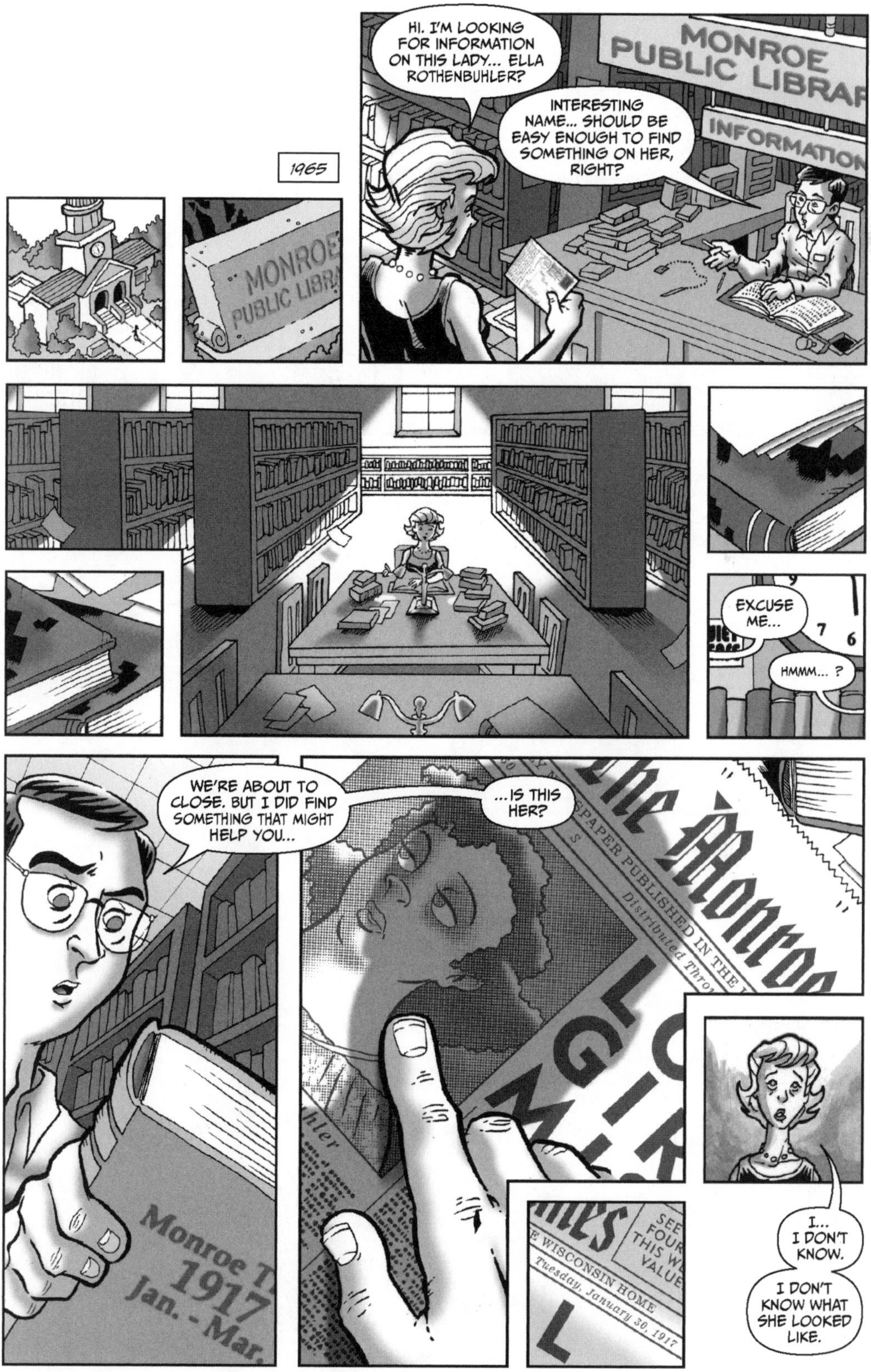
1965
MONROE PUBLIC LIBRA
HI. I'M LOOKING FOR INFORMATION ON THIS LADY... ELLA ROTHENBUHLER?
MONROE PUBLIC LIBRAR
INFORMATION
INTERESTING NAME... SHOULD BE EASY ENOUGH TO FIND SOMETHING ON HER, RIGHT?
EXCUSE ME...
HMMM... ?
WE'RE ABOUT TO CLOSE. BUT I DID FIND SOMETHING THAT MIGHT HELP YOU...
...IS THIS HER?
Monroe T
1917
Jan. - Mar.
I... I DON'T KNOW.
I DON'T KNOW WHAT SHE LOOKED LIKE.

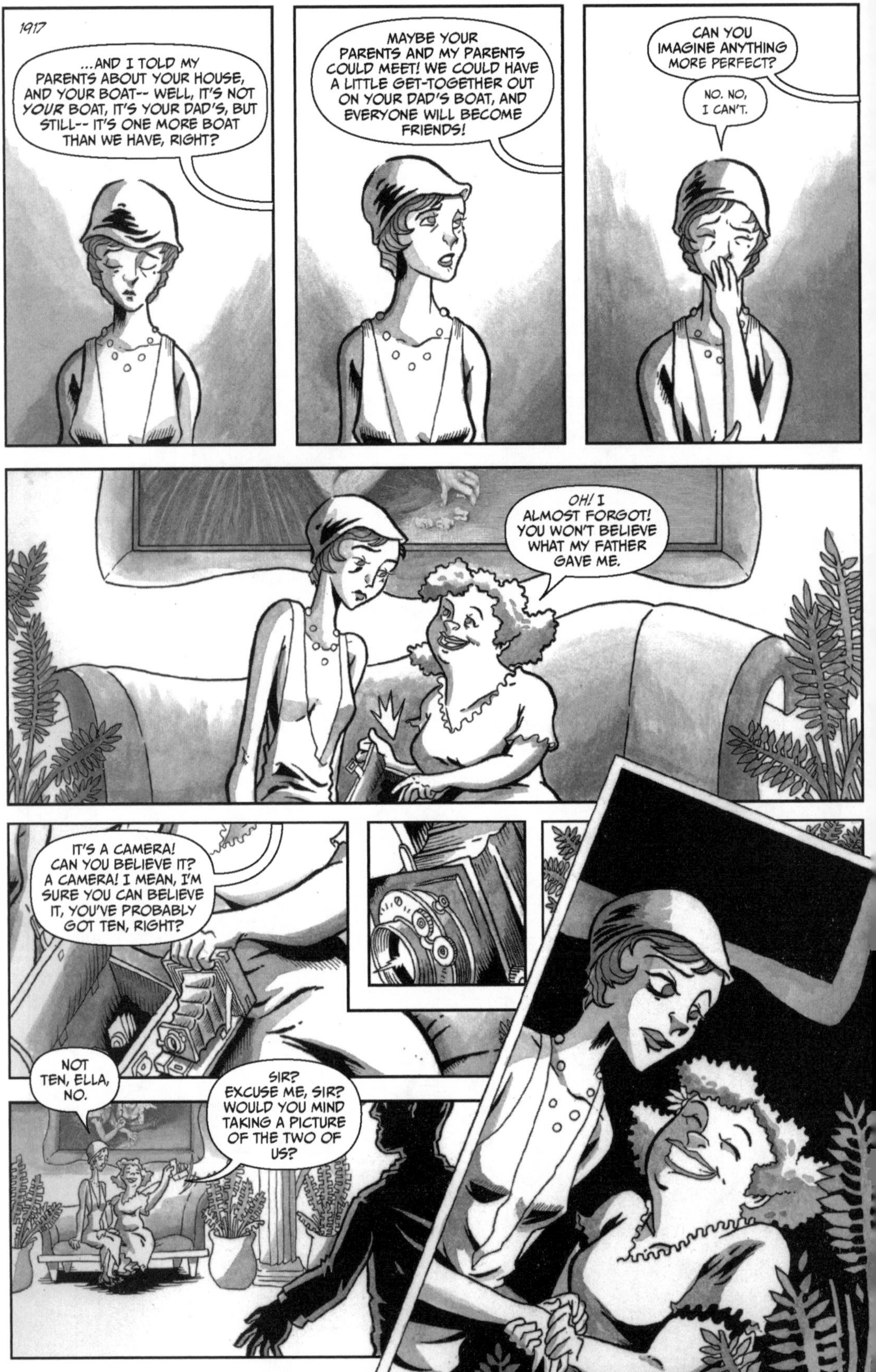
1917
...AND I TOLD MY PARENTS ABOUT YOUR HOUSE, AND YOUR BOAT-- WELL, IT'S NOT *YOUR* BOAT, IT'S YOUR DAD'S, BUT STILL-- IT'S ONE MORE BOAT THAN WE HAVE, RIGHT?
MAYBE YOUR PARENTS AND MY PARENTS COULD MEET! WE COULD HAVE A LITTLE GET-TOGETHER OUT ON YOUR DAD'S BOAT, AND EVERYONE WILL BECOME FRIENDS!
CAN YOU IMAGINE ANYTHING MORE PERFECT?
NO. NO, I CAN'T.
OH! I ALMOST FORGOT! YOU WON'T BELIEVE WHAT MY FATHER GAVE ME.
IT'S A CAMERA! CAN YOU BELIEVE IT? A CAMERA! I MEAN, I'M SURE YOU CAN BELIEVE IT, YOU'VE PROBABLY GOT TEN, RIGHT?
NOT TEN, ELLA, NO.
SIR? EXCUSE ME, SIR? WOULD YOU MIND TAKING A PICTURE OF THE TWO OF US?

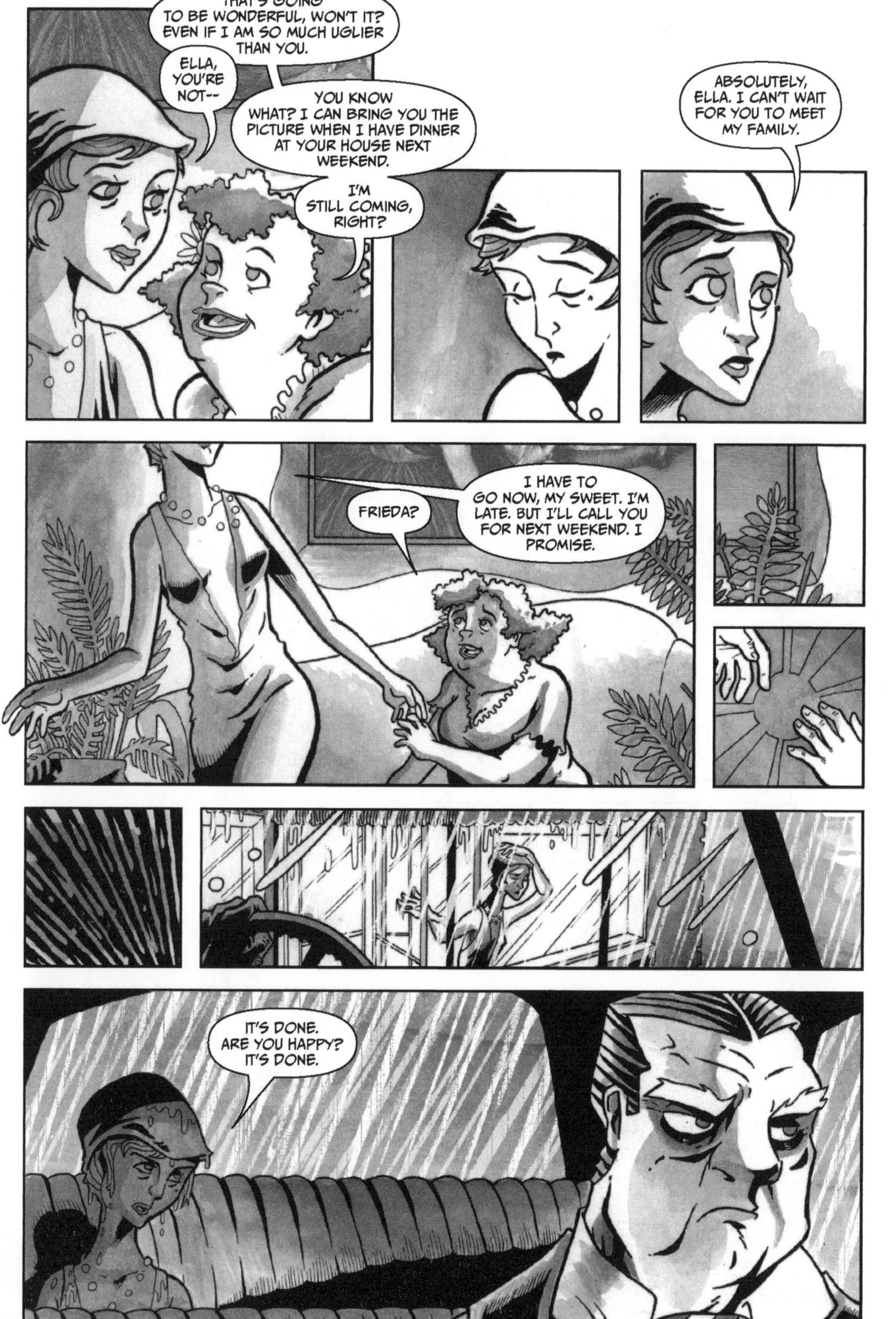
THAT'S GOING TO BE WONDERFUL, WON'T IT? EVEN IF I AM SO MUCH UGLIER THAN YOU.
ELLA, YOU'RE NOT--
YOU KNOW WHAT? I CAN BRING YOU THE PICTURE WHEN I HAVE DINNER AT YOUR HOUSE NEXT WEEKEND.
I'M STILL COMING, RIGHT?
ABSOLUTELY, ELLA. I CAN'T WAIT FOR YOU TO MEET MY FAMILY.
FRIEDA?
I HAVE TO GO NOW, MY SWEET. I'M LATE. BUT I'LL CALL YOU FOR NEXT WEEKEND. I PROMISE.
IT'S DONE. ARE YOU HAPPY? IT'S DONE.

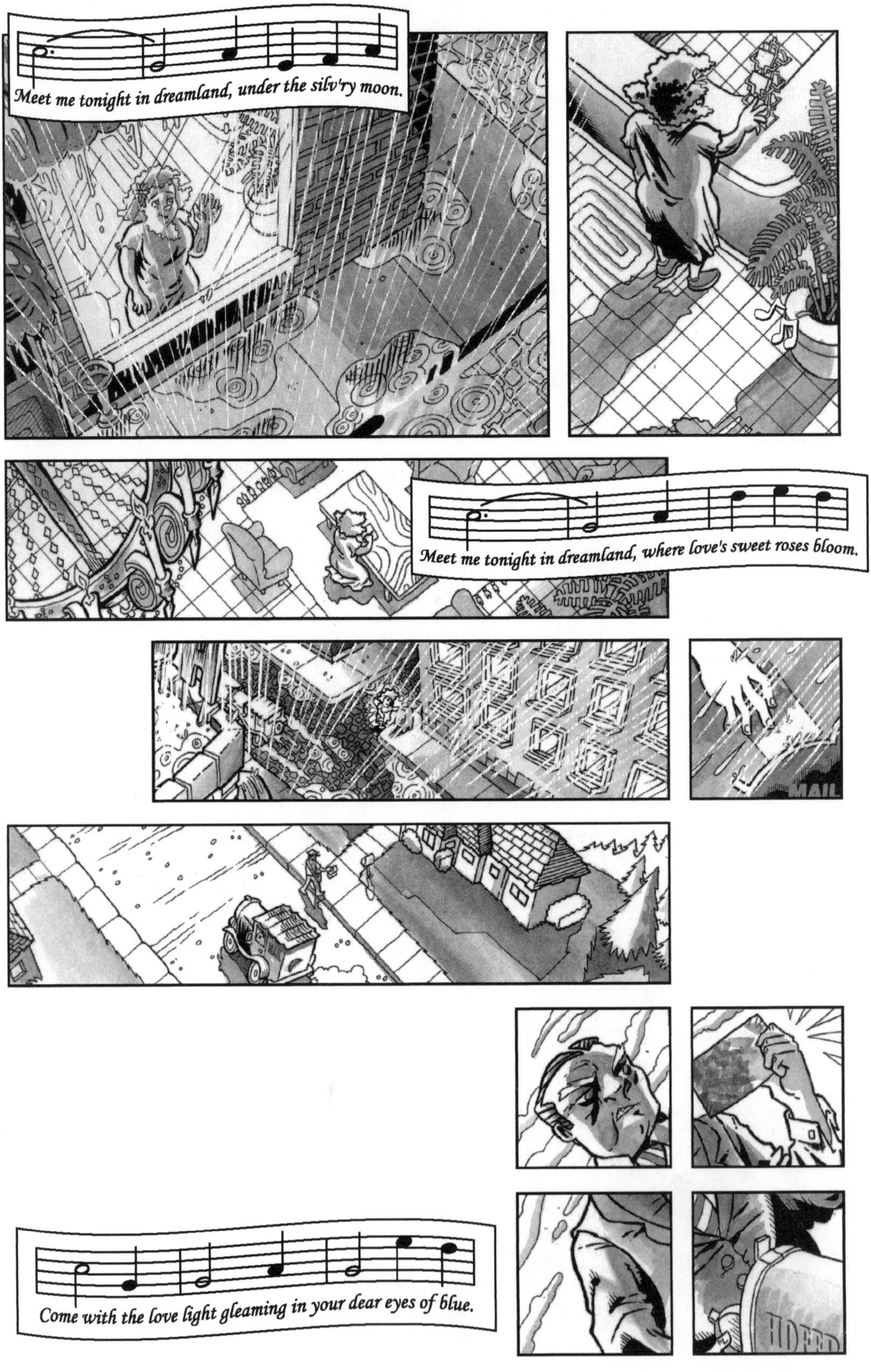
Meet me tonight in dreamland, under the silv'ry moon.
Meet me tonight in dreamland, where love's sweet roses bloom.
MAIL
Come with the love light gleaming in your dear eyes of blue.

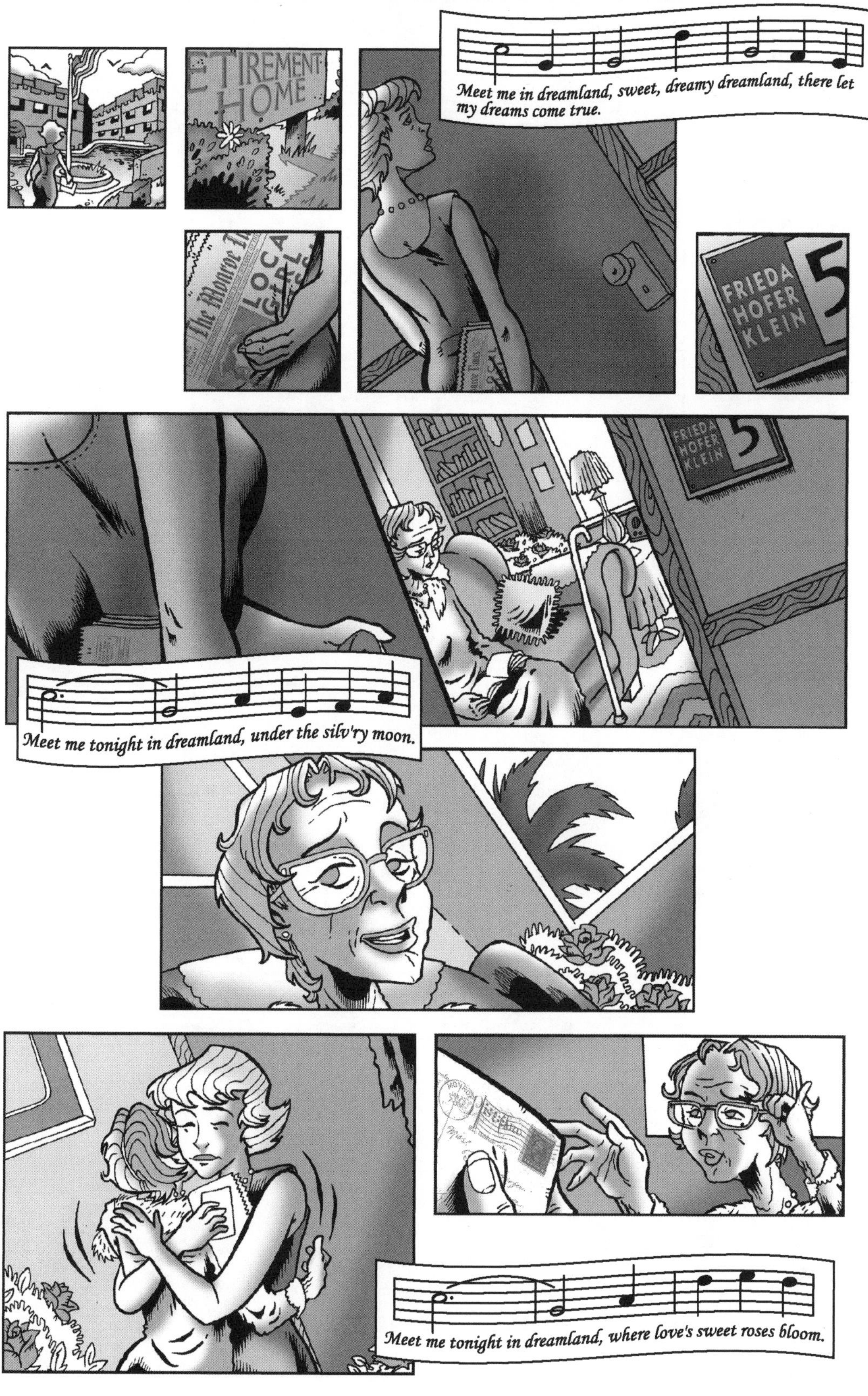
ETIREMENT
HOME
Meet me in dreamland, sweet, dreamy dreamland, there let my dreams come true.
FRIEDA HOFER KLEIN 5
FRIEDA HOFER KLEIN 5
Meet me tonight in dreamland, under the silv'ry moon.
Meet me tonight in dreamland, where love's sweet roses bloom.

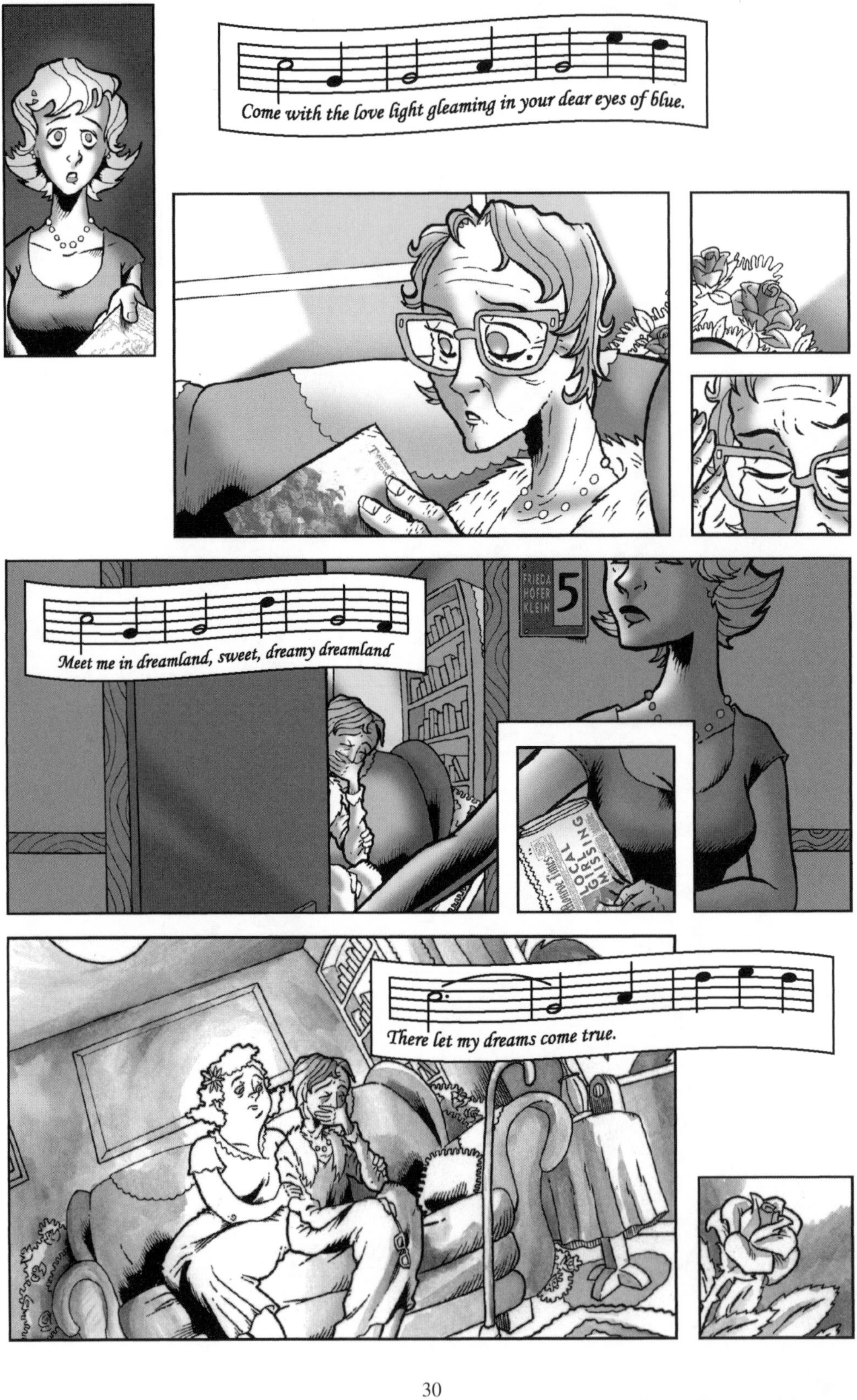
Come with the love light gleaming in your dear eyes of blue.
FRIEDA HOFER KLEIN
5
Meet me in dreamland, sweet, dreamy dreamland
LOCAL GIRL MISSING
There let my dreams come true.

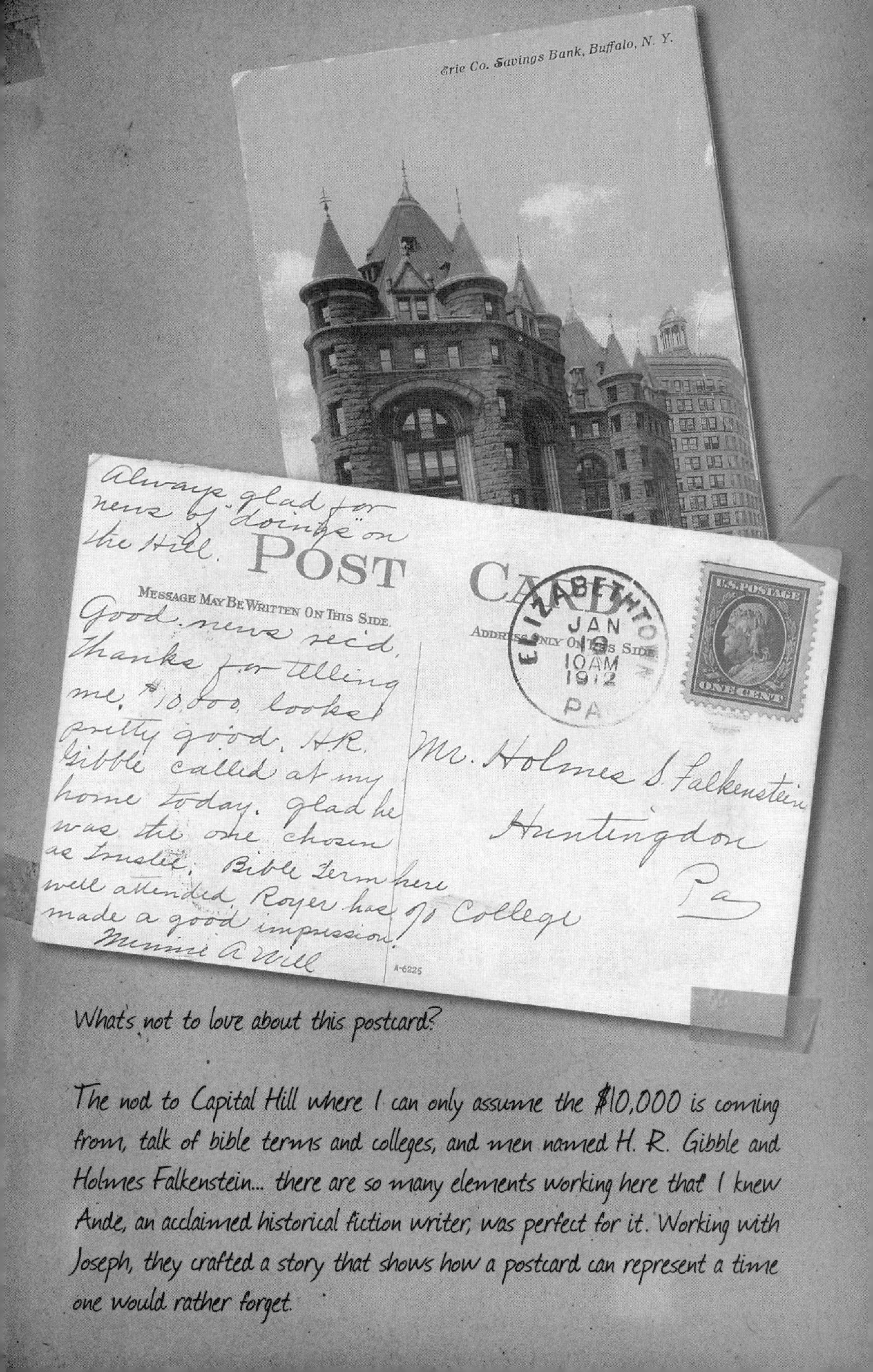
Erie Co. Savings Bank, Buffalo, N. Y.
Always glad for news of doings on the Hill.
POST CARD
MESSAGE MAY BE WRITTEN ON THIS SIDE.
Good news recd. thanks for telling me. $10,000 looks pretty good. H.R. Gibble called at my home today. glad he was the one chosen as Trustee. Bible Term here well attended, Royer has made a good impression.
Minnie A Will
ADDRESS ONLY ON THIS SIDE.
ELIZABETHTOWN JAN 19 10AM 1912 PA
U.S. POSTAGE
ONE CENT
Mr. Holmes S. Falkenstein
Huntingdon
Pa
Jo College
A-6225

What's not to love about this postcard?

The nod to Capital Hill where I can only assume the $10,000 is coming from, talk of bible terms and colleges, and men named H. R. Gibble and Holmes Falkenstein... there are so many elements working here that I knew Ande, an acclaimed historical fiction writer, was perfect for it. Working with Joseph, they crafted a story that shows how a postcard can represent a time one would rather forget.

Taken on Faith

Story by ANDE PARKS
Illustrated by JOSEPH BERGIN III

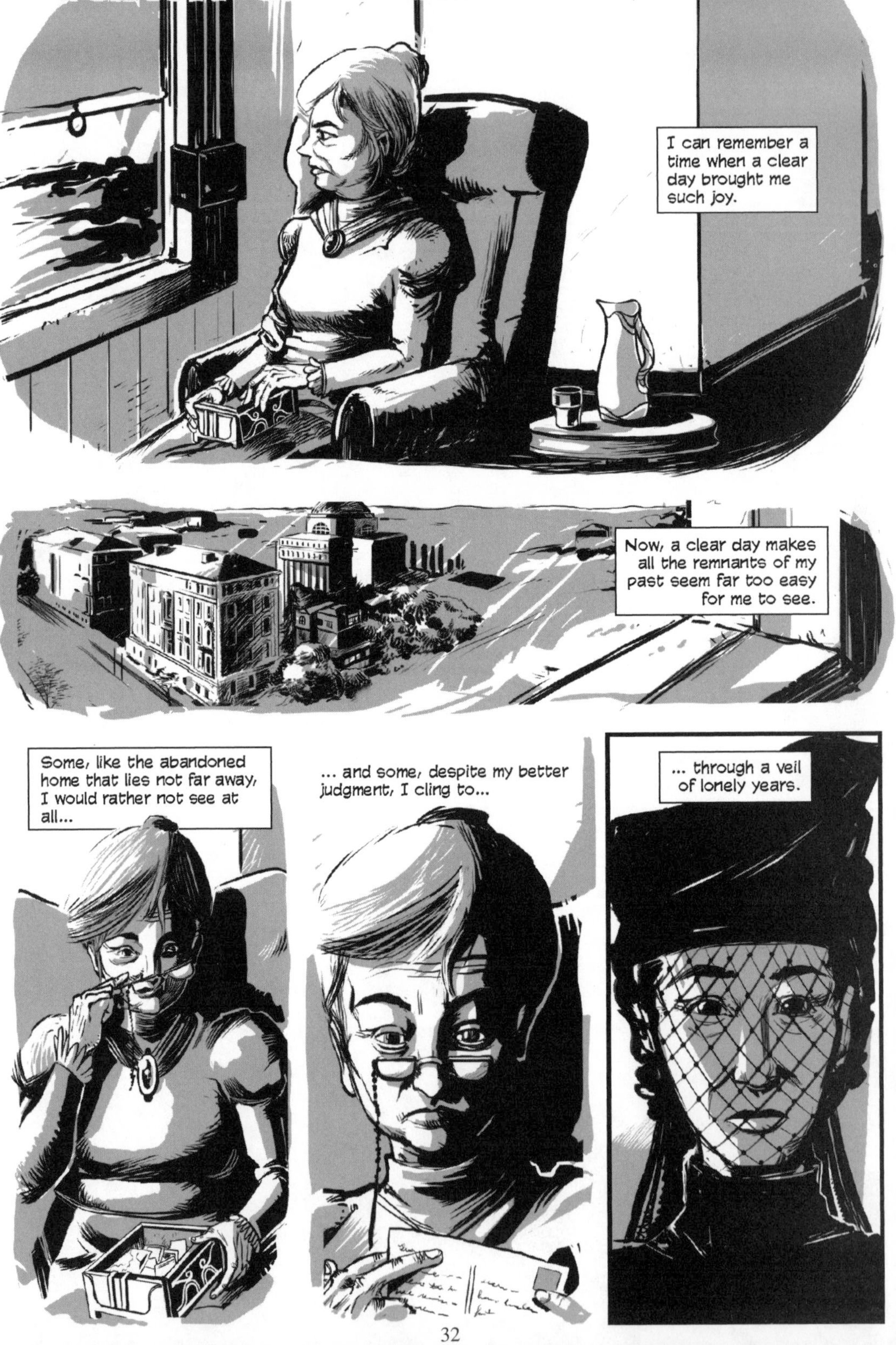
I can remember a time when a clear day brought me such joy.
Now, a clear day makes all the remnants of my past seem far too easy for me to see.
Some, like the abandoned home that lies not far away, I would rather not see at all...
... and some, despite my better judgment, I cling to...
... through a veil of lonely years.

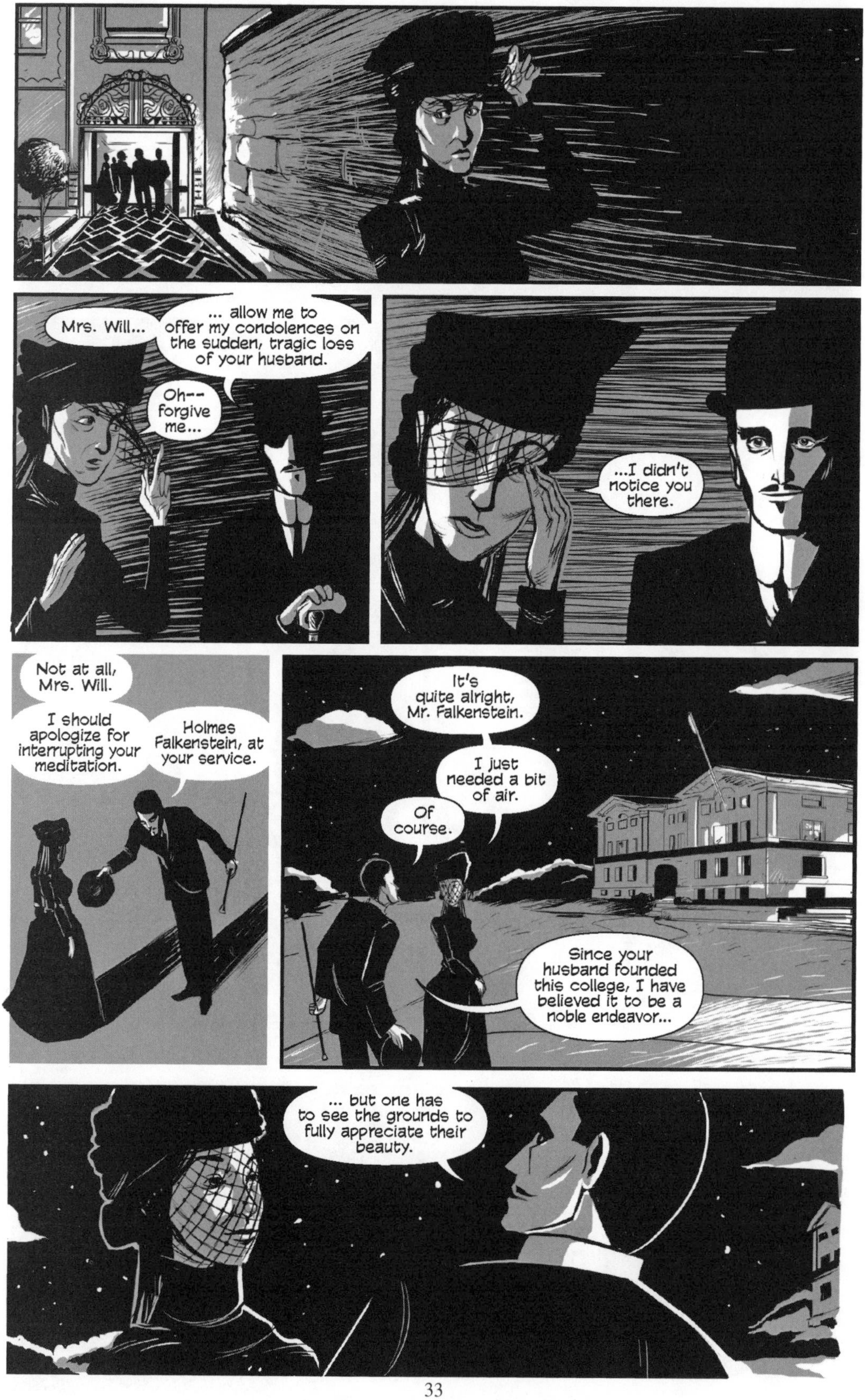

Mrs. Will...
... allow me to offer my condolences on the sudden, tragic loss of your husband.
Oh-- forgive me...
...I didn't notice you there.
Not at all, Mrs. Will.
I should apologize for interrupting your meditation.
Holmes Falkenstein, at your service.
It's quite alright, Mr. Falkenstein.
I just needed a bit of air.
Of course.
Since your husband founded this college, I have believed it to be a noble endeavor...
... but one has to see the grounds to fully appreciate their beauty.

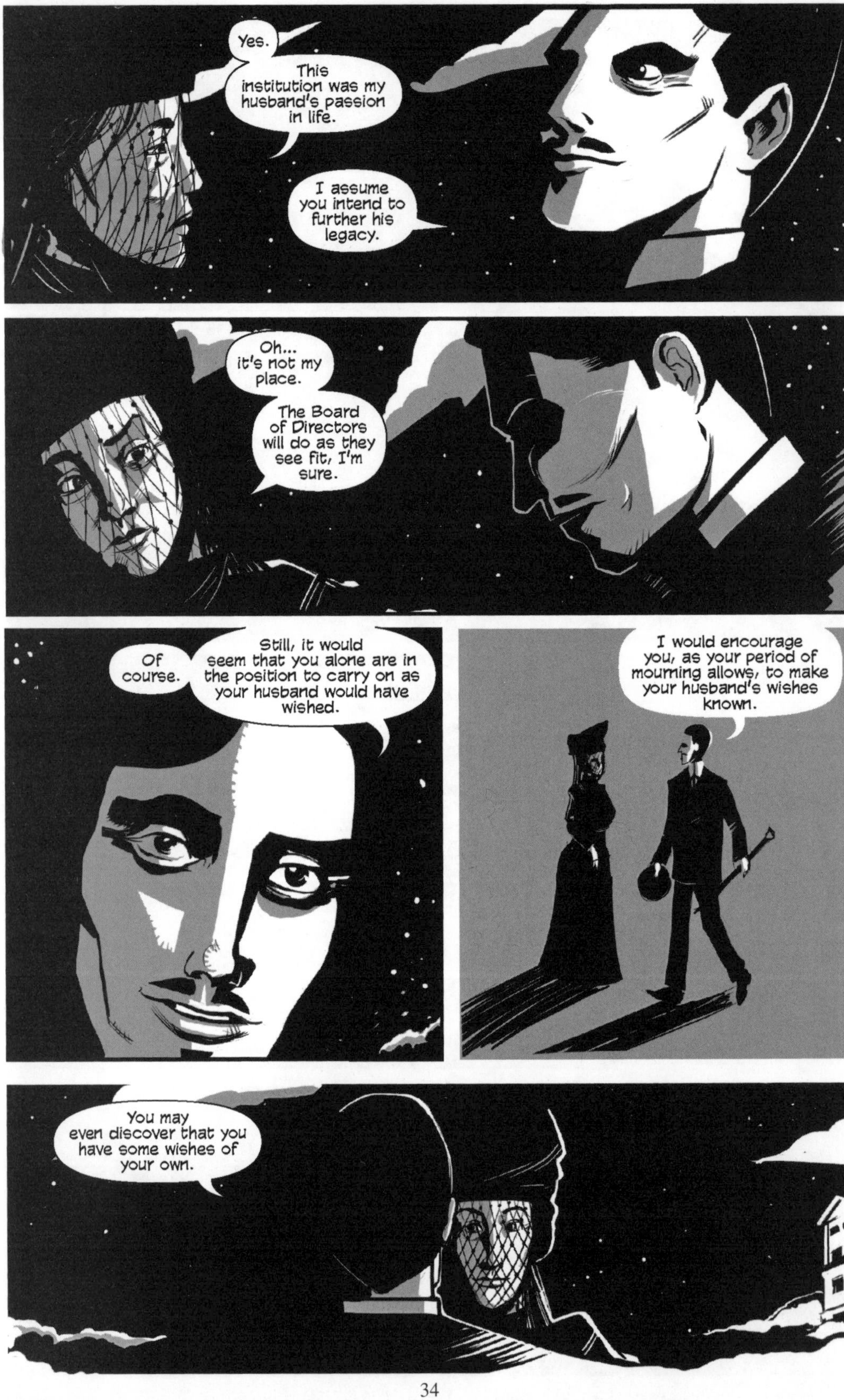
Yes.
This institution was my husband's passion in life.
I assume you intend to further his legacy.
Oh... it's not my place.
The Board of Directors will do as they see fit, I'm sure.
Of course.
Still, it would seem that you alone are in the position to carry on as your husband would have wished.
I would encourage you, as your period of mourning allows, to make your husband's wishes known.
You may even discover that you have some wishes of your own.

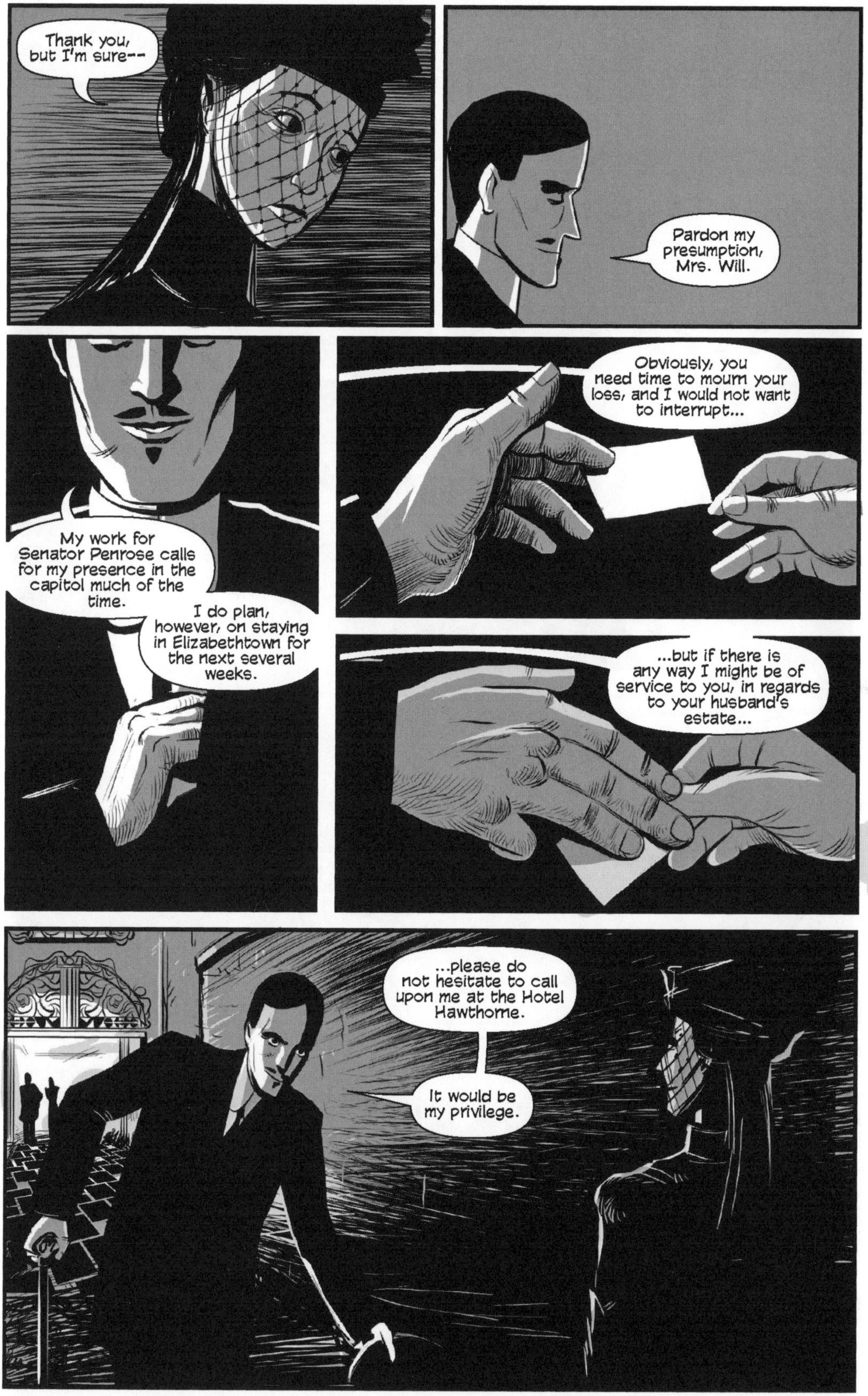
Thank you, but I'm sure--
Pardon my presumption, Mrs. Will.
My work for Senator Penrose calls for my presence in the capitol much of the time.
I do plan, however, on staying in Elizabethtown for the next several weeks.
Obviously, you need time to mourn your loss, and I would not want to interrupt...
...but if there is any way I might be of service to you, in regards to your husband's estate...
...please do not hesitate to call upon me at the Hotel Hawthorne.
It would be my privilege.

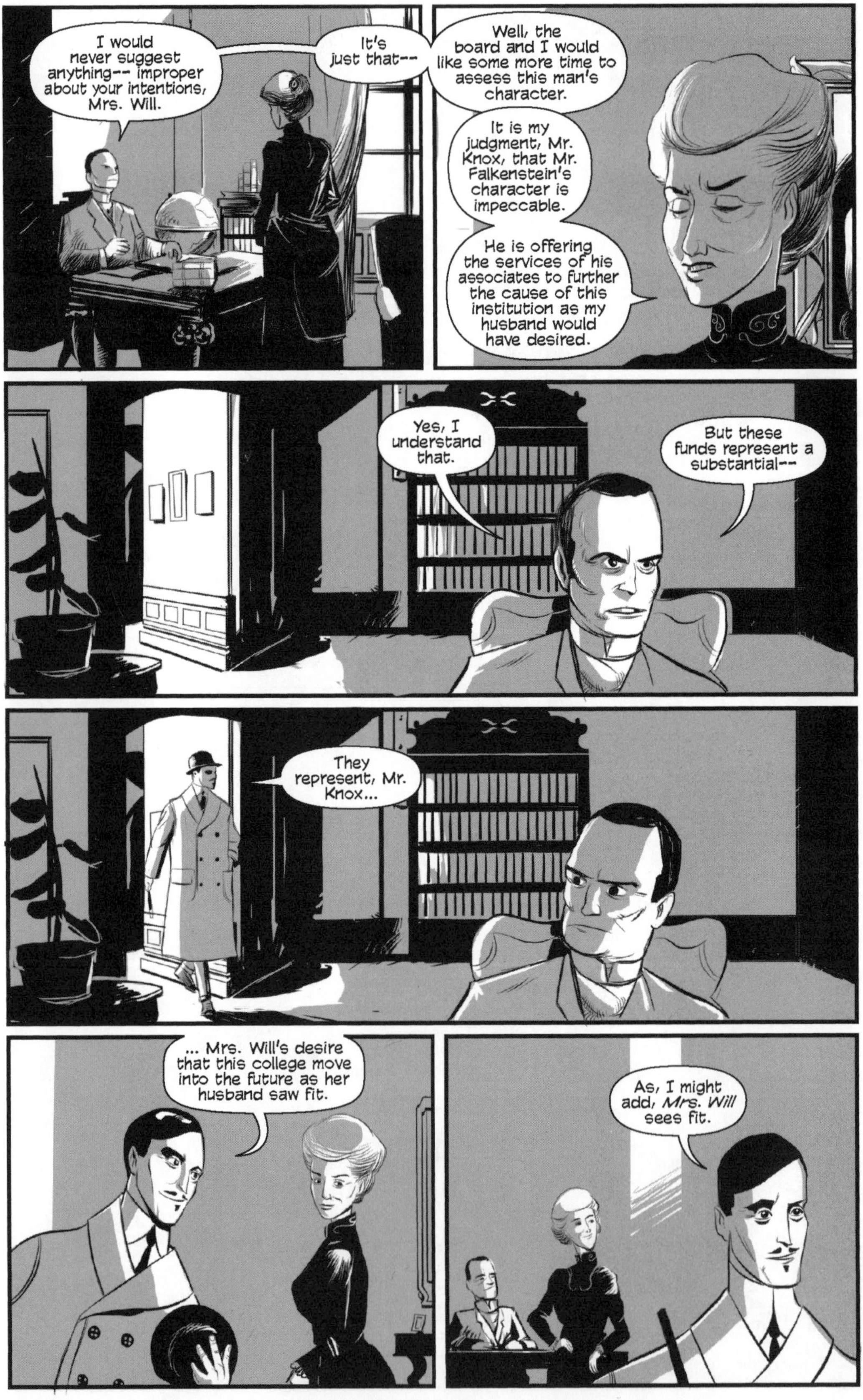
I would never suggest anything-- improper about your intentions, Mrs. Will.
It's just that--
Well, the board and I would like some more time to assess this man's character.
It is my judgment, Mr. Knox, that Mr. Falkenstein's character is impeccable.
He is offering the services of his associates to further the cause of this institution as my husband would have desired.
Yes, I understand that.
But these funds represent a substantial--
They represent, Mr. Knox...
... Mrs. Will's desire that this college move into the future as her husband saw fit.
As, I might add, *Mrs. Will* sees fit.

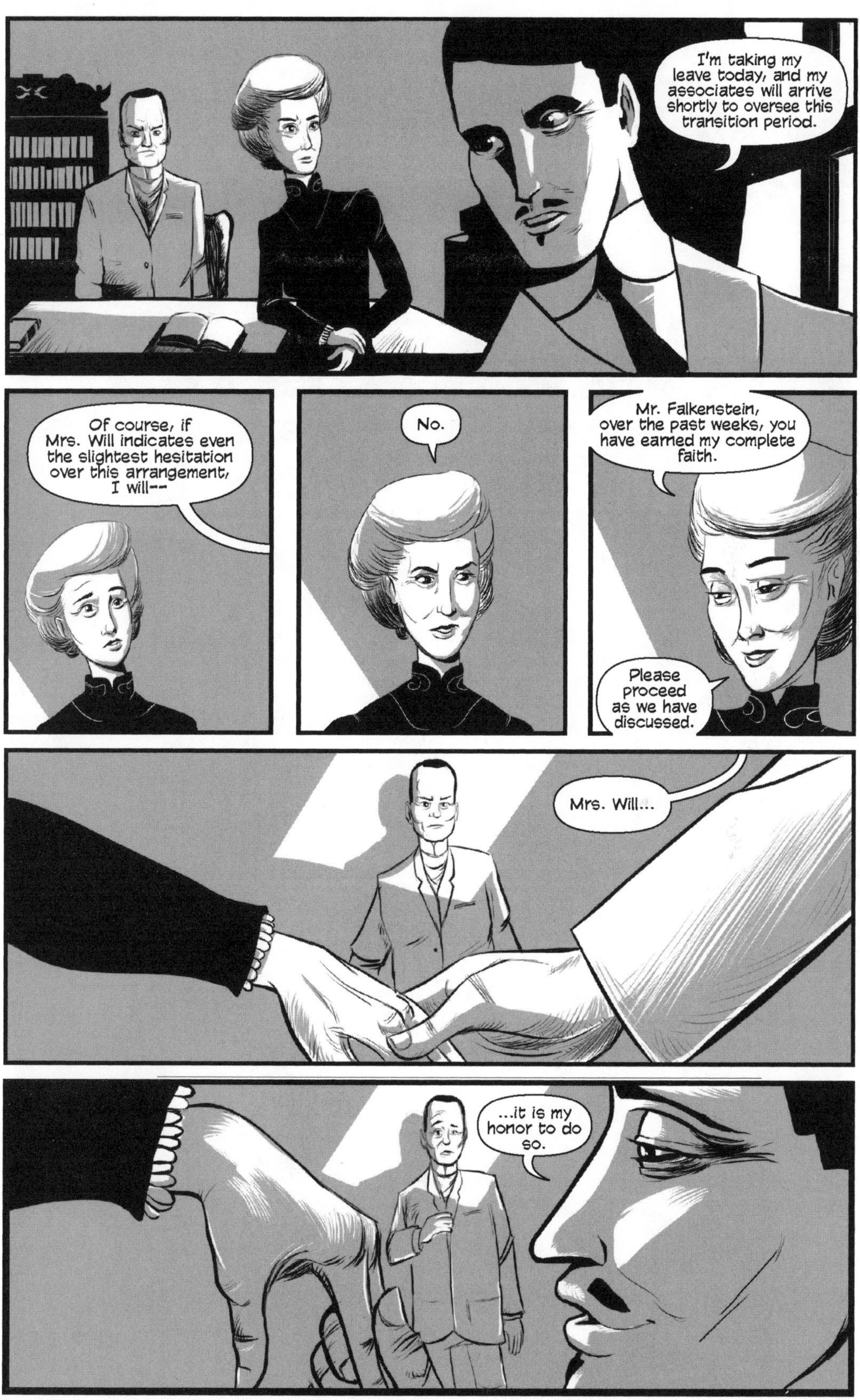
I'm taking my leave today, and my associates will arrive shortly to oversee this transition period.
Of course, if Mrs. Will indicates even the slightest hesitation over this arrangement, I will--
No.
Mr. Falkenstein, over the past weeks, you have earned my complete faith.
Please proceed as we have discussed.
Mrs. Will...
...it is my honor to do so.

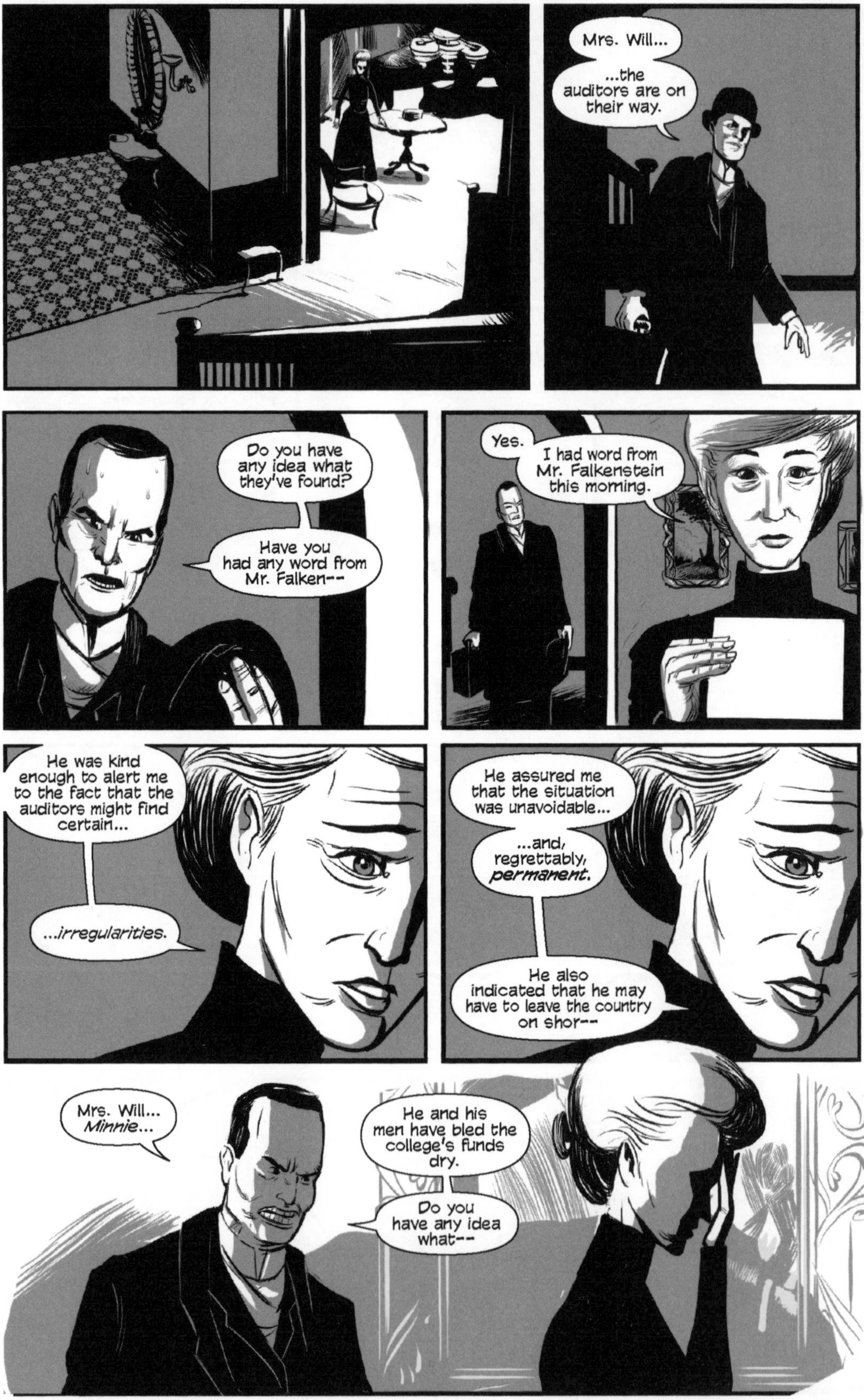
Mrs. Will...
...the auditors are on their way.
Do you have any idea what they've found?
Have you had any word from Mr. Falken--
Yes.
I had word from Mr. Falkenstein this morning.
He was kind enough to alert me to the fact that the auditors might find certain...
...*irregularities*.
He assured me that the situation was unavoidable...
...and, regrettably, *permanent*.
He also indicated that he may have to leave the country on shor--
Mrs. Will... *Minnie*...
He and his men have bled the college's funds dry.
Do you have any idea what--

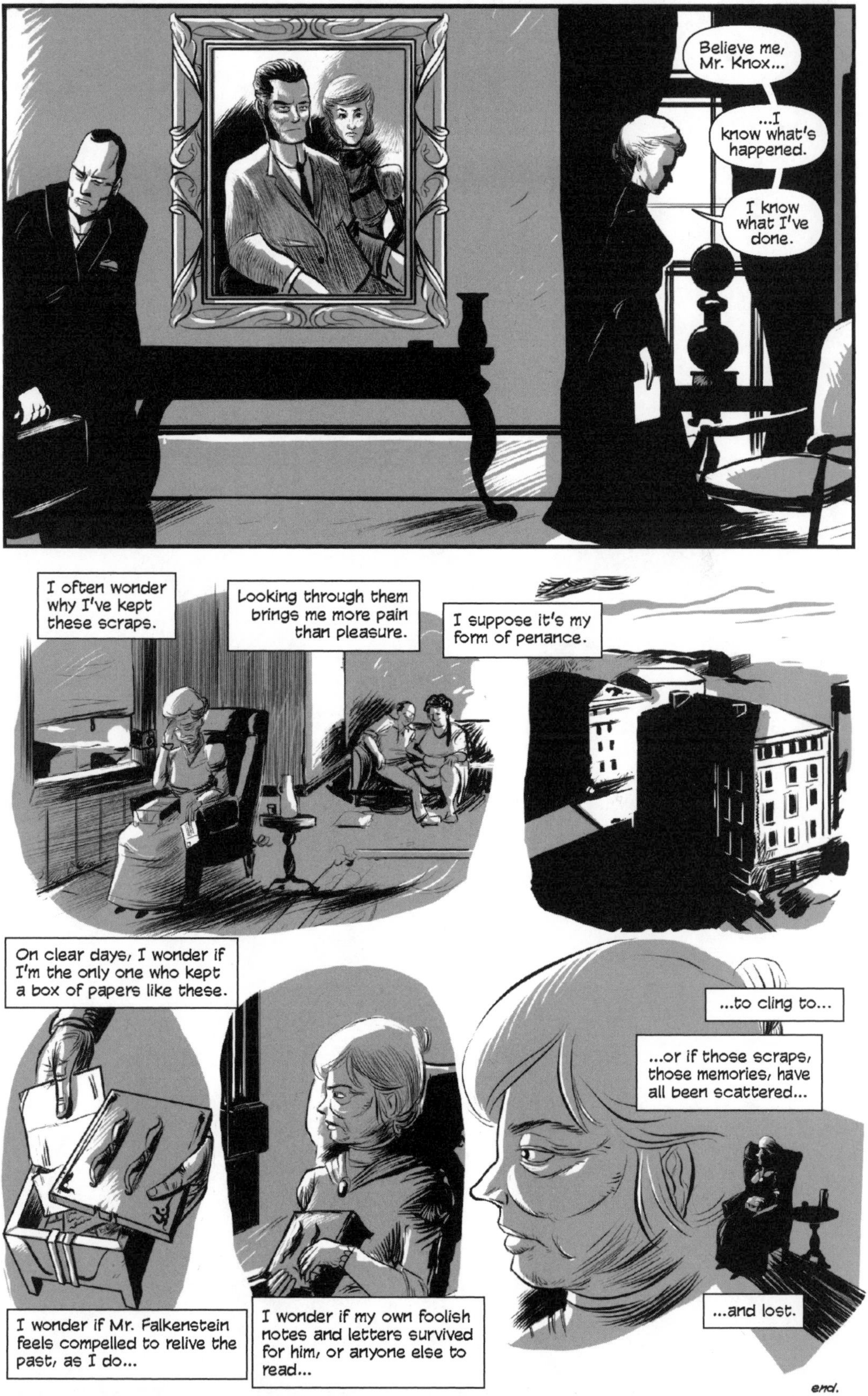
Believe me, Mr. Knox...
...I know what's happened.
I know what I've done.
I often wonder why I've kept these scraps.
Looking through them brings me more pain than pleasure.
I suppose it's my form of penance.
On clear days, I wonder if I'm the only one who kept a box of papers like these.
I wonder if Mr. Falkenstein feels compelled to relive the past, as I do...
I wonder if my own foolish notes and letters survived for him, or anyone else to read...
...to cling to...
...or if those scraps, those memories, have all been scattered...
...and lost.
end.

"If you get a chance soon or come down send Louis his underwear..." I couldn't wait to see what somebody did with this one, but little did I know the story behind the seemingly comical sign-off could be so dark and frightening. Matt and Jason show us how a postcard can capture sheer horror just as easily as it captures moments of levity.

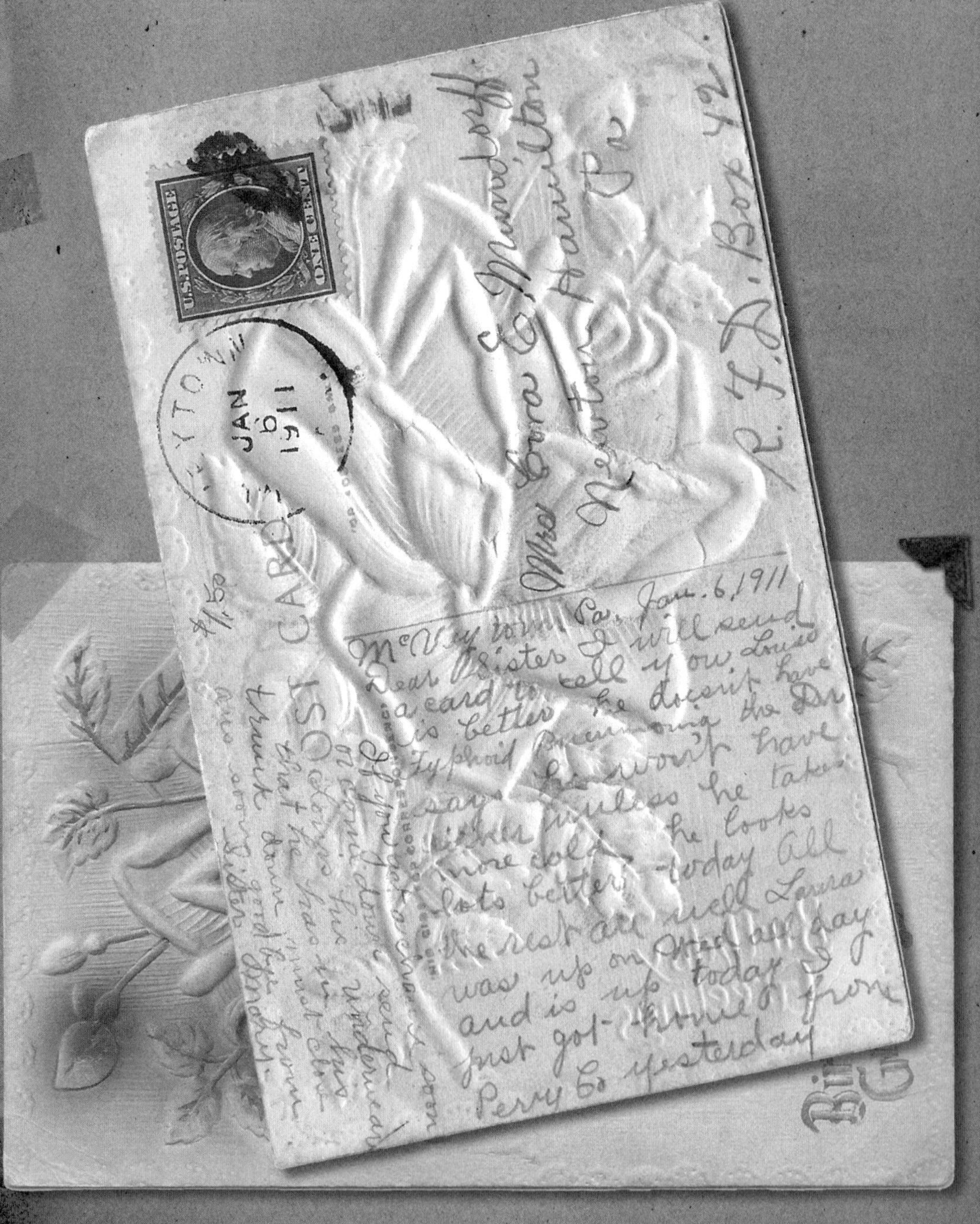

U.S. POSTAGE
ONE CENT
JAN
1911
POST CARD
McVeytown Pa. Jan. 6, 1911
Dear Sister I will send
a card to tell you Louis
is better he doesn't have
Typhoid Pneumonia the Dr
says he won't have
unless he takes
more cold he looks
lots better today All
the rest are well Laura
was up
and is up today I
just got home from
Perry Co. yesterday

SEND LOUIS HIS UNDERWEAR

STORY BY MATT DEMBICKI
ILLUSTRATED BY JASON COPLAND

NEWTON HAMILTON, PA DEC. 30, 1910

DEAR MARY,

SORRY YOU COULDN'T MAKE IT UP FOR CHRISTMAS, BUT I UNDERSTAND. THE HOLIDAYS ARE A TIME FOR FAMILY, AFTER ALL, AND IT SOUNDS AS IF YOURS NEEDS YOU AT HOME RIGHT NOW. I HOPE LOUIS IS FEELING BETTER.

I'M SURE HIS SICKNESS COMES FROM ALL THE STRESS OF A NEW HOUSE, NEW LIFE, RETIREMENT. IT TAKES ITS TOLL ON A BODY.

IF HIS CONDITION WORSENS, PLEASE LET US KNOW AND WE'LL COME SOONER. OTHERWISE, WE'LL SEE YOU AT EASTER.

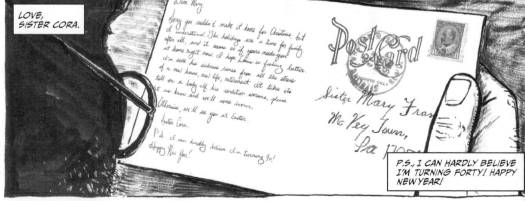

LOVE, SISTER CORA.

P.S., I CAN HARDLY BELIEVE I'M TURNING FORTY! HAPPY NEW YEAR!

41

MCVEY TOWN PA.
JAN 6, 1911

DEAR SISTER

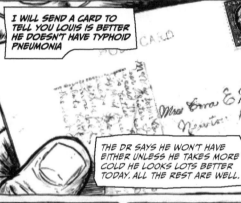

I WILL SEND A CARD TO TELL YOU LOUIS IS BETTER HE DOESN'T HAVE TYPHOID PNEUMONIA

THE DR SAYS HE WON'T HAVE EITHER UNLESS HE TAKES MORE COLD HE LOOKS LOTS BETTER TODAY. ALL THE REST ARE WELL.

LAURA WAS UP ON WED ALL DAY AND IS UP TODAY. I JUST GOT HOME FROM PERRY CO YESTERDAY.

42

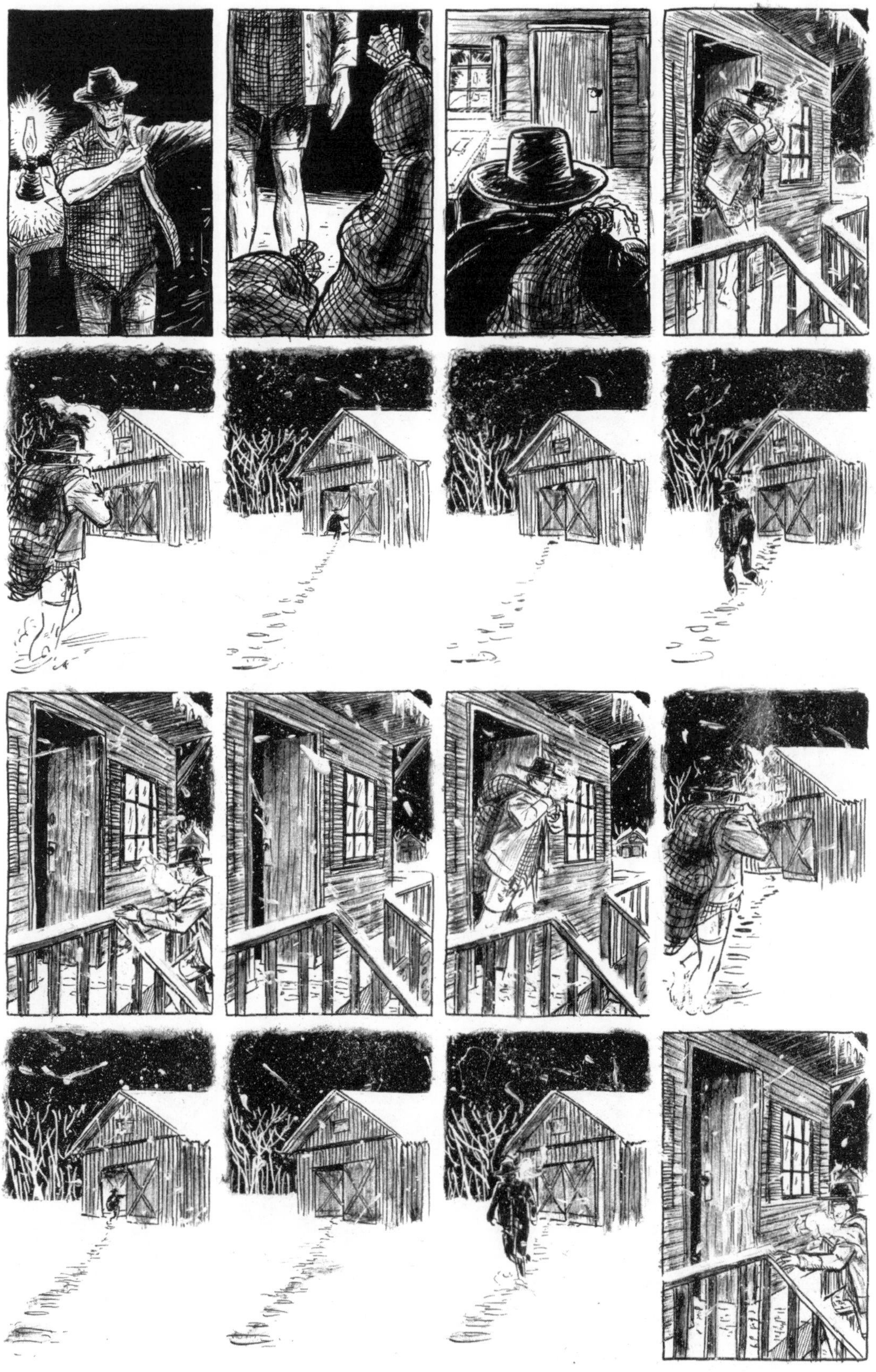

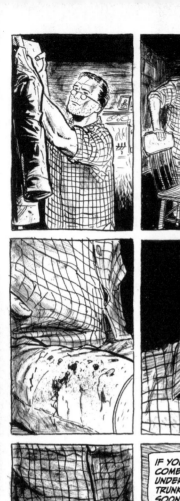

IF YOU GET A CHANCE SOON OR COME DOWN SEND LOUIS HIS UNDERWEAR THAT HE HAS IN HIS TRUNK DOWN MUST CLOSE ANS SOON, GOODBYE FROM SISTER MARY

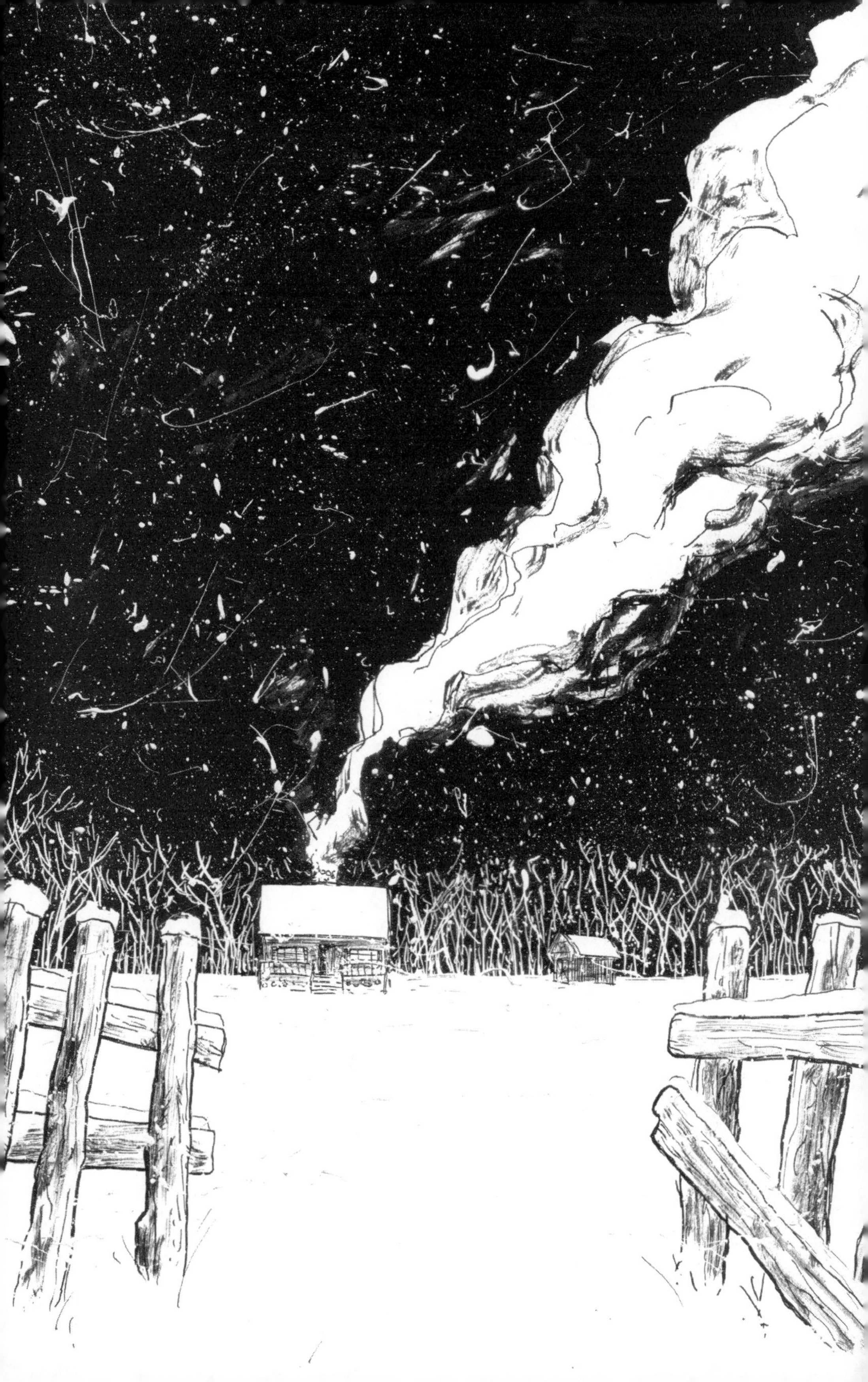

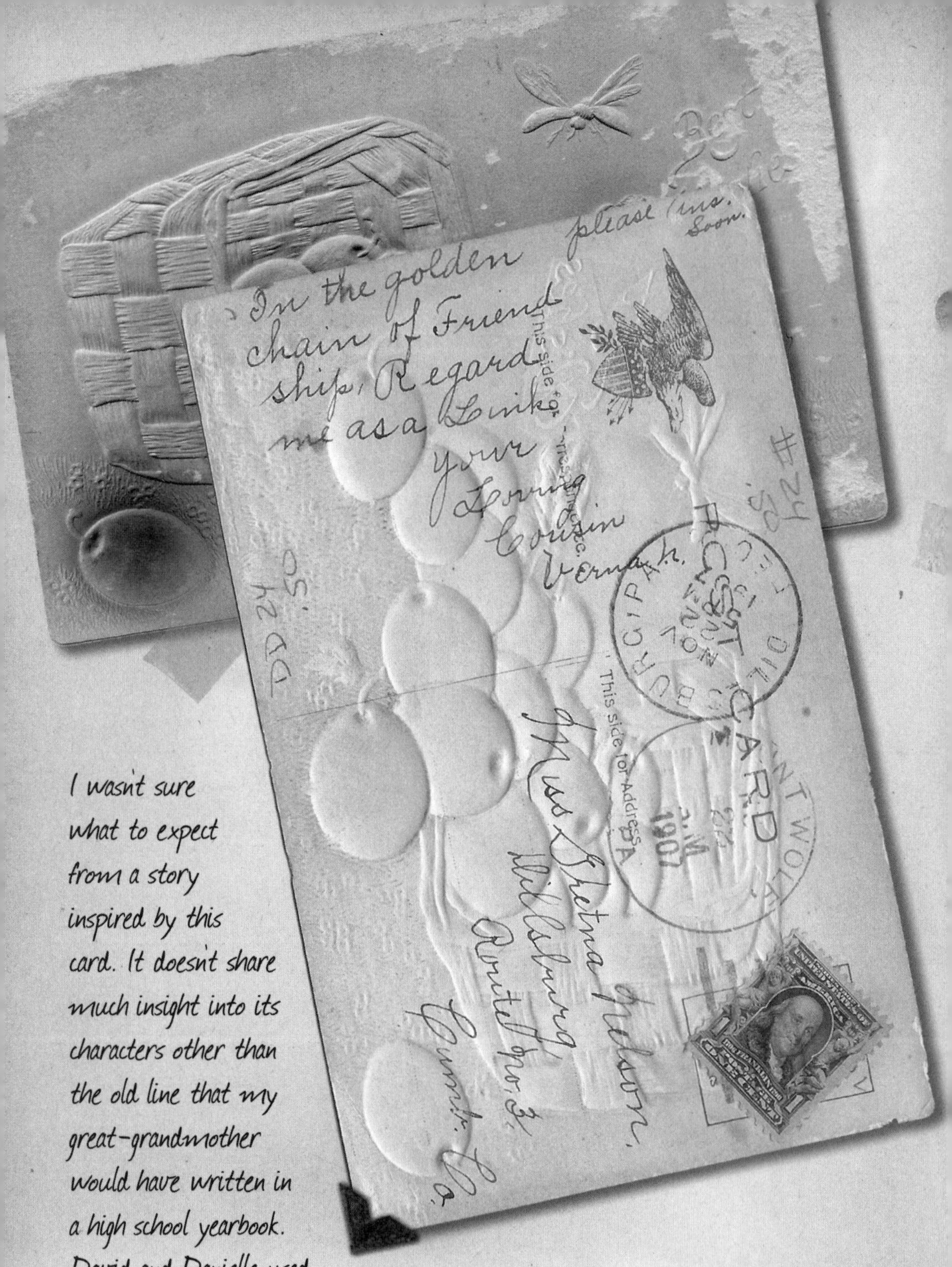
In the golden chain of Friendship, Regard me as a Link your Loving Cousin Verna.
please Ans. Soon.
This side for Address
CARD
1907

I wasn't sure what to expect from a story inspired by this card. It doesn't share much insight into its characters other than the old line that my great-grandmother would have written in a high school yearbook. David and Danielle used the subtext of the card, talk of chains and friendships, to show how a postcard can represent epiphanies, freedoms, and missed opportunities.

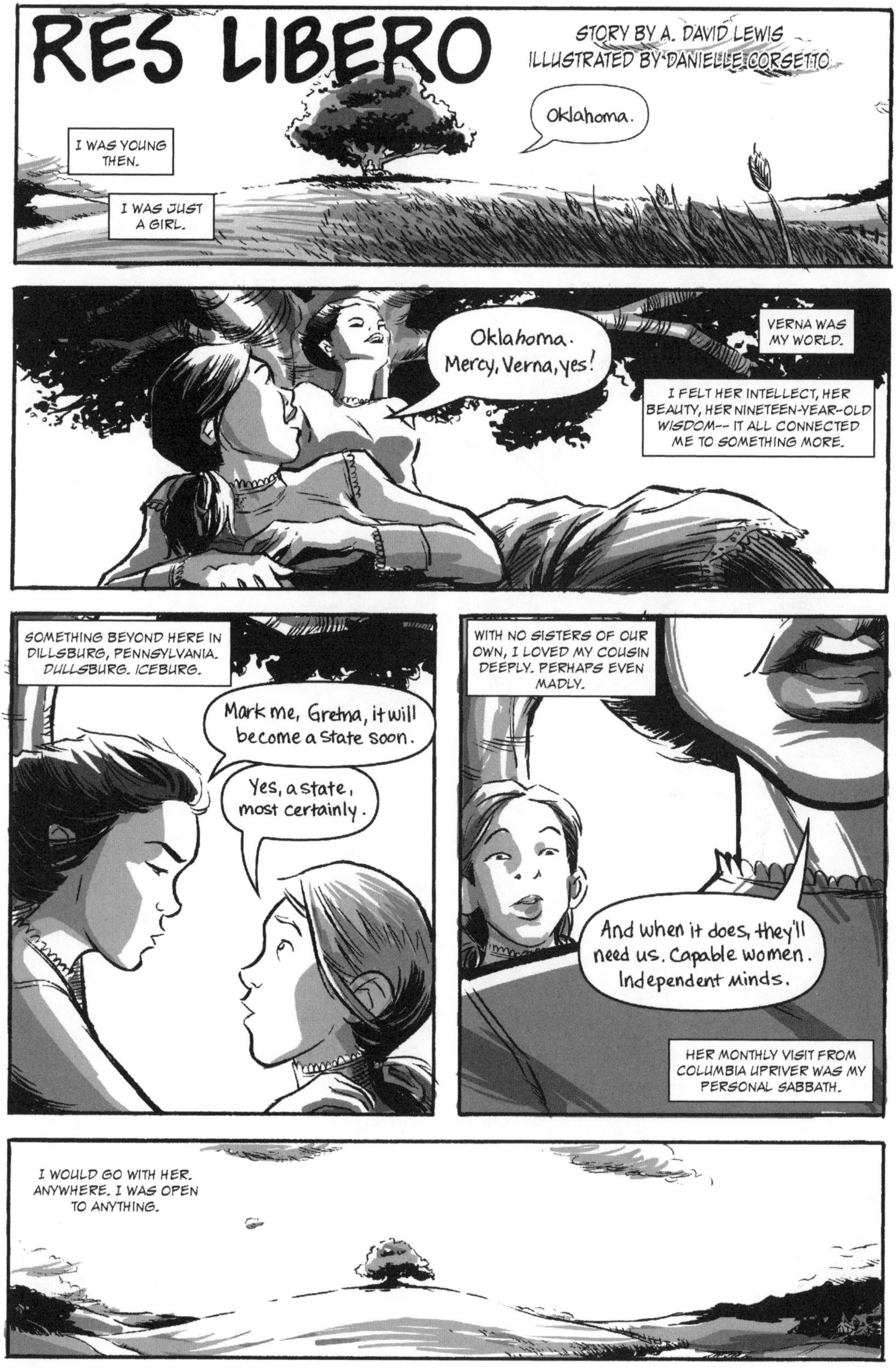
RES LIBERO
STORY BY A. DAVID LEWIS
ILLUSTRATED BY DANIELLE CORSETTO
I WAS YOUNG THEN.
I WAS JUST A GIRL.
Oklahoma.
Oklahoma. Mercy, Verna, yes!
VERNA WAS MY WORLD.
I FELT HER INTELLECT, HER BEAUTY, HER NINETEEN-YEAR-OLD WISDOM-- IT ALL CONNECTED ME TO SOMETHING MORE.
SOMETHING BEYOND HERE IN DILLSBURG, PENNSYLVANIA. DULLSBURG. ICEBURG.
Mark me, Gretna, it will become a state soon.
Yes, a state, most certainly.
WITH NO SISTERS OF OUR OWN, I LOVED MY COUSIN DEEPLY. PERHAPS EVEN MADLY.
And when it does, they'll need us. Capable women. Independent minds.
HER MONTHLY VISIT FROM COLUMBIA UPRIVER WAS MY PERSONAL SABBATH.
I WOULD GO WITH HER. ANYWHERE. I WAS OPEN TO ANYTHING.

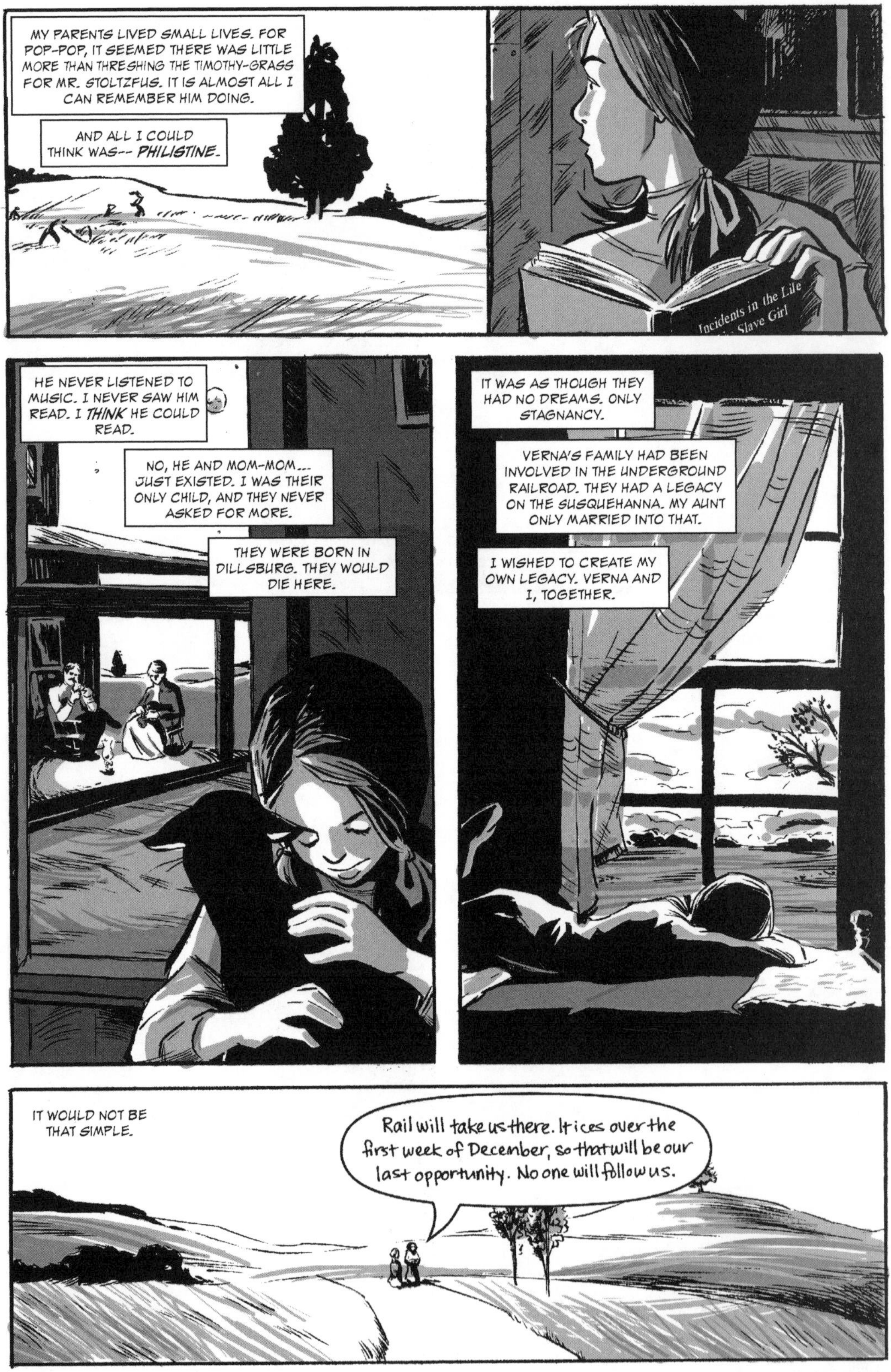
MY PARENTS LIVED SMALL LIVES. FOR POP-POP, IT SEEMED THERE WAS LITTLE MORE THAN THRESHING THE TIMOTHY-GRASS FOR MR. STOLTZFUS. IT IS ALMOST ALL I CAN REMEMBER HIM DOING.
AND ALL I COULD THINK WAS-- *PHILISTINE*.
Incidents in the Life
Slave Girl
HE NEVER LISTENED TO MUSIC. I NEVER SAW HIM READ. I *THINK* HE COULD READ.
NO, HE AND MOM-MOM... JUST EXISTED. I WAS THEIR ONLY CHILD, AND THEY NEVER ASKED FOR MORE.
THEY WERE BORN IN DILLSBURG. THEY WOULD DIE HERE.
IT WAS AS THOUGH THEY HAD NO DREAMS. ONLY STAGNANCY.
VERNA'S FAMILY HAD BEEN INVOLVED IN THE UNDERGROUND RAILROAD. THEY HAD A LEGACY ON THE SUSQUEHANNA. MY AUNT ONLY MARRIED INTO THAT.
I WISHED TO CREATE MY OWN LEGACY. VERNA AND I, TOGETHER.
IT WOULD NOT BE THAT SIMPLE.
Rail will take us there. It ices over the first week of December, so that will be our last opportunity. No one will follow us.

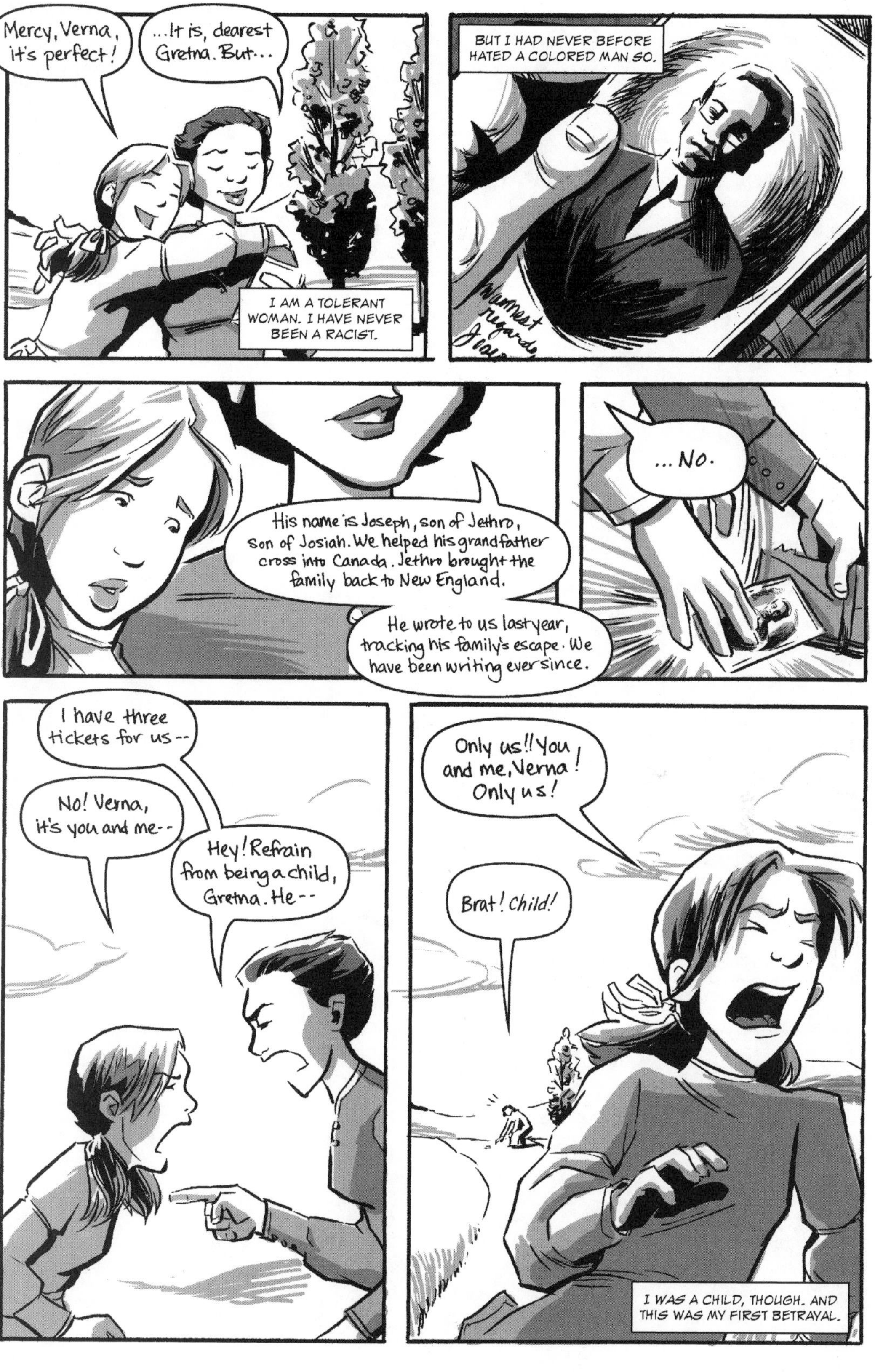

Mercy, Verna, it's perfect!
...It is, dearest Gretna. But...
I AM A TOLERANT WOMAN. I HAVE NEVER BEEN A RACIST.
BUT I HAD NEVER BEFORE HATED A COLORED MAN SO.
His name is Joseph, son of Jethro, son of Josiah. We helped his grandfather cross into Canada. Jethro brought the family back to New England.
He wrote to us last year, tracking his family's escape. We have been writing ever since.
...No.
I have three tickets for us--
No! Verna, it's you and me--
Hey! Refrain from being a child, Gretna. He--
Only us!! You and me, Verna! Only us!
Brat! Child!
I WAS A CHILD, THOUGH. AND THIS WAS MY FIRST BETRAYAL.

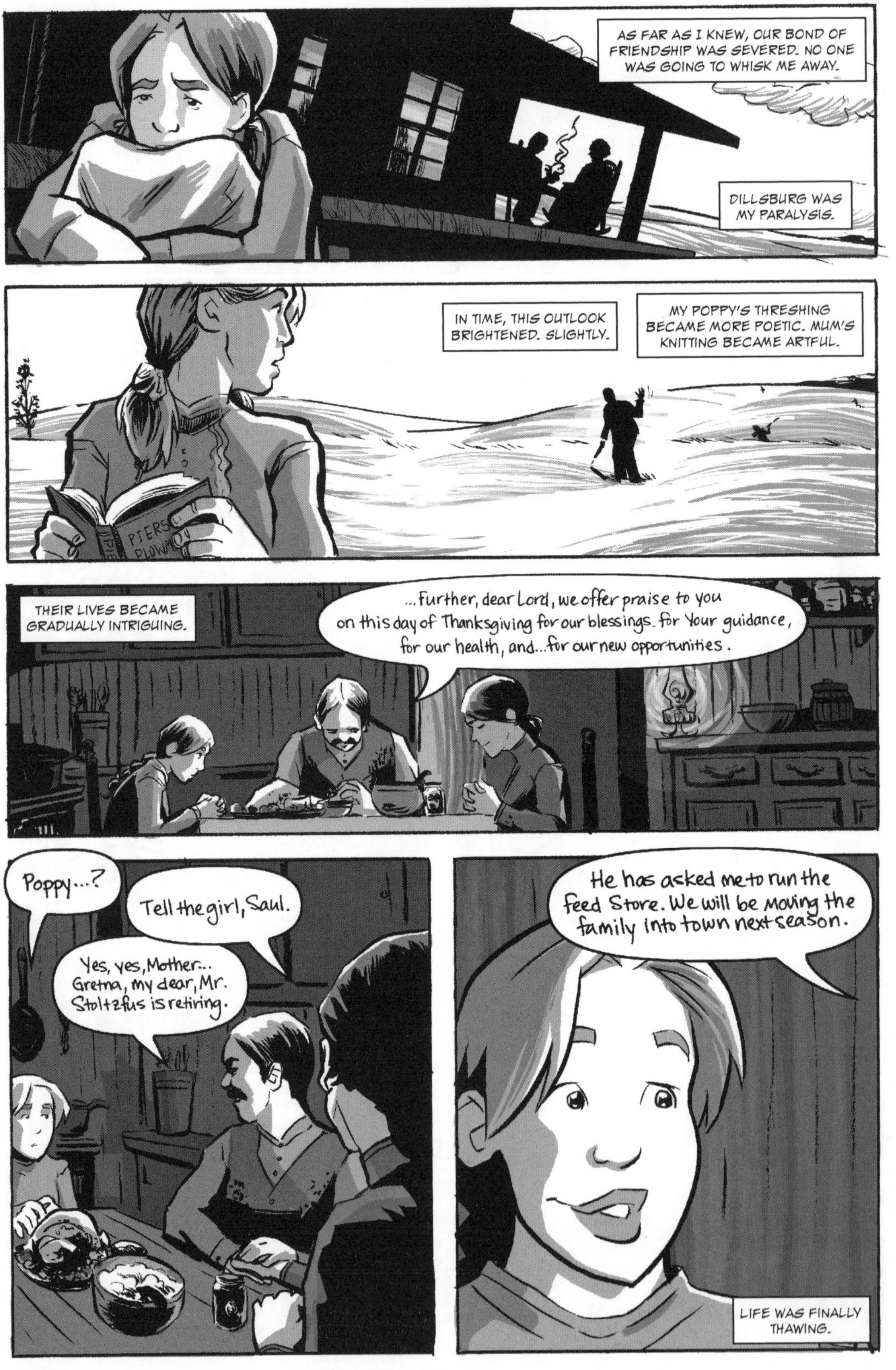
AS FAR AS I KNEW, OUR BOND OF FRIENDSHIP WAS SEVERED. NO ONE WAS GOING TO WHISK ME AWAY.
DILLSBURG WAS MY PARALYSIS.
IN TIME, THIS OUTLOOK BRIGHTENED. SLIGHTLY.
MY POPPY'S THRESHING BECAME MORE POETIC. MUM'S KNITTING BECAME ARTFUL.
PIERS PLOWM
THEIR LIVES BECAME GRADUALLY INTRIGUING.
...Further, dear Lord, we offer praise to you on this day of Thanksgiving for our blessings. for Your guidance, for our health, and...for our new opportunities.
Poppy...?
Tell the girl, Saul.
Yes, yes, Mother... Gretna, my dear, Mr. Stoltzfus is retiring.
He has asked me to run the feed Store. We will be moving the family into town next season.
LIFE WAS FINALLY THAWING.

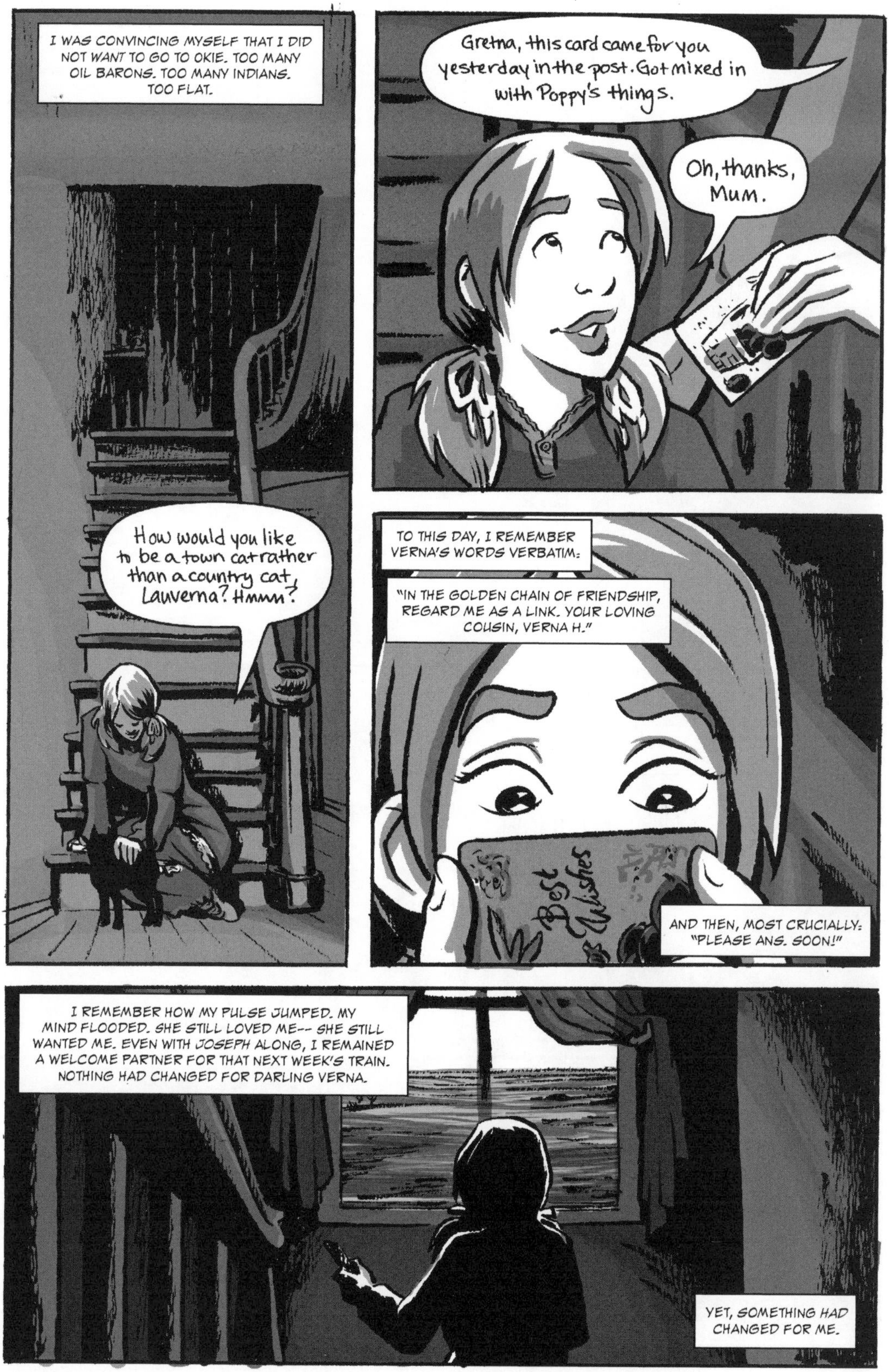
I WAS CONVINCING MYSELF THAT I DID NOT WANT TO GO TO OKIE. TOO MANY OIL BARONS. TOO MANY INDIANS. TOO FLAT.
Gretna, this card came for you yesterday in the post. Got mixed in with Poppy's things.
Oh, thanks, Mum.
How would you like to be a town cat rather than a country cat, Lauverna? Hmmm?
TO THIS DAY, I REMEMBER VERNA'S WORDS VERBATIM:
"IN THE GOLDEN CHAIN OF FRIENDSHIP, REGARD ME AS A LINK. YOUR LOVING COUSIN, VERNA H."
Best Wishes
AND THEN, MOST CRUCIALLY: "PLEASE ANS. SOON!"
I REMEMBER HOW MY PULSE JUMPED. MY MIND FLOODED. SHE STILL LOVED ME-- SHE STILL WANTED ME. EVEN WITH JOSEPH ALONG, I REMAINED A WELCOME PARTNER FOR THAT NEXT WEEK'S TRAIN. NOTHING HAD CHANGED FOR DARLING VERNA.
YET, SOMETHING HAD CHANGED FOR ME.

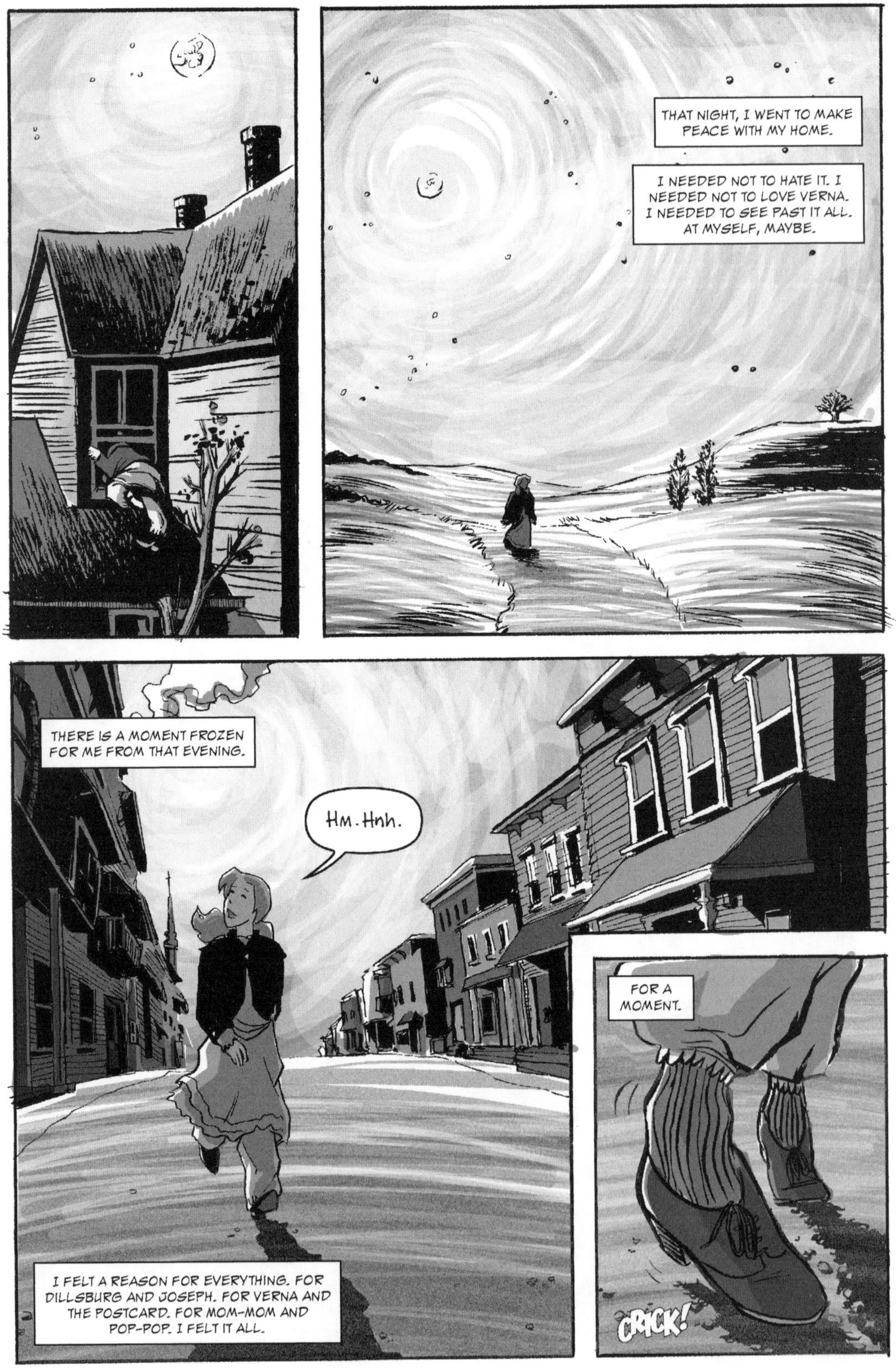
THAT NIGHT, I WENT TO MAKE PEACE WITH MY HOME.
I NEEDED NOT TO HATE IT. I NEEDED NOT TO LOVE VERNA. I NEEDED TO SEE PAST IT ALL. AT MYSELF, MAYBE.
THERE IS A MOMENT FROZEN FOR ME FROM THAT EVENING.
Hm. Hnh.
I FELT A REASON FOR EVERYTHING. FOR DILLSBURG AND JOSEPH. FOR VERNA AND THE POSTCARD. FOR MOM-MOM AND POP-POP. I FELT IT ALL.
FOR A MOMENT.
CRICK!

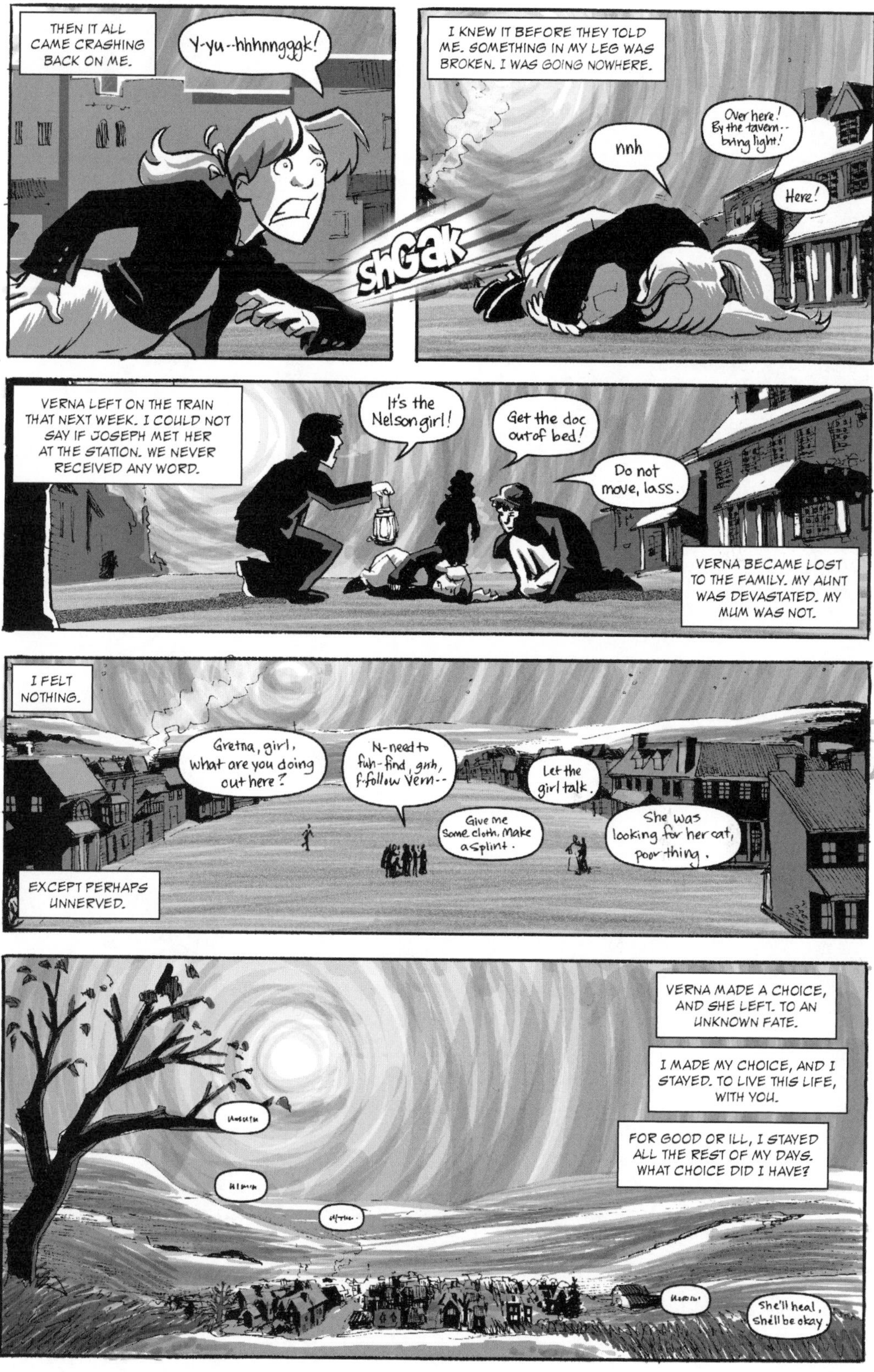
THEN IT ALL CAME CRASHING BACK ON ME.
Y-yu--hhhnngggk!
shGak
I KNEW IT BEFORE THEY TOLD ME. SOMETHING IN MY LEG WAS BROKEN. I WAS GOING NOWHERE.
nnh
Over here! By the tavern-- bring light!
Here!
VERNA LEFT ON THE TRAIN THAT NEXT WEEK. I COULD NOT SAY IF JOSEPH MET HER AT THE STATION. WE NEVER RECEIVED ANY WORD.
It's the Nelson girl!
Get the doc out of bed!
Do not move, lass.
VERNA BECAME LOST TO THE FAMILY. MY AUNT WAS DEVASTATED. MY MUM WAS NOT.
I FELT NOTHING.
Gretna, girl, what are you doing out here?
N-need to fuh-find, gnh, f-follow Vern--
Let the girl talk.
Give me some cloth. Make a splint.
She was looking for her cat, poor thing.
EXCEPT PERHAPS UNNERVED.
VERNA MADE A CHOICE, AND SHE LEFT. TO AN UNKNOWN FATE.
I MADE MY CHOICE, AND I STAYED. TO LIVE THIS LIFE, WITH YOU.
FOR GOOD OR ILL, I STAYED ALL THE REST OF MY DAYS. WHAT CHOICE DID I HAVE?
She'll heal, she'll be okay.

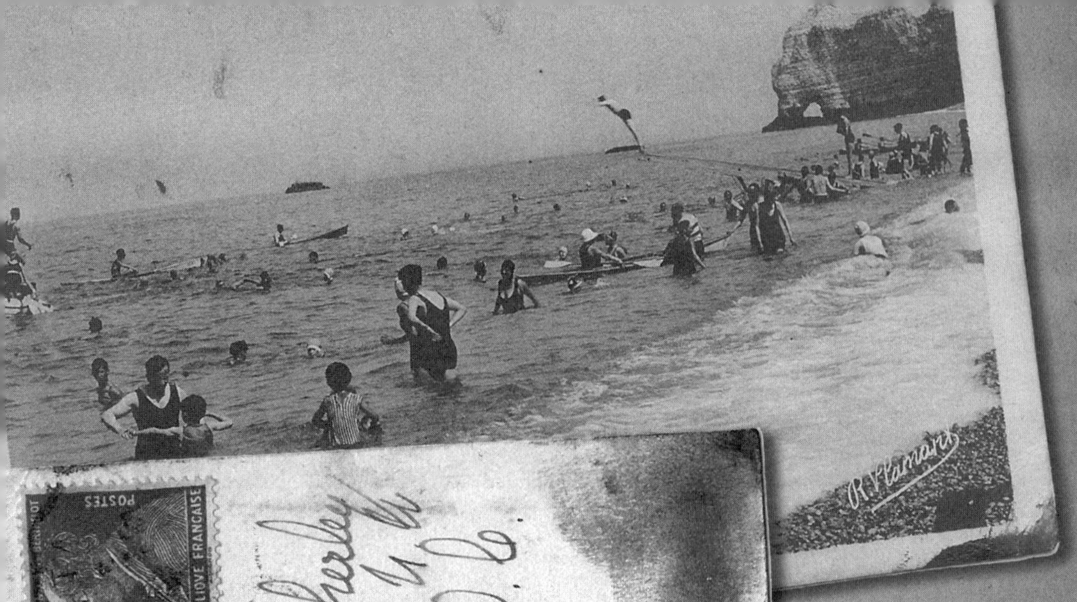
R. V. Flamant

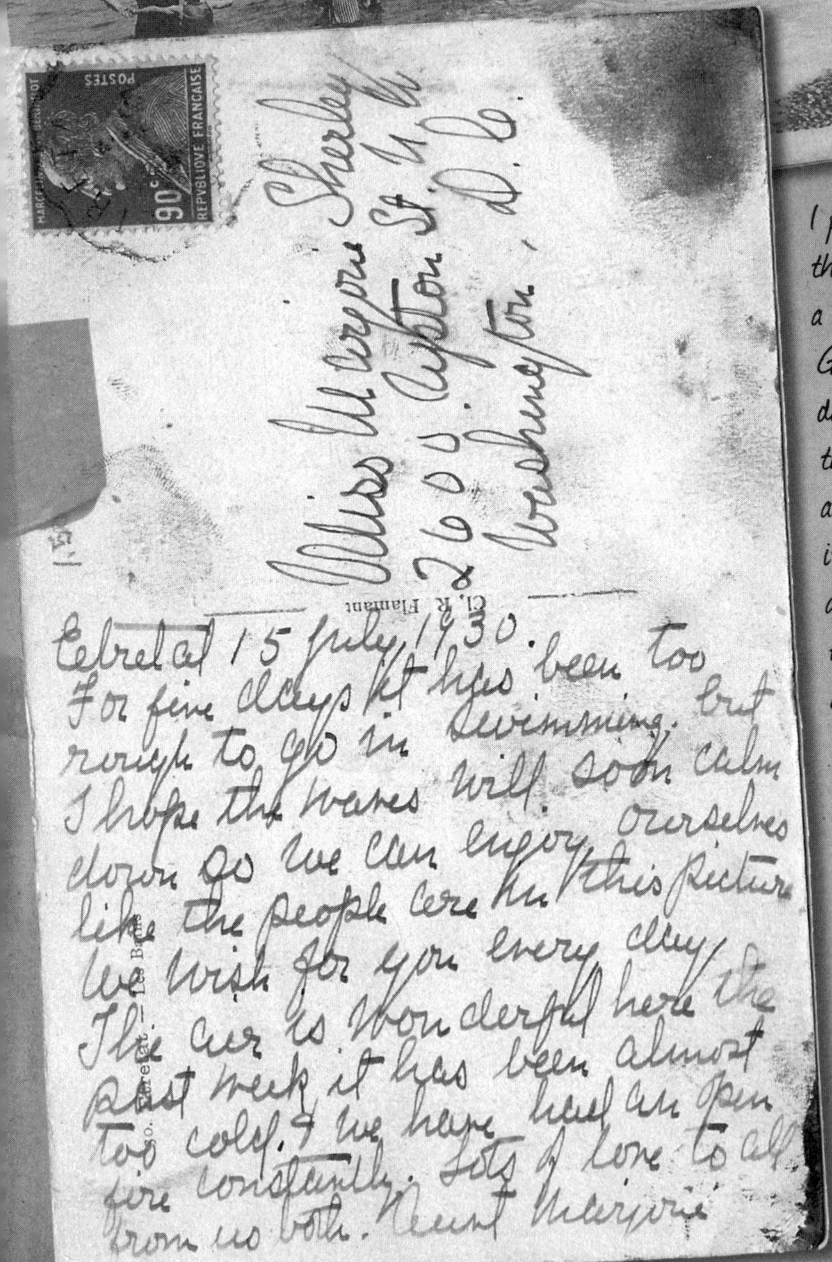
REPUBLIQUE FRANCAISE
POSTES
90c
Miss M. Gregory Sherley
1600 Upton St N.W.
Washington, D.C.
Cl. R. Flamant
Etretat — Les Bains
Etretat 15 July 1930.
For five days it has been too
rough to go in swimming. but
I hope the waves will soon calm
down so we can enjoy ourselves
like the people are in this picture.
We wish for you every day. The
The air is wonderful here the
past week it has been almost
too cold. & we have had an open
fire constantly. Lots of love to all
from us both. Aunt Marjorie

I purchased this postcard at a flea market in Georgetown for the desperation I felt in the words. Joshua and Micah realized it was written by an American in France at the start of the Great Depression, complaining about the weather, and created a story that shows how a postcard can represent an attempt to mask the grievances that lie beneath.

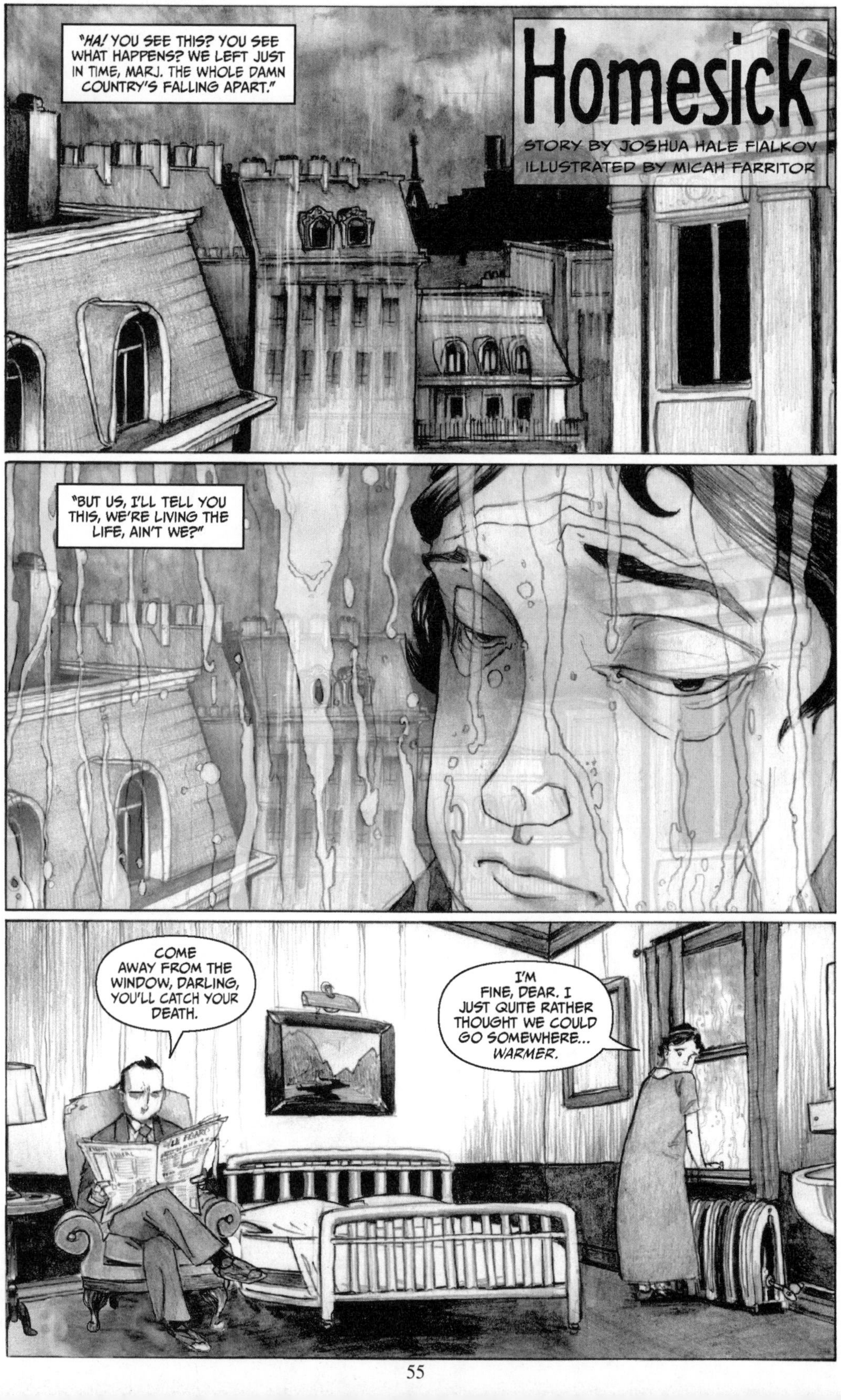
Homesick
STORY BY JOSHUA HALE FIALKOV
ILLUSTRATED BY MICAH FARRITOR
"HA! YOU SEE THIS? YOU SEE WHAT HAPPENS? WE LEFT JUST IN TIME, MARJ. THE WHOLE DAMN COUNTRY'S FALLING APART."
"BUT US, I'LL TELL YOU THIS, WE'RE LIVING THE LIFE, AIN'T WE?"
COME AWAY FROM THE WINDOW, DARLING, YOU'LL CATCH YOUR DEATH.
I'M FINE, DEAR. I JUST QUITE RATHER THOUGHT WE COULD GO SOMEWHERE... WARMER.

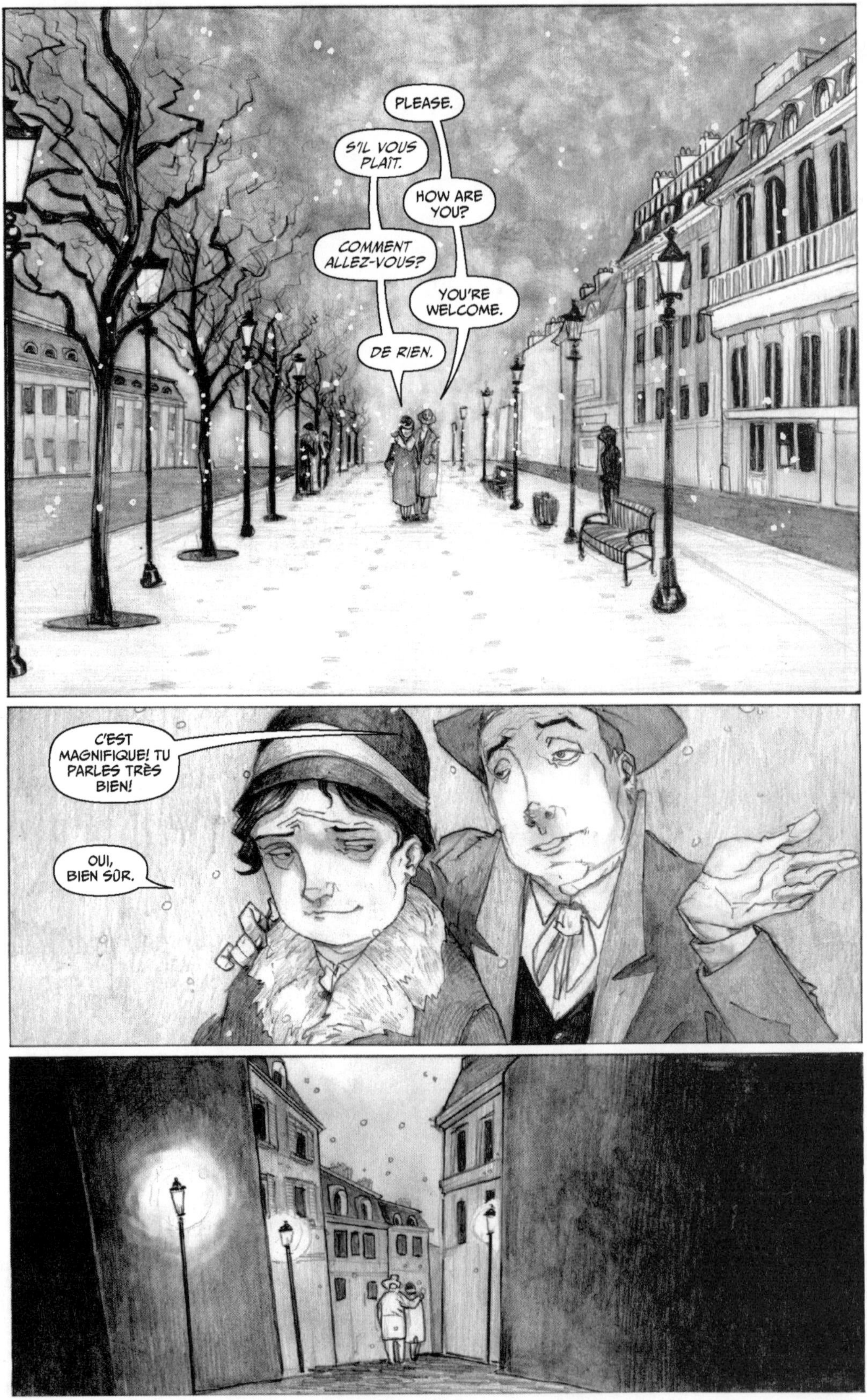
PLEASE.
S'IL VOUS PLAÎT.
HOW ARE YOU?
COMMENT ALLEZ-VOUS?
YOU'RE WELCOME.
DE RIEN.
C'EST MAGNIFIQUE! TU PARLES TRÈS BIEN!
OUI, BIEN SÛR.

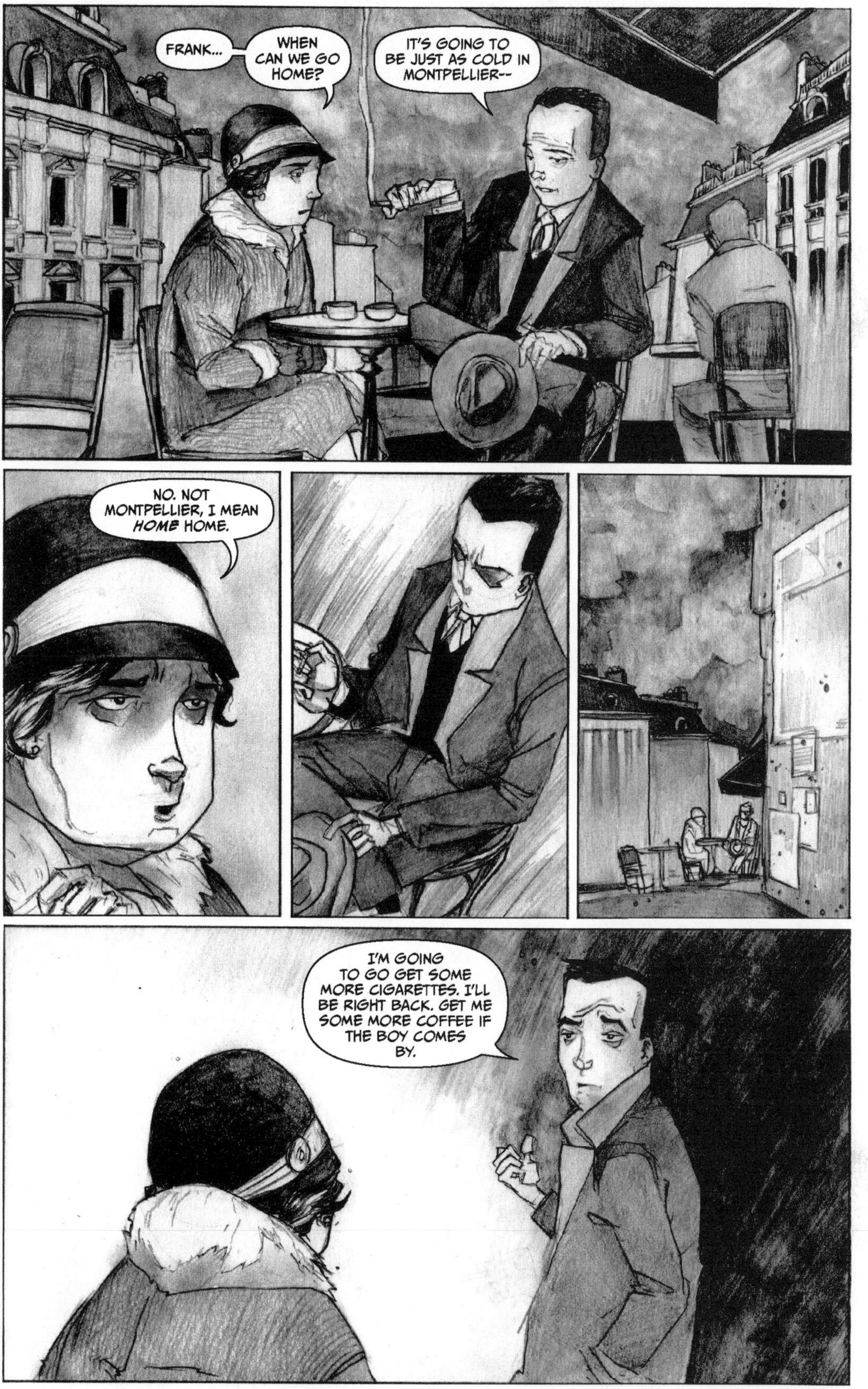
FRANK...
WHEN CAN WE GO HOME?
IT'S GOING TO BE JUST AS COLD IN MONTPELLIER--
NO. NOT MONTPELLIER, I MEAN *HOME* HOME.
I'M GOING TO GO GET SOME MORE CIGARETTES. I'LL BE RIGHT BACK. GET ME SOME MORE COFFEE IF THE BOY COMES BY.

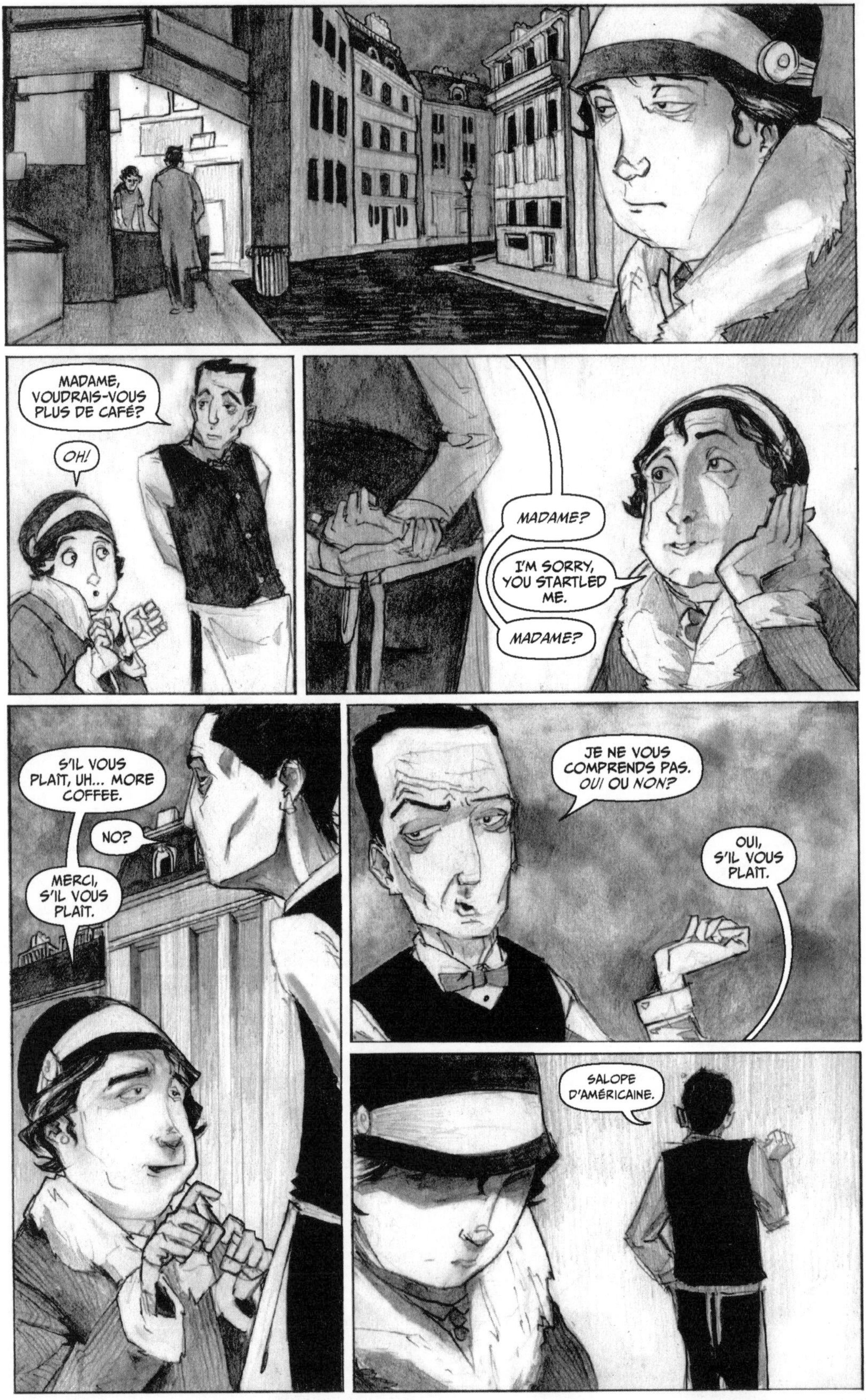
MADAME, VOUDRAIS-VOUS PLUS DE CAFÉ?
OH!
MADAME?
I'M SORRY, YOU STARTLED ME.
MADAME?
S'IL VOUS PLAIT, UH... MORE COFFEE.
NO?
MERCI, S'IL VOUS PLAIT.
JE NE VOUS COMPRENDS PAS. OUI OU NON?
OUI, S'IL VOUS PLAIT.
SALOPE D'AMÉRICAINE.

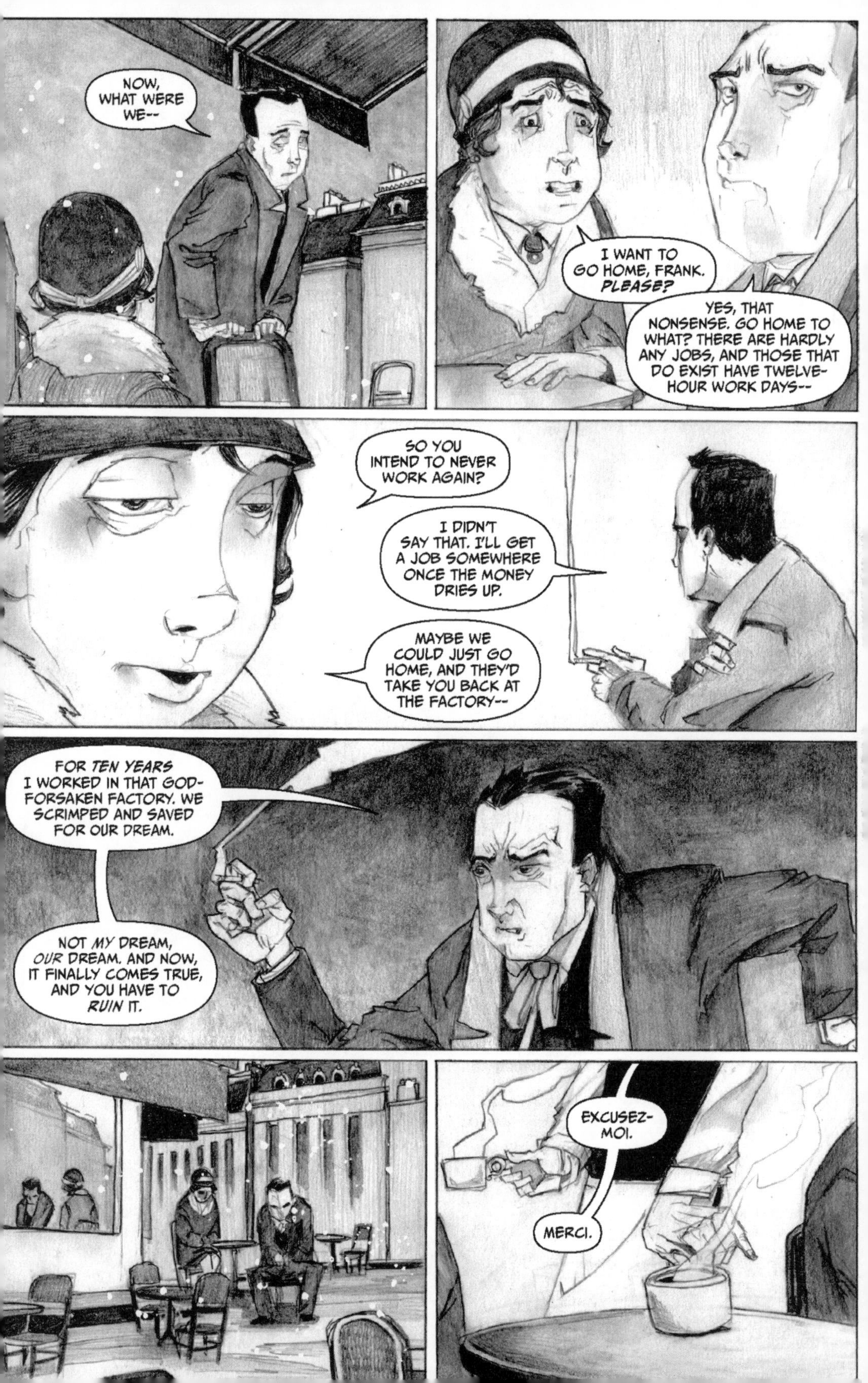
NOW, WHAT WERE WE--
I WANT TO GO HOME, FRANK. *PLEASE?*
YES, THAT NONSENSE. GO HOME TO WHAT? THERE ARE HARDLY ANY JOBS, AND THOSE THAT DO EXIST HAVE TWELVE-HOUR WORK DAYS--
SO YOU INTEND TO NEVER WORK AGAIN?
I DIDN'T SAY THAT. I'LL GET A JOB SOMEWHERE ONCE THE MONEY DRIES UP.
MAYBE WE COULD JUST GO HOME, AND THEY'D TAKE YOU BACK AT THE FACTORY--
FOR *TEN YEARS* I WORKED IN THAT GOD-FORSAKEN FACTORY. WE SCRIMPED AND SAVED FOR OUR DREAM.
NOT *MY* DREAM, *OUR* DREAM. AND NOW, IT FINALLY COMES TRUE, AND YOU HAVE TO *RUIN* IT.
EXCUSEZ-MOI.
MERCI.

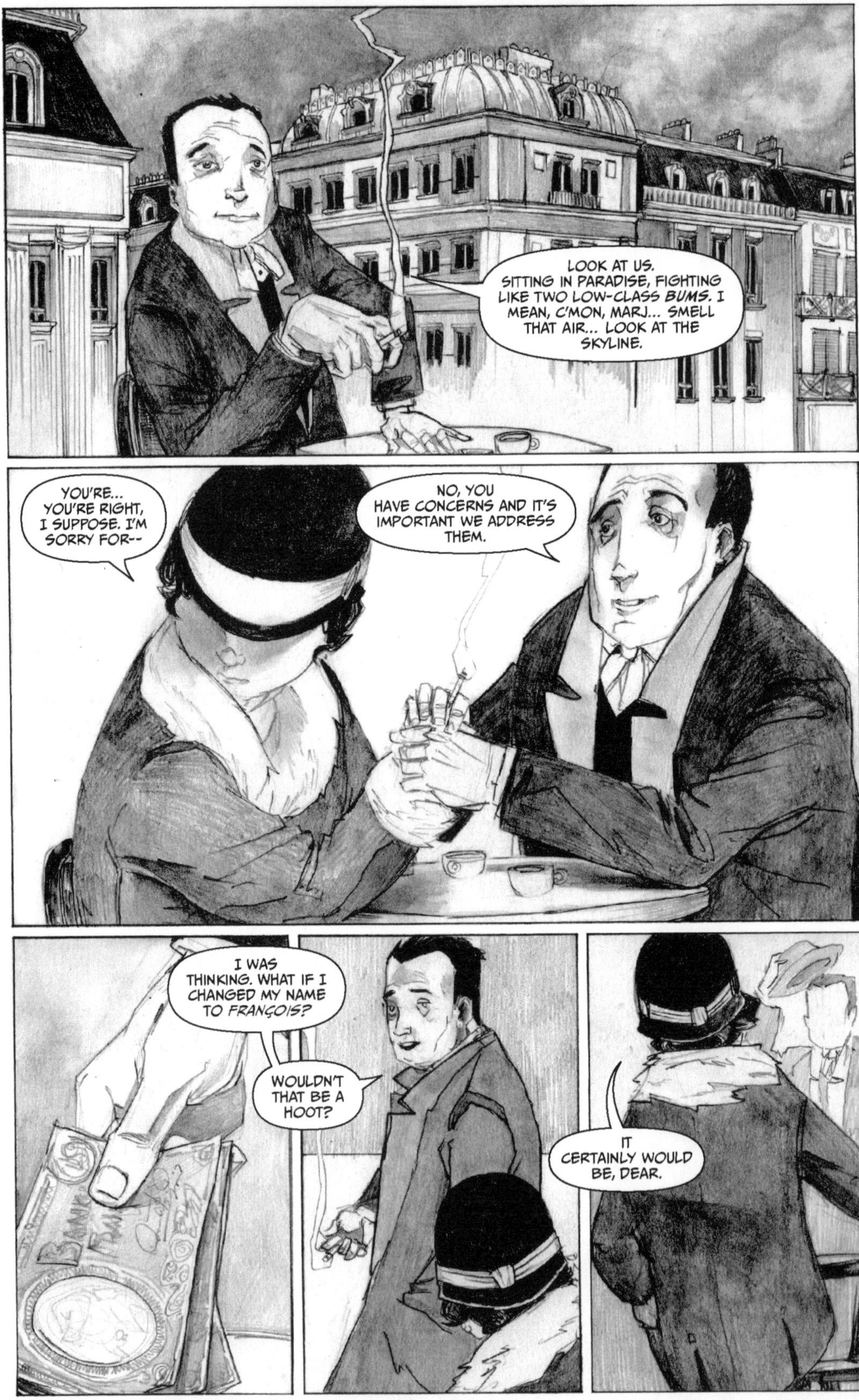
LOOK AT US. SITTING IN PARADISE, FIGHTING LIKE TWO LOW-CLASS *BUMS*. I MEAN, C'MON, MARJ... SMELL THAT AIR... LOOK AT THE SKYLINE.
YOU'RE... YOU'RE RIGHT, I SUPPOSE. I'M SORRY FOR--
NO, YOU HAVE CONCERNS AND IT'S IMPORTANT WE ADDRESS THEM.
I WAS THINKING. WHAT IF I CHANGED MY NAME TO *FRANÇOIS*?
WOULDN'T THAT BE A HOOT?
IT CERTAINLY WOULD BE, DEAR.

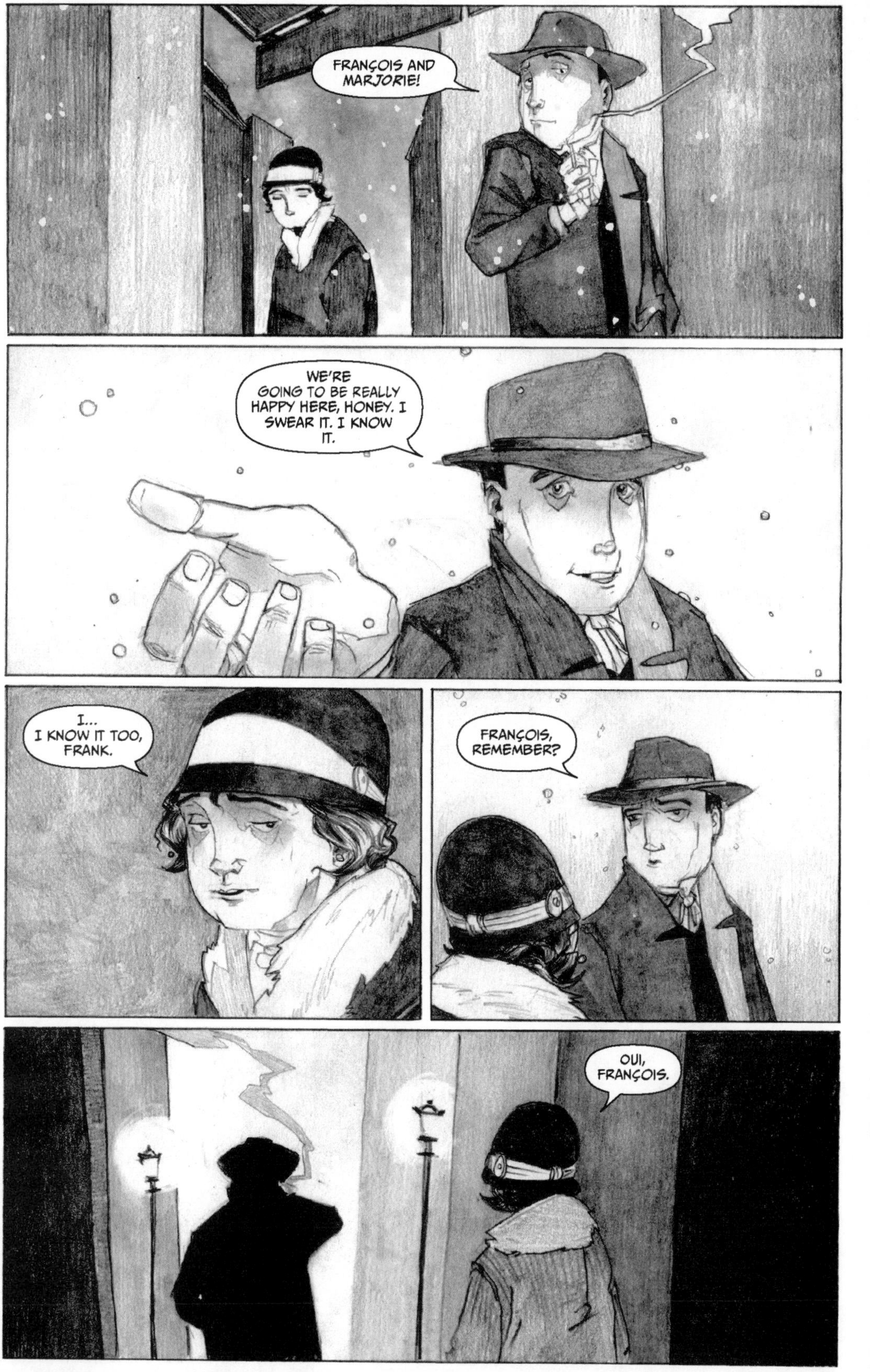
FRANÇOIS AND MARJORIE!
WE'RE GOING TO BE REALLY HAPPY HERE, HONEY. I SWEAR IT. I KNOW IT.
I... I KNOW IT TOO, FRANK.
FRANÇOIS, REMEMBER?
OUI, FRANÇOIS.

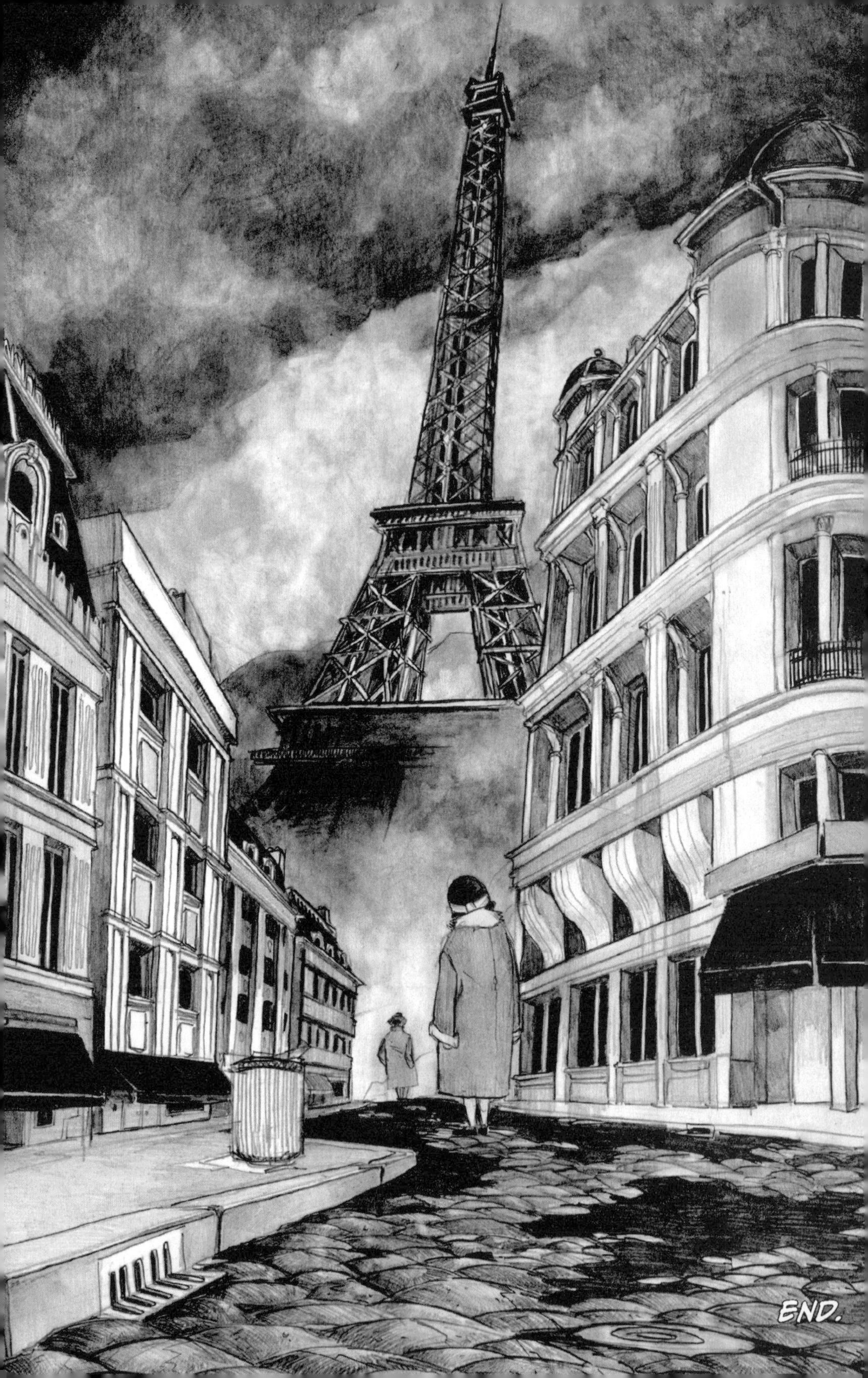
END.

James requested this postcard from the many samples I showed him. I was curious to see what he had planned since to me this card was really nothing more than an example of how postcards were the turn-of-the-century equivalent of modern-day text messages. James saw more than that; he and Drew show how a postcard can represent the loss of innocence.

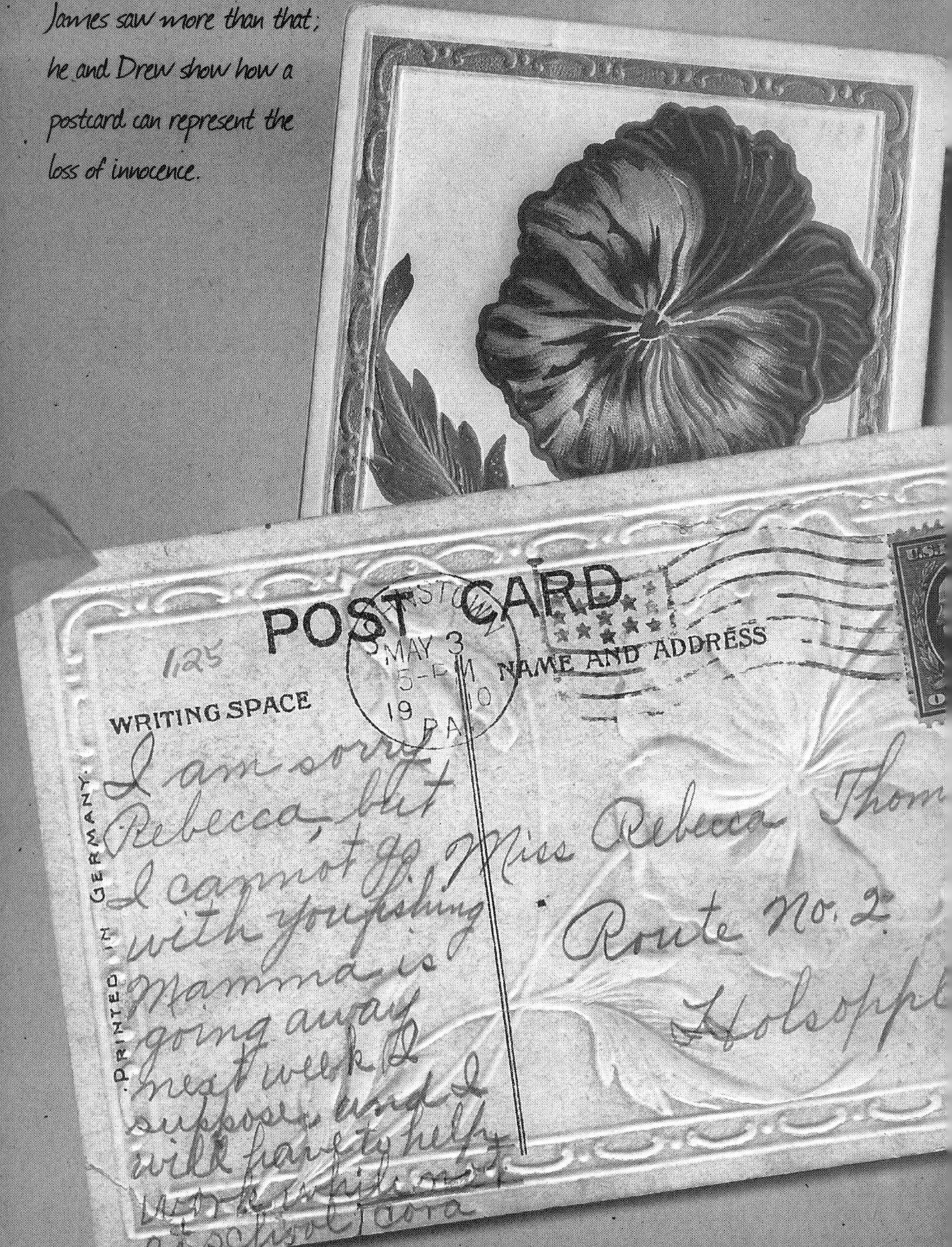
POST CARD
NAME AND ADDRESS
WRITING SPACE
PRINTED IN GERMANY
1.25
MAY 3
5-PM
1910
PA
I am sorry
Rebecca, but
I cannot go
with you fishing
Mamma is
going away
Miss Rebecca Thom
Route No. 2
Holsopp

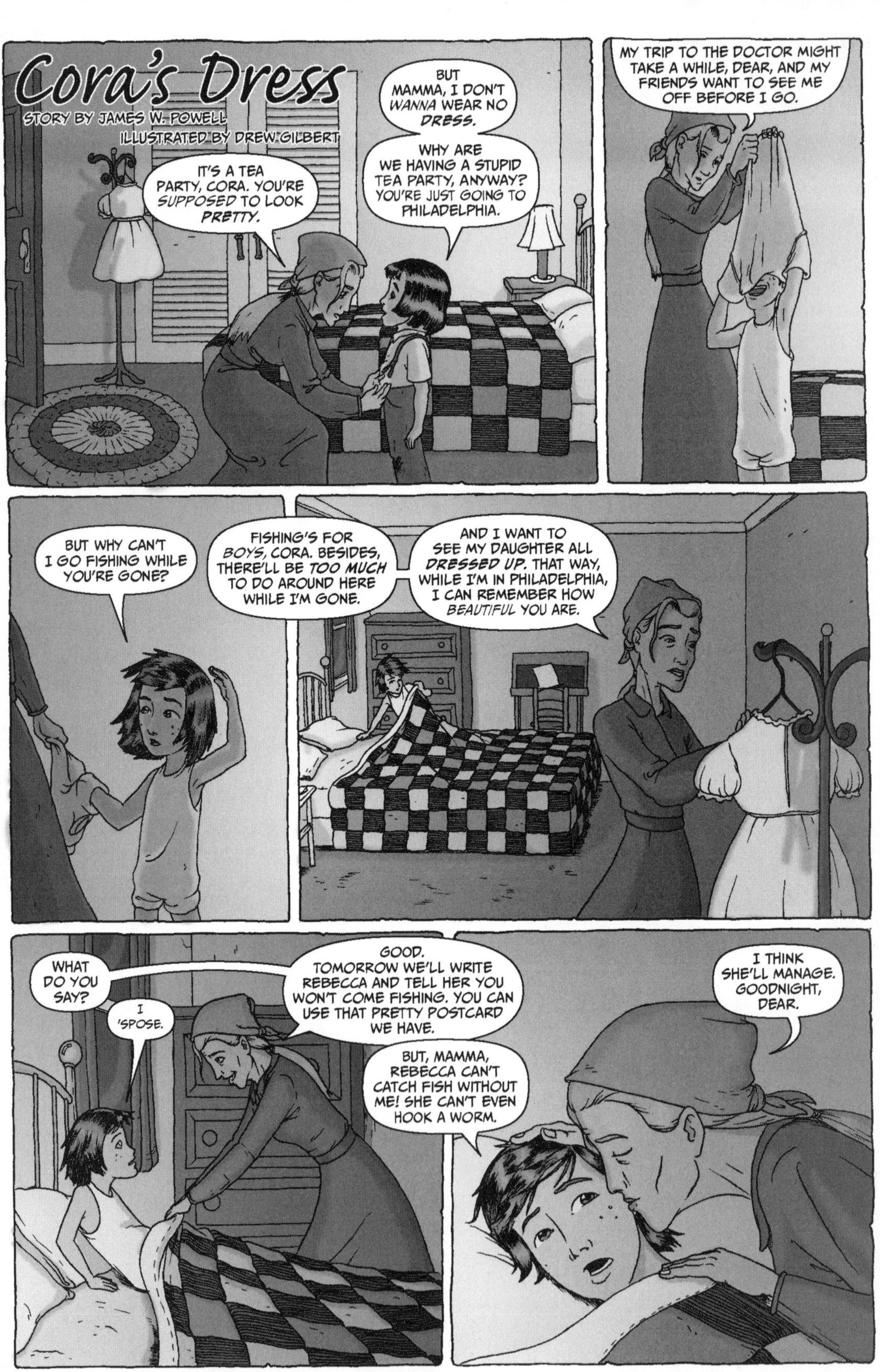

Cora's Dress
STORY BY JAMES W. POWELL
ILLUSTRATED BY DREW GILBERT
IT'S A TEA PARTY, CORA. YOU'RE SUPPOSED TO LOOK PRETTY.
BUT MAMMA, I DON'T WANNA WEAR NO DRESS.
WHY ARE WE HAVING A STUPID TEA PARTY, ANYWAY? YOU'RE JUST GOING TO PHILADELPHIA.
MY TRIP TO THE DOCTOR MIGHT TAKE A WHILE, DEAR, AND MY FRIENDS WANT TO SEE ME OFF BEFORE I GO.
BUT WHY CAN'T I GO FISHING WHILE YOU'RE GONE?
FISHING'S FOR BOYS, CORA. BESIDES, THERE'LL BE TOO MUCH TO DO AROUND HERE WHILE I'M GONE.
AND I WANT TO SEE MY DAUGHTER ALL DRESSED UP. THAT WAY, WHILE I'M IN PHILADELPHIA, I CAN REMEMBER HOW BEAUTIFUL YOU ARE.
WHAT DO YOU SAY?
I 'SPOSE.
GOOD. TOMORROW WE'LL WRITE REBECCA AND TELL HER YOU WON'T COME FISHING. YOU CAN USE THAT PRETTY POSTCARD WE HAVE.
BUT, MAMMA, REBECCA CAN'T CATCH FISH WITHOUT ME! SHE CAN'T EVEN HOOK A WORM.
I THINK SHE'LL MANAGE. GOODNIGHT, DEAR.

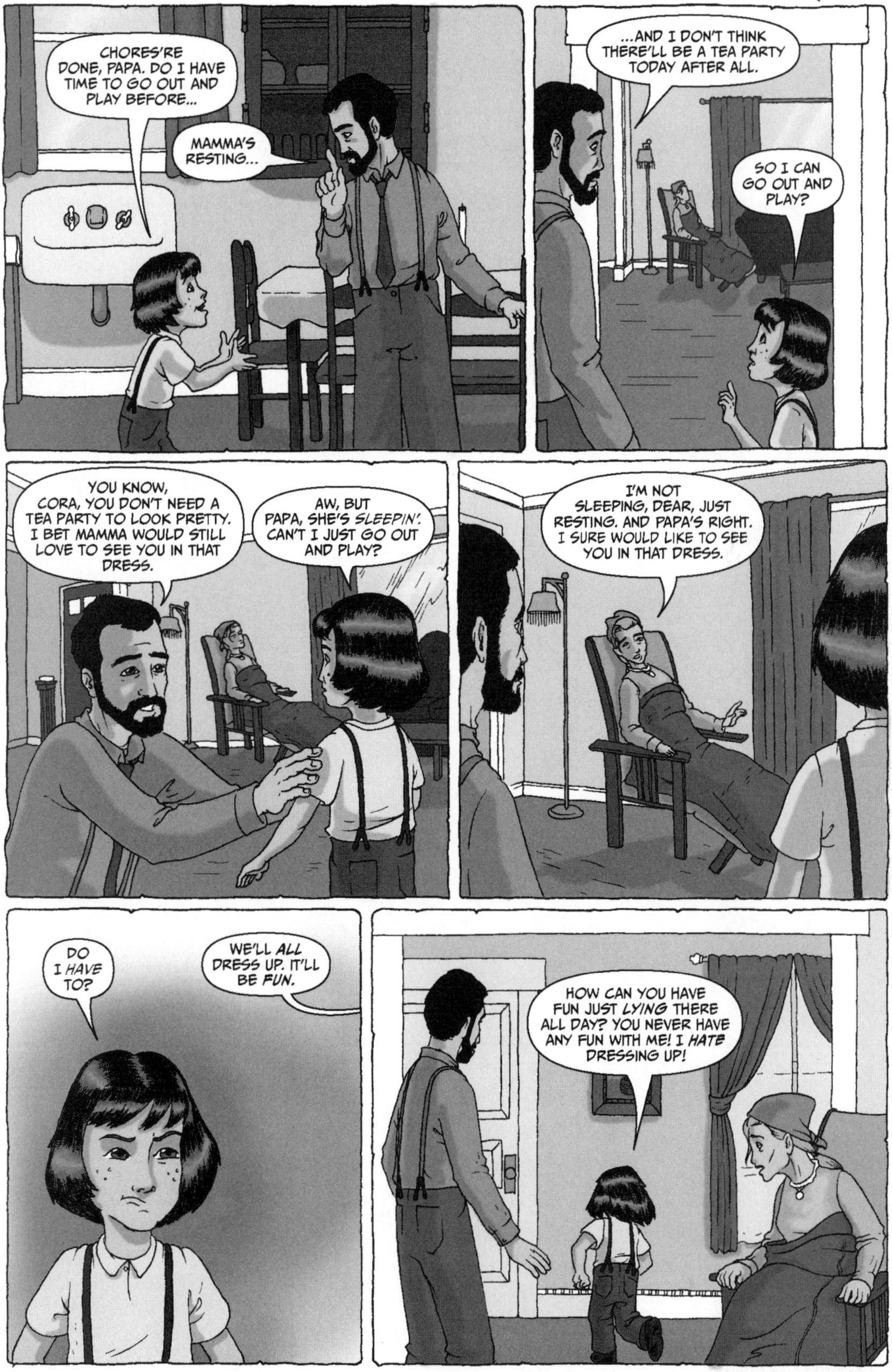
CHORES'RE DONE, PAPA. DO I HAVE TIME TO GO OUT AND PLAY BEFORE...
MAMMA'S RESTING...
...AND I DON'T THINK THERE'LL BE A TEA PARTY TODAY AFTER ALL.
SO I CAN GO OUT AND PLAY?
YOU KNOW, CORA, YOU DON'T NEED A TEA PARTY TO LOOK PRETTY. I BET MAMMA WOULD STILL LOVE TO SEE YOU IN THAT DRESS.
AW, BUT PAPA, SHE'S *SLEEPIN'.* CAN'T I JUST GO OUT AND PLAY?
I'M NOT SLEEPING, DEAR, JUST RESTING. AND PAPA'S RIGHT. I SURE WOULD LIKE TO SEE YOU IN THAT DRESS.
DO I *HAVE* TO?
WE'LL *ALL* DRESS UP. IT'LL BE *FUN.*
HOW CAN YOU HAVE FUN JUST *LYING* THERE ALL DAY? YOU NEVER HAVE ANY FUN WITH ME! I *HATE* DRESSING UP!

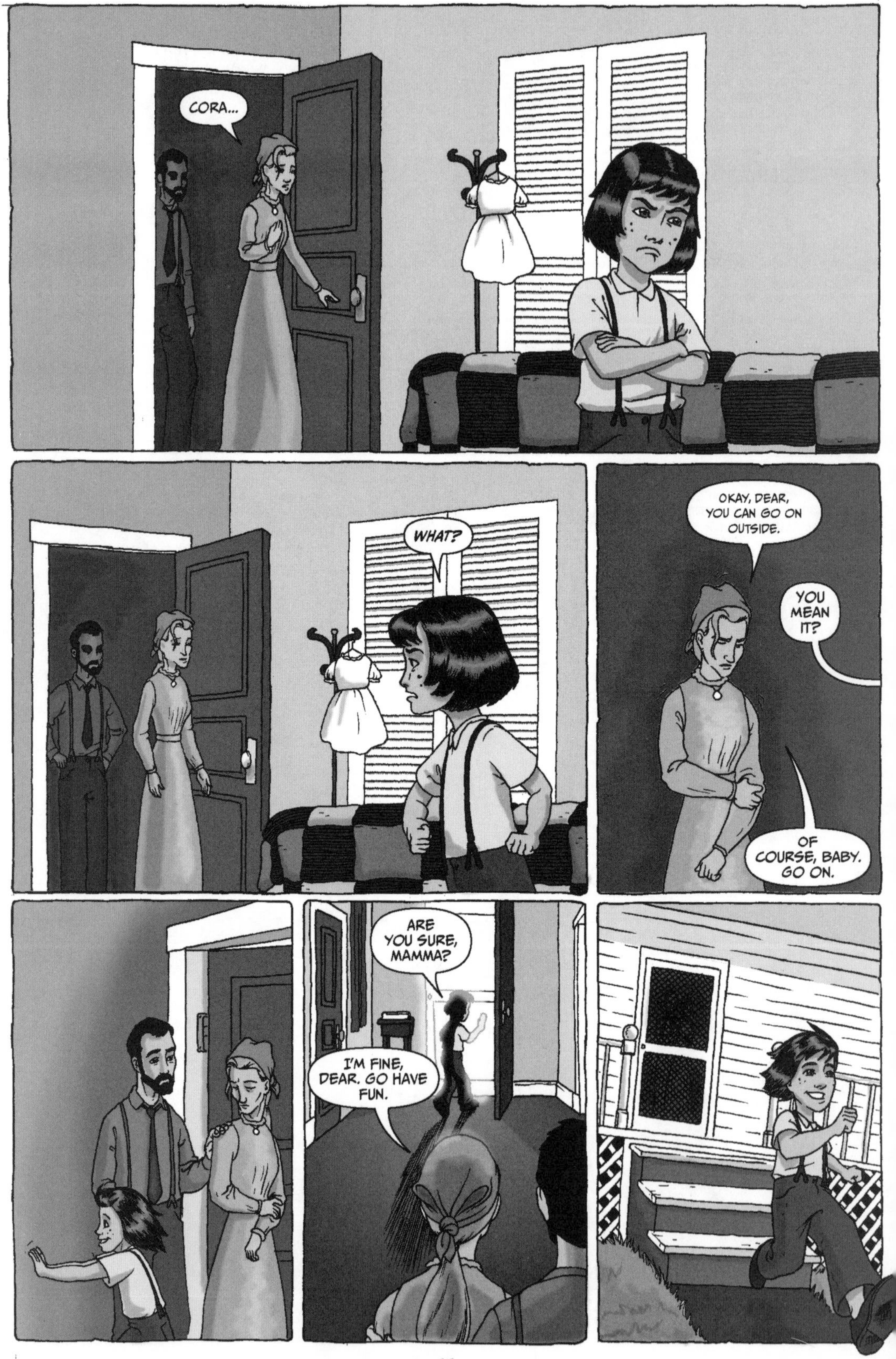
CORA...
WHAT?
OKAY, DEAR, YOU CAN GO ON OUTSIDE.
YOU MEAN IT?
OF COURSE, BABY. GO ON.
ARE YOU SURE, MAMMA?
I'M FINE, DEAR. GO HAVE FUN.

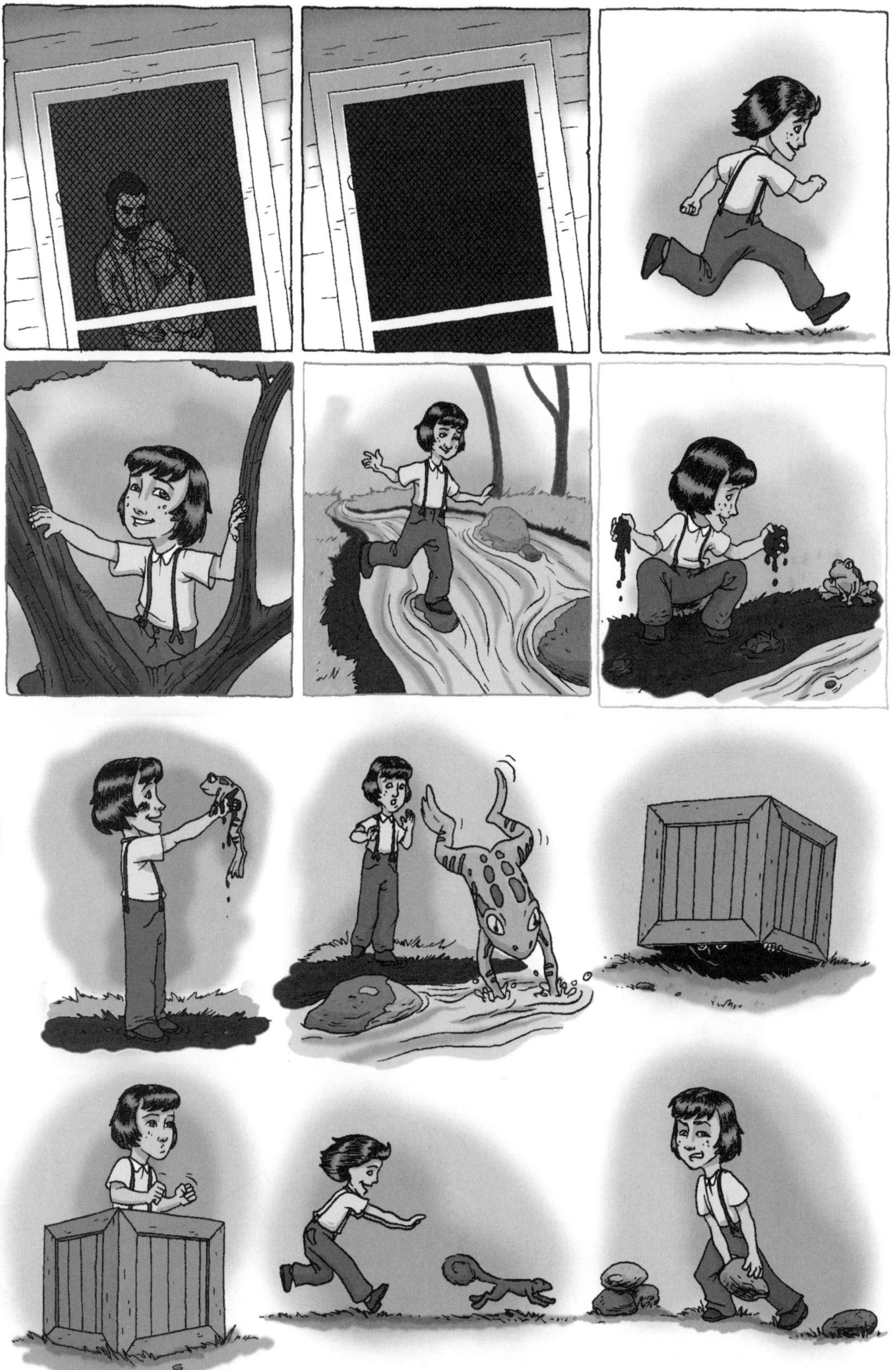

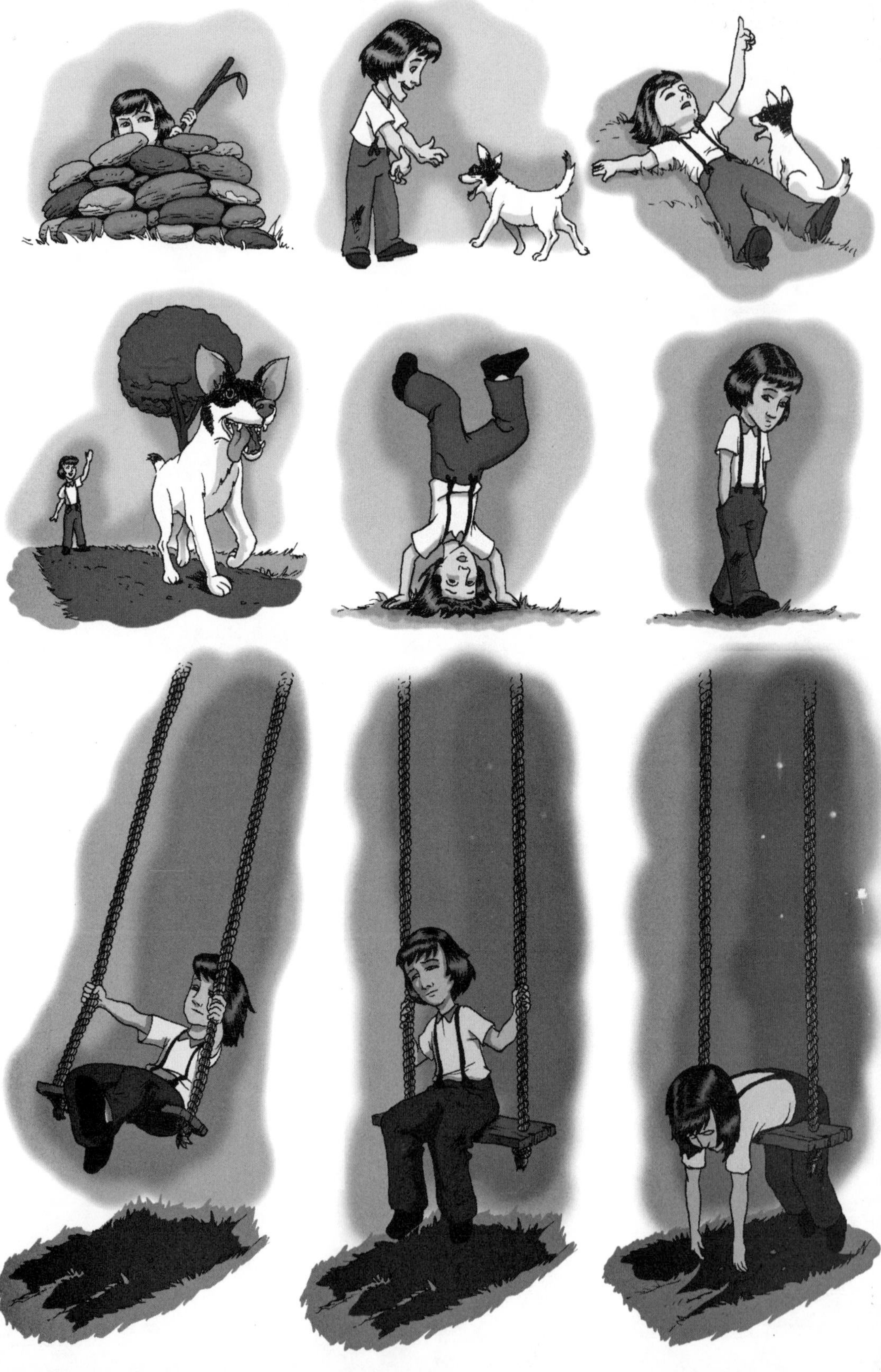

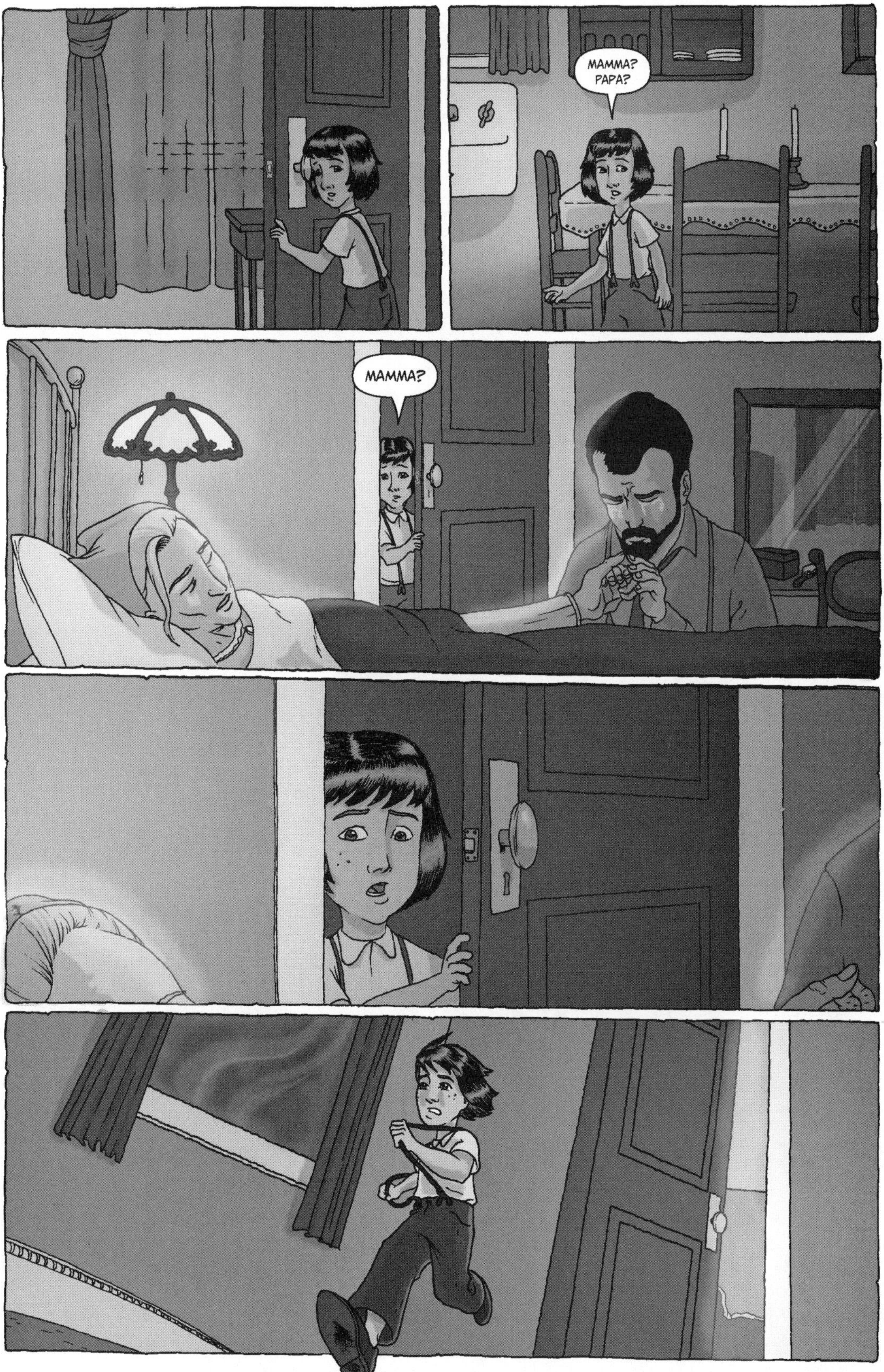
MAMMA?
PAPA?
MAMMA?

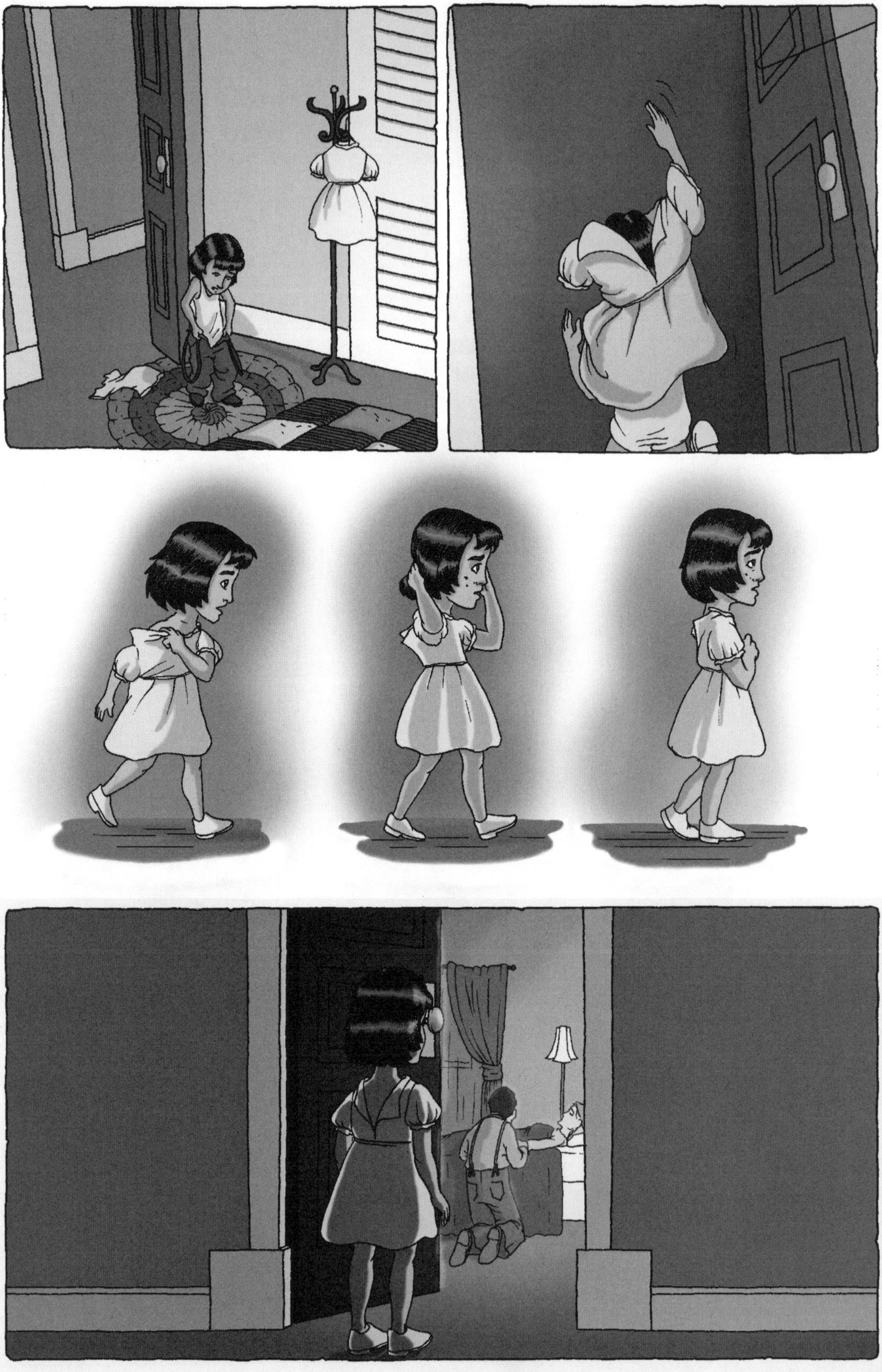

"Someone from Adams Co told the girls that you married a man who had a boy 12 yrs. old..." Scandalous. I gave this card to Phil expecting a story of gossip and hearsay. Instead he shows us how a postcard can mark a turning point, a moment of desperation with unintended consequences that resonates over the course of a lifetime.

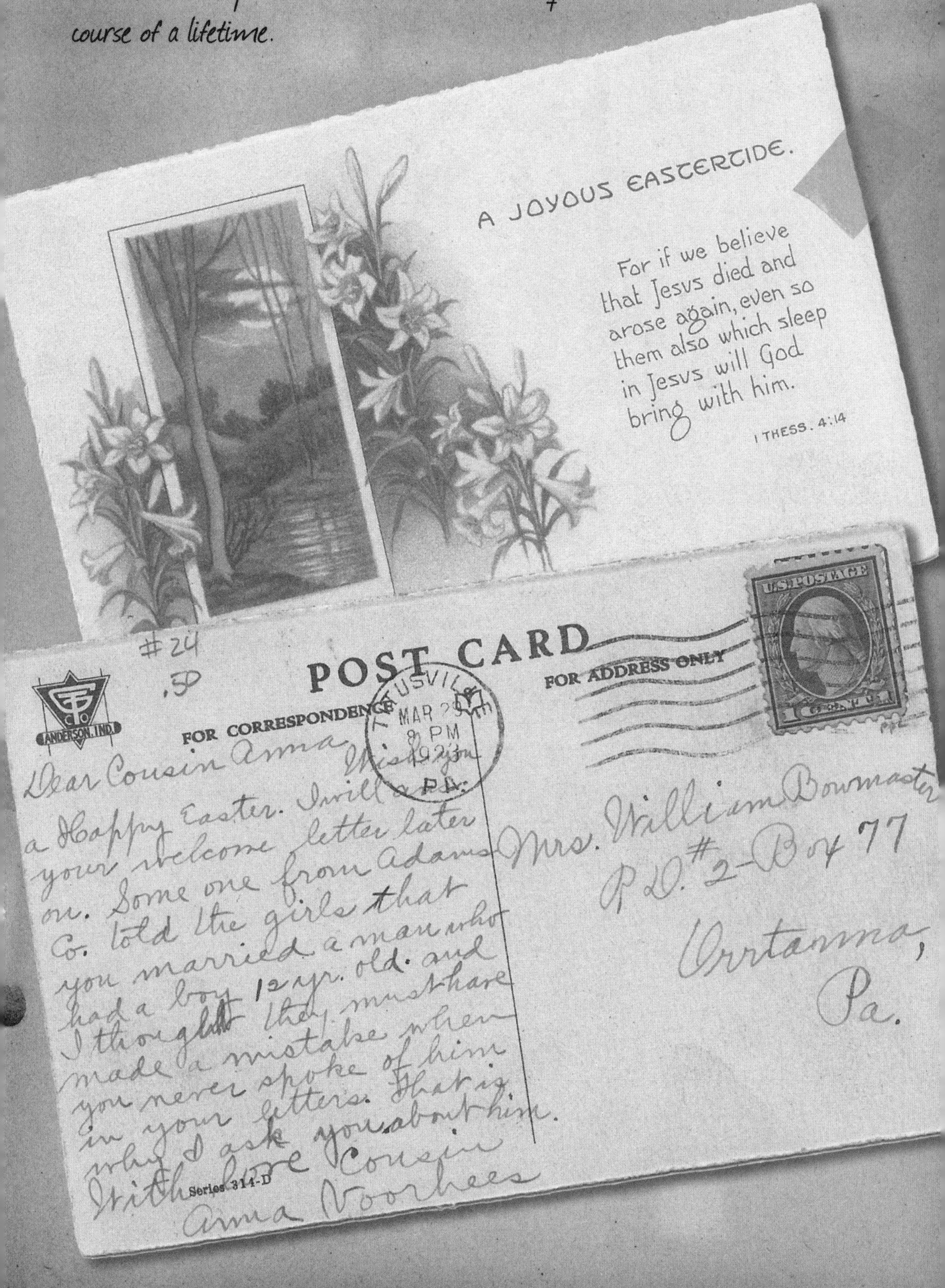

A JOYOUS EASTERTIDE.
For if we believe that Jesus died and arose again, even so them also which sleep in Jesus will God bring with him.
I THESS. 4:14
#24
.50
POST CARD
FOR CORRESPONDENCE
FOR ADDRESS ONLY
ANDERSON, IND.
U.S. POSTAGE
MAR 29
8 PM
PA.
Dear Cousin Anna,
Wish you
a Happy Easter. I will answer
your welcome letter later
on. Some one from Adams
Co. told the girls that
you married a man who
had a boy 12 yr. old. and
I thought they must have
made a mistake when
you never spoke of him
in your letters. That is
why I ask you about him.
With love Cousin
Anna Voorhees
Series 314-D
Mrs. William Bowmaster
R.D. #2 - Box 77
Orrtanna,
Pa.

A Joyous Eastertide

Story and Illustration by

Phillip Hester

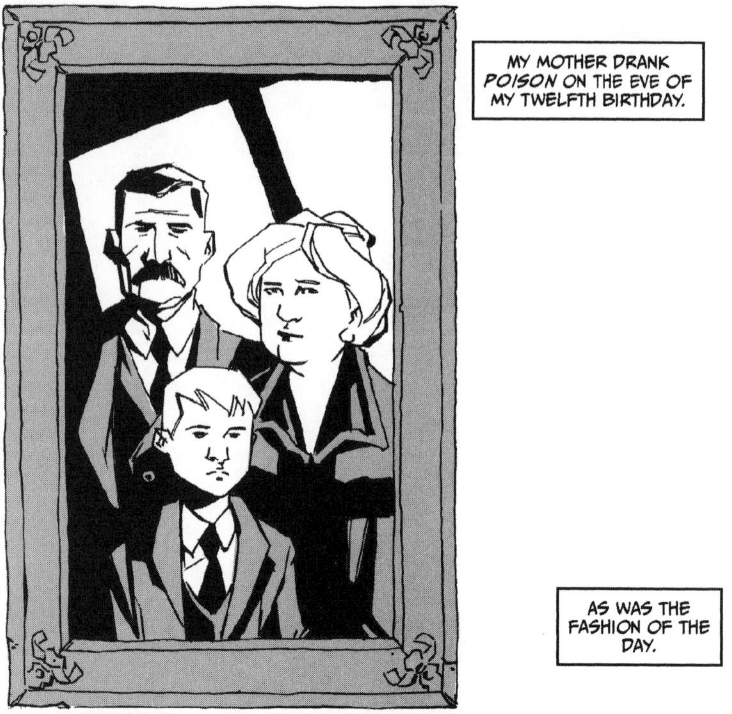

MY MOTHER DRANK POISON ON THE EVE OF MY TWELFTH BIRTHDAY.
AS WAS THE FASHION OF THE DAY.

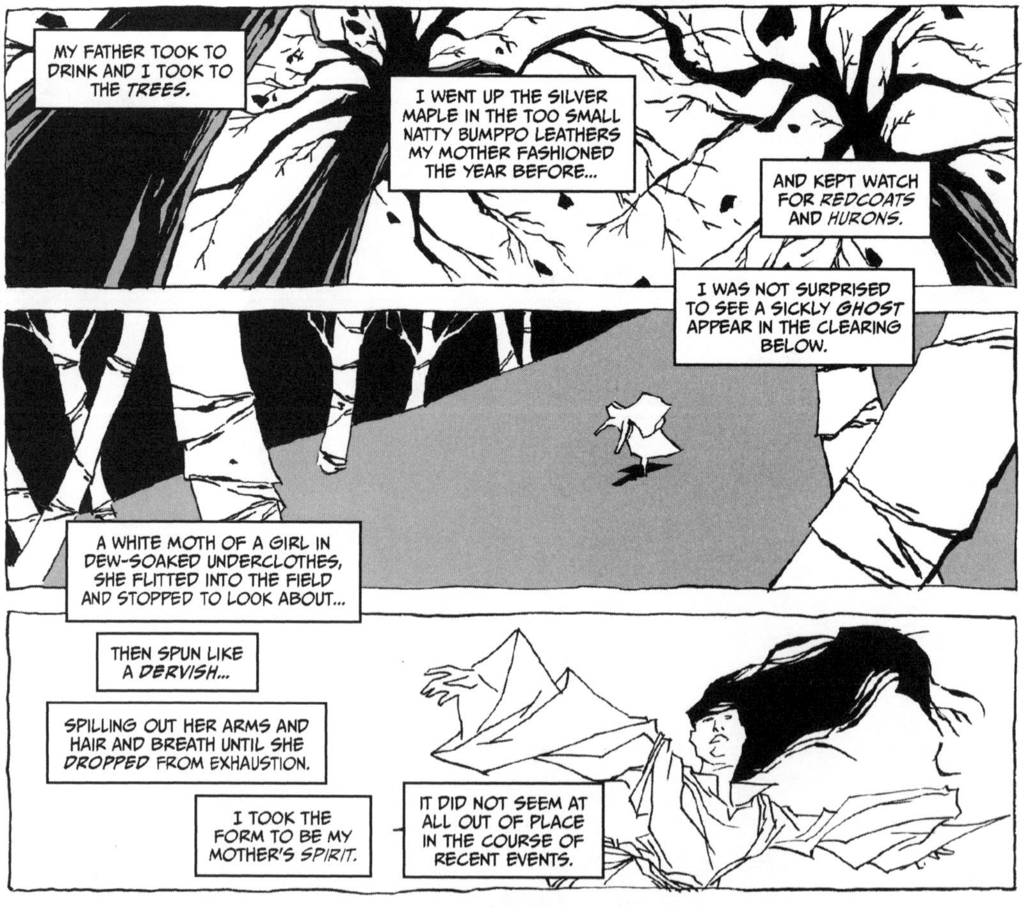

MY FATHER TOOK TO DRINK AND I TOOK TO THE TREES.
I WENT UP THE SILVER MAPLE IN THE TOO SMALL NATTY BUMPPO LEATHERS MY MOTHER FASHIONED THE YEAR BEFORE...
AND KEPT WATCH FOR REDCOATS AND HURONS.
I WAS NOT SURPRISED TO SEE A SICKLY GHOST APPEAR IN THE CLEARING BELOW.
A WHITE MOTH OF A GIRL IN DEW-SOAKED UNDERCLOTHES, SHE FLITTED INTO THE FIELD AND STOPPED TO LOOK ABOUT...
THEN SPUN LIKE A DERVISH...
SPILLING OUT HER ARMS AND HAIR AND BREATH UNTIL SHE DROPPED FROM EXHAUSTION.
I TOOK THE FORM TO BE MY MOTHER'S SPIRIT.
IT DID NOT SEEM AT ALL OUT OF PLACE IN THE COURSE OF RECENT EVENTS.

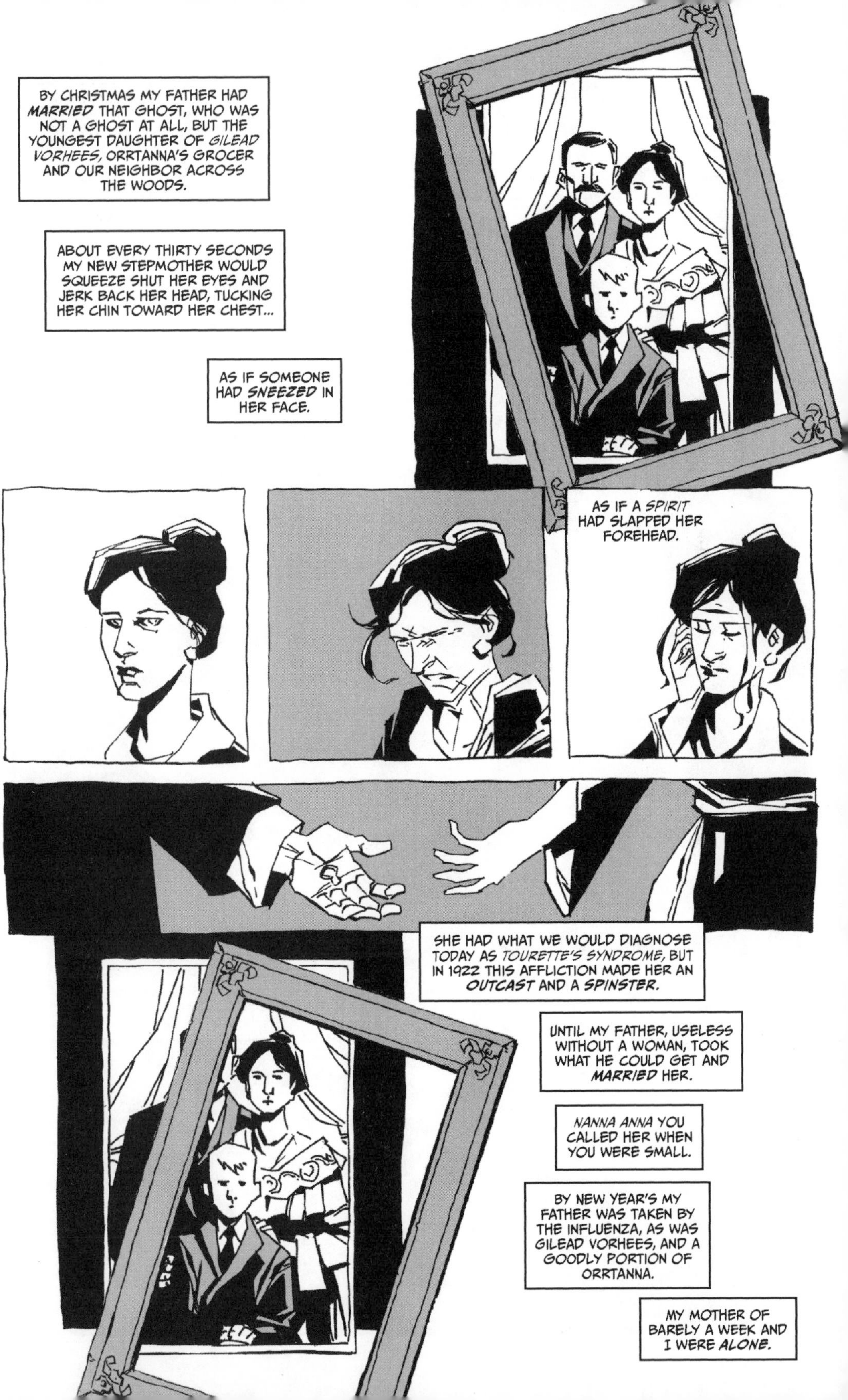
BY CHRISTMAS MY FATHER HAD *MARRIED* THAT GHOST, WHO WAS NOT A GHOST AT ALL, BUT THE YOUNGEST DAUGHTER OF *GILEAD VORHEES*, ORRTANNA'S GROCER AND OUR NEIGHBOR ACROSS THE WOODS.
ABOUT EVERY THIRTY SECONDS MY NEW STEPMOTHER WOULD SQUEEZE SHUT HER EYES AND JERK BACK HER HEAD, TUCKING HER CHIN TOWARD HER CHEST...
AS IF SOMEONE HAD *SNEEZED* IN HER FACE.
AS IF A *SPIRIT* HAD SLAPPED HER FOREHEAD.
SHE HAD WHAT WE WOULD DIAGNOSE TODAY AS *TOURETTE'S SYNDROME*, BUT IN 1922 THIS AFFLICTION MADE HER AN *OUTCAST* AND A *SPINSTER*.
UNTIL MY FATHER, USELESS WITHOUT A WOMAN, TOOK WHAT HE COULD GET AND *MARRIED* HER.
NANNA ANNA YOU CALLED HER WHEN YOU WERE SMALL.
BY NEW YEAR'S MY FATHER WAS TAKEN BY THE INFLUENZA, AS WAS GILEAD VORHEES, AND A GOODLY PORTION OF ORRTANNA.
MY MOTHER OF BARELY A WEEK AND I WERE *ALONE*.

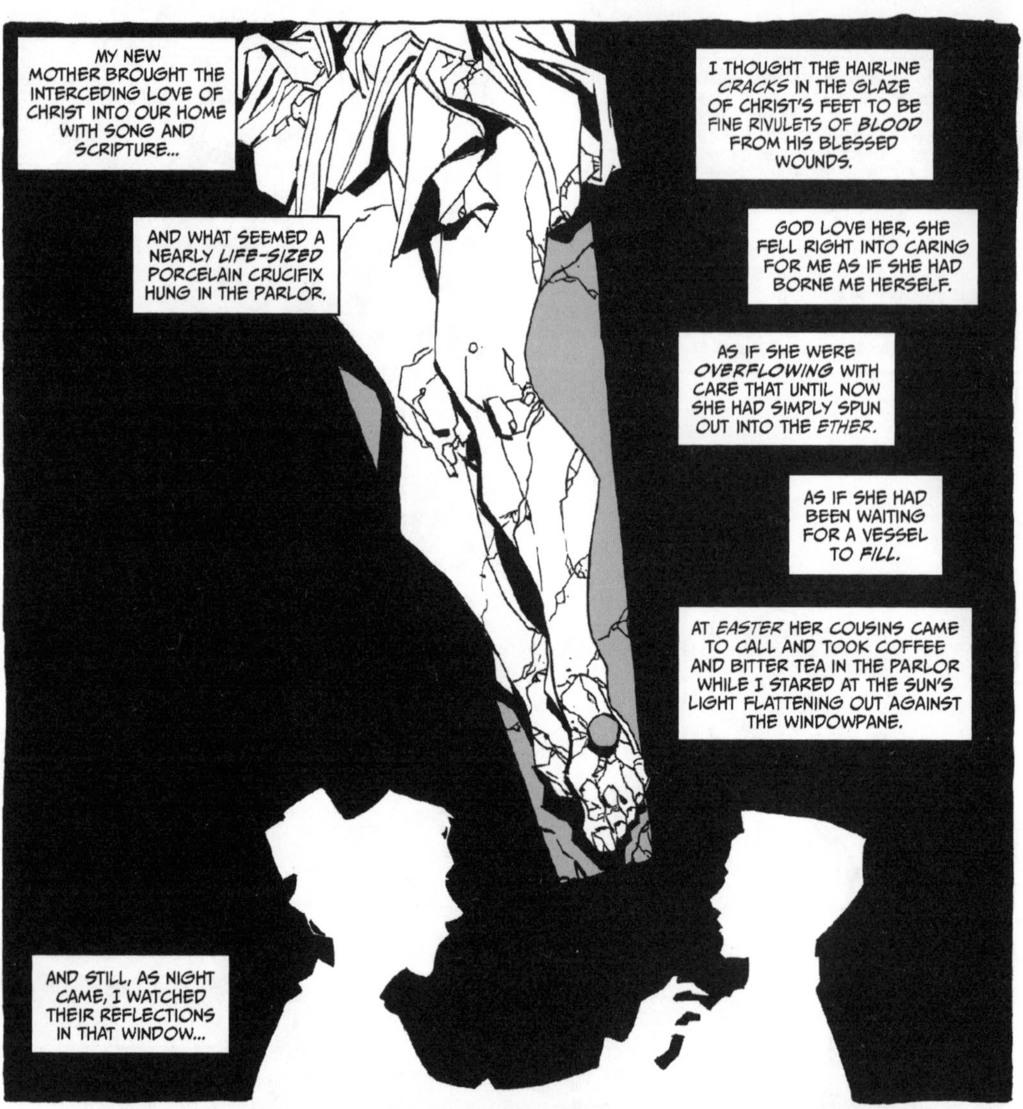
MY NEW MOTHER BROUGHT THE INTERCEDING LOVE OF CHRIST INTO OUR HOME WITH SONG AND SCRIPTURE...
AND WHAT SEEMED A NEARLY *LIFE-SIZED* PORCELAIN CRUCIFIX HUNG IN THE PARLOR.
I THOUGHT THE HAIRLINE *CRACKS* IN THE GLAZE OF CHRIST'S FEET TO BE FINE RIVULETS OF *BLOOD* FROM HIS BLESSED WOUNDS.
GOD LOVE HER, SHE FELL RIGHT INTO CARING FOR ME AS IF SHE HAD BORNE ME HERSELF.
AS IF SHE WERE *OVERFLOWING* WITH CARE THAT UNTIL NOW SHE HAD SIMPLY SPUN OUT INTO THE *ETHER*.
AS IF SHE HAD BEEN WAITING FOR A VESSEL TO *FILL*.
AT *EASTER* HER COUSINS CAME TO CALL AND TOOK COFFEE AND BITTER TEA IN THE PARLOR WHILE I STARED AT THE SUN'S LIGHT FLATTENING OUT AGAINST THE WINDOWPANE.
AND STILL, AS NIGHT CAME, I WATCHED THEIR REFLECTIONS IN THAT WINDOW...

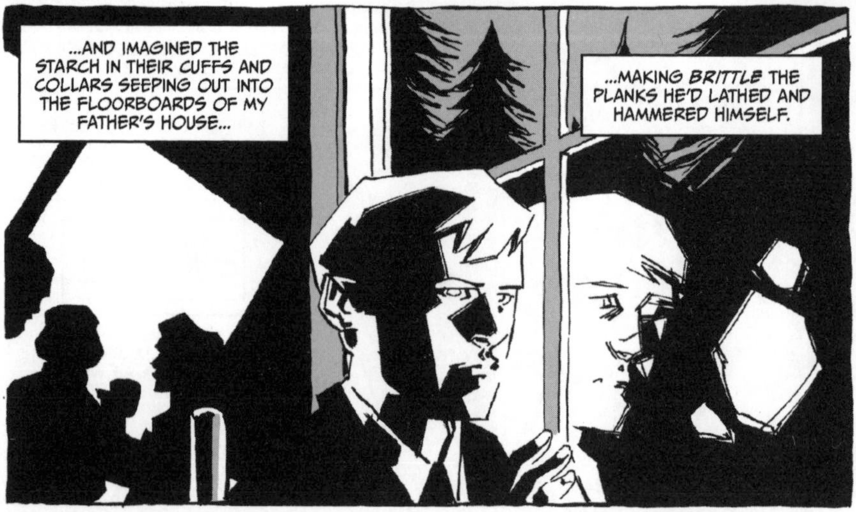
...AND IMAGINED THE STARCH IN THEIR CUFFS AND COLLARS SEEPING OUT INTO THE FLOORBOARDS OF MY FATHER'S HOUSE...
...MAKING *BRITTLE* THE PLANKS HE'D LATHED AND HAMMERED HIMSELF.

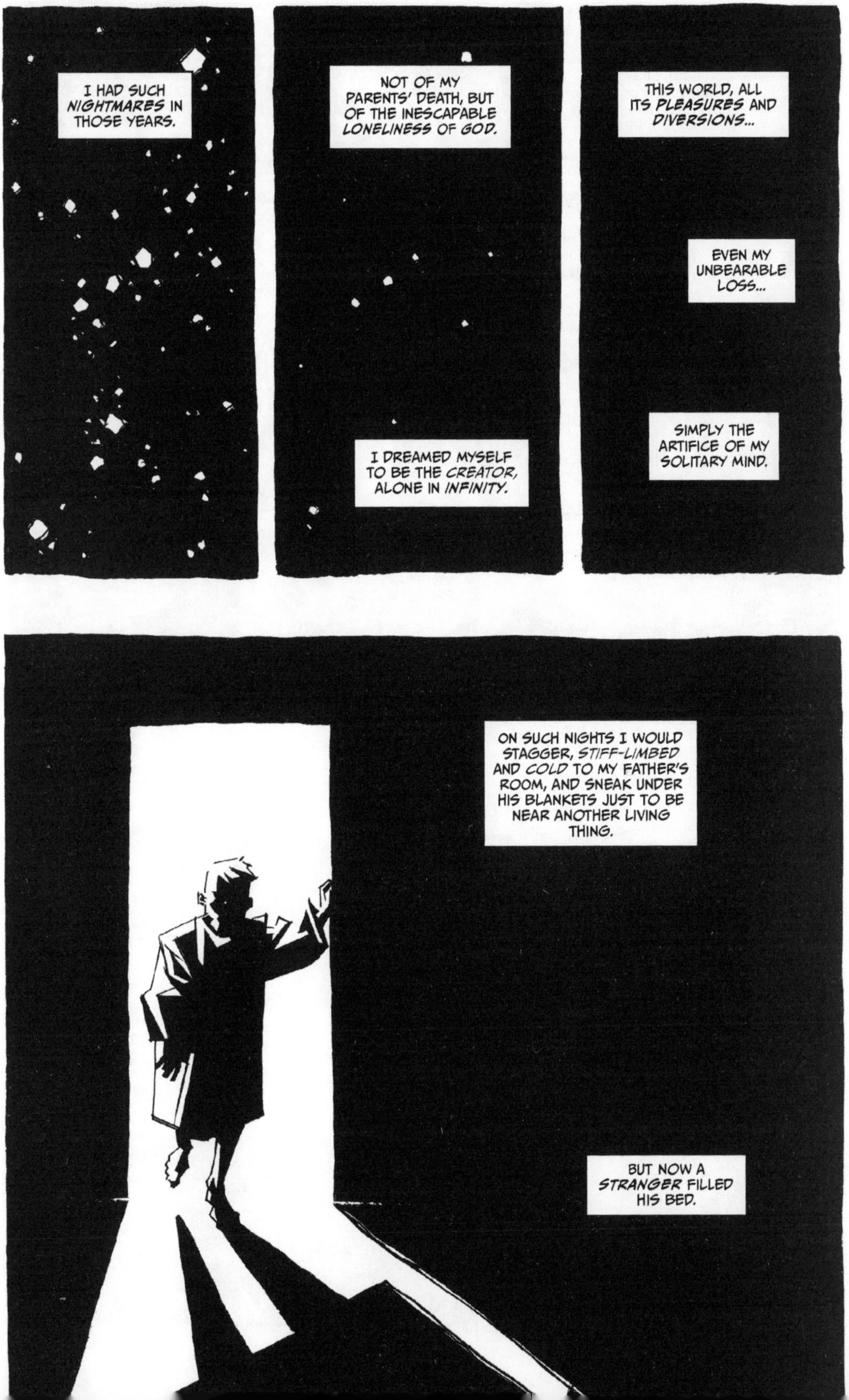
I HAD SUCH *NIGHTMARES* IN THOSE YEARS.
NOT OF MY PARENTS' DEATH, BUT OF THE INESCAPABLE *LONELINESS* OF *GOD.*
I DREAMED MYSELF TO BE THE *CREATOR,* ALONE IN *INFINITY.*
THIS WORLD, ALL ITS *PLEASURES* AND *DIVERSIONS*...
EVEN MY UNBEARABLE LOSS...
SIMPLY THE ARTIFICE OF MY SOLITARY MIND.
ON SUCH NIGHTS I WOULD STAGGER, *STIFF-LIMBED* AND *COLD* TO MY FATHER'S ROOM, AND SNEAK UNDER HIS BLANKETS JUST TO BE NEAR ANOTHER LIVING THING.
BUT NOW A *STRANGER* FILLED HIS BED.

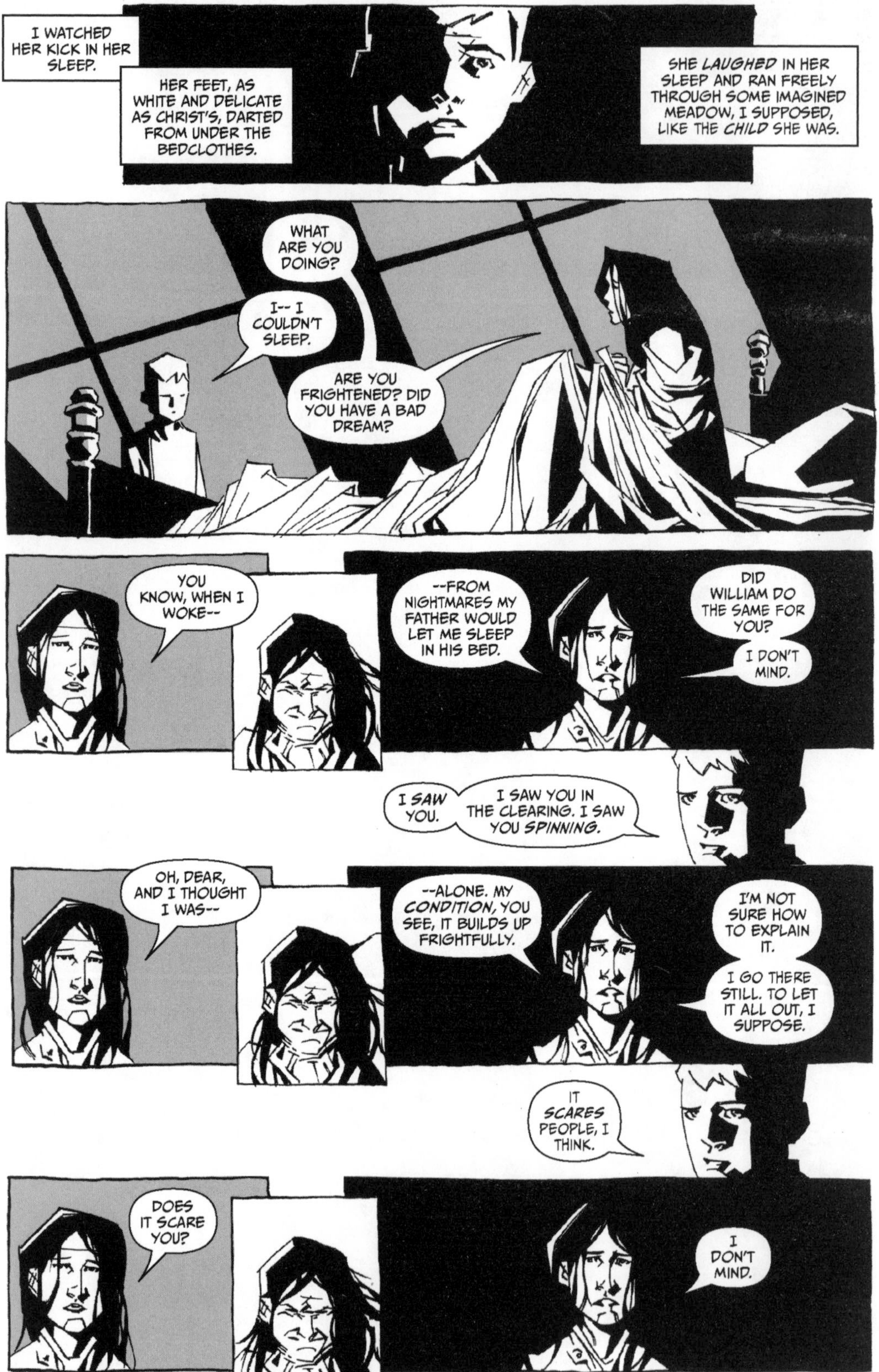
I WATCHED HER KICK IN HER SLEEP.
HER FEET, AS WHITE AND DELICATE AS CHRIST'S, DARTED FROM UNDER THE BEDCLOTHES.
SHE *LAUGHED* IN HER SLEEP AND RAN FREELY THROUGH SOME IMAGINED MEADOW, I SUPPOSED, LIKE THE *CHILD* SHE WAS.
WHAT ARE YOU DOING?
I-- I COULDN'T SLEEP.
ARE YOU FRIGHTENED? DID YOU HAVE A BAD DREAM?
YOU KNOW, WHEN I WOKE--
--FROM NIGHTMARES MY FATHER WOULD LET ME SLEEP IN HIS BED.
DID WILLIAM DO THE SAME FOR YOU?
I DON'T MIND.
I *SAW* YOU.
I SAW YOU IN THE CLEARING. I SAW YOU *SPINNING.*
OH, DEAR, AND I THOUGHT I WAS--
--ALONE. MY *CONDITION,* YOU SEE, IT BUILDS UP FRIGHTFULLY.
I'M NOT SURE HOW TO EXPLAIN IT.
I GO THERE STILL. TO LET IT ALL OUT, I SUPPOSE.
IT *SCARES* PEOPLE, I THINK.
DOES IT SCARE YOU?
I DON'T MIND.

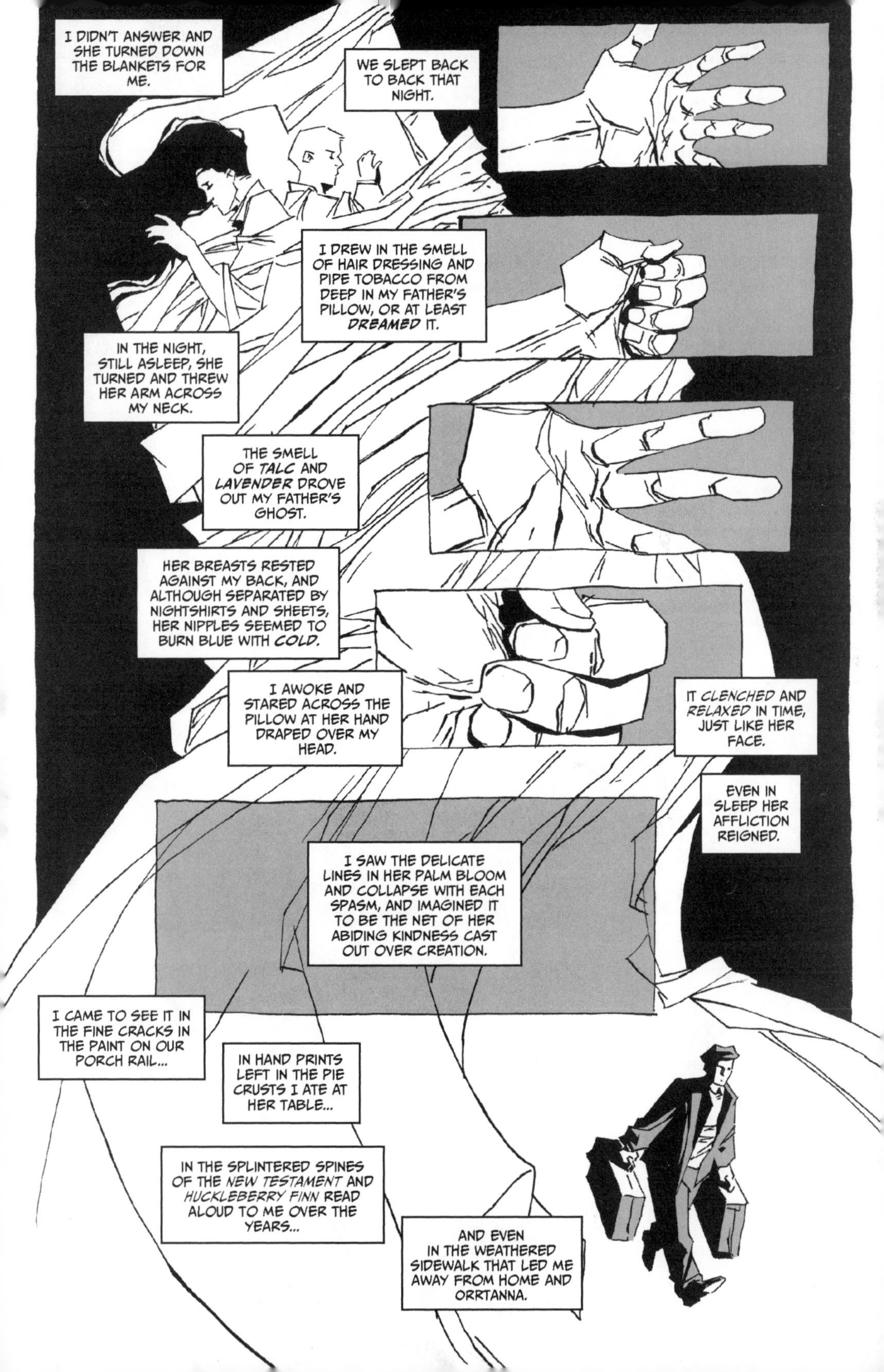
I DIDN'T ANSWER AND SHE TURNED DOWN THE BLANKETS FOR ME.
WE SLEPT BACK TO BACK THAT NIGHT.
I DREW IN THE SMELL OF HAIR DRESSING AND PIPE TOBACCO FROM DEEP IN MY FATHER'S PILLOW, OR AT LEAST *DREAMED* IT.
IN THE NIGHT, STILL ASLEEP, SHE TURNED AND THREW HER ARM ACROSS MY NECK.
THE SMELL OF *TALC* AND *LAVENDER* DROVE OUT MY FATHER'S GHOST.
HER BREASTS RESTED AGAINST MY BACK, AND ALTHOUGH SEPARATED BY NIGHTSHIRTS AND SHEETS, HER NIPPLES SEEMED TO BURN BLUE WITH *COLD*.
I AWOKE AND STARED ACROSS THE PILLOW AT HER HAND DRAPED OVER MY HEAD.
IT *CLENCHED* AND *RELAXED* IN TIME, JUST LIKE HER FACE.
EVEN IN SLEEP HER AFFLICTION REIGNED.
I SAW THE DELICATE LINES IN HER PALM BLOOM AND COLLAPSE WITH EACH SPASM, AND IMAGINED IT TO BE THE NET OF HER ABIDING KINDNESS CAST OUT OVER CREATION.
I CAME TO SEE IT IN THE FINE CRACKS IN THE PAINT ON OUR PORCH RAIL...
IN HAND PRINTS LEFT IN THE PIE CRUSTS I ATE AT HER TABLE...
IN THE SPLINTERED SPINES OF THE *NEW TESTAMENT* AND *HUCKLEBERRY FINN* READ ALOUD TO ME OVER THE YEARS...
AND EVEN IN THE WEATHERED SIDEWALK THAT LED ME AWAY FROM HOME AND ORRTANNA.

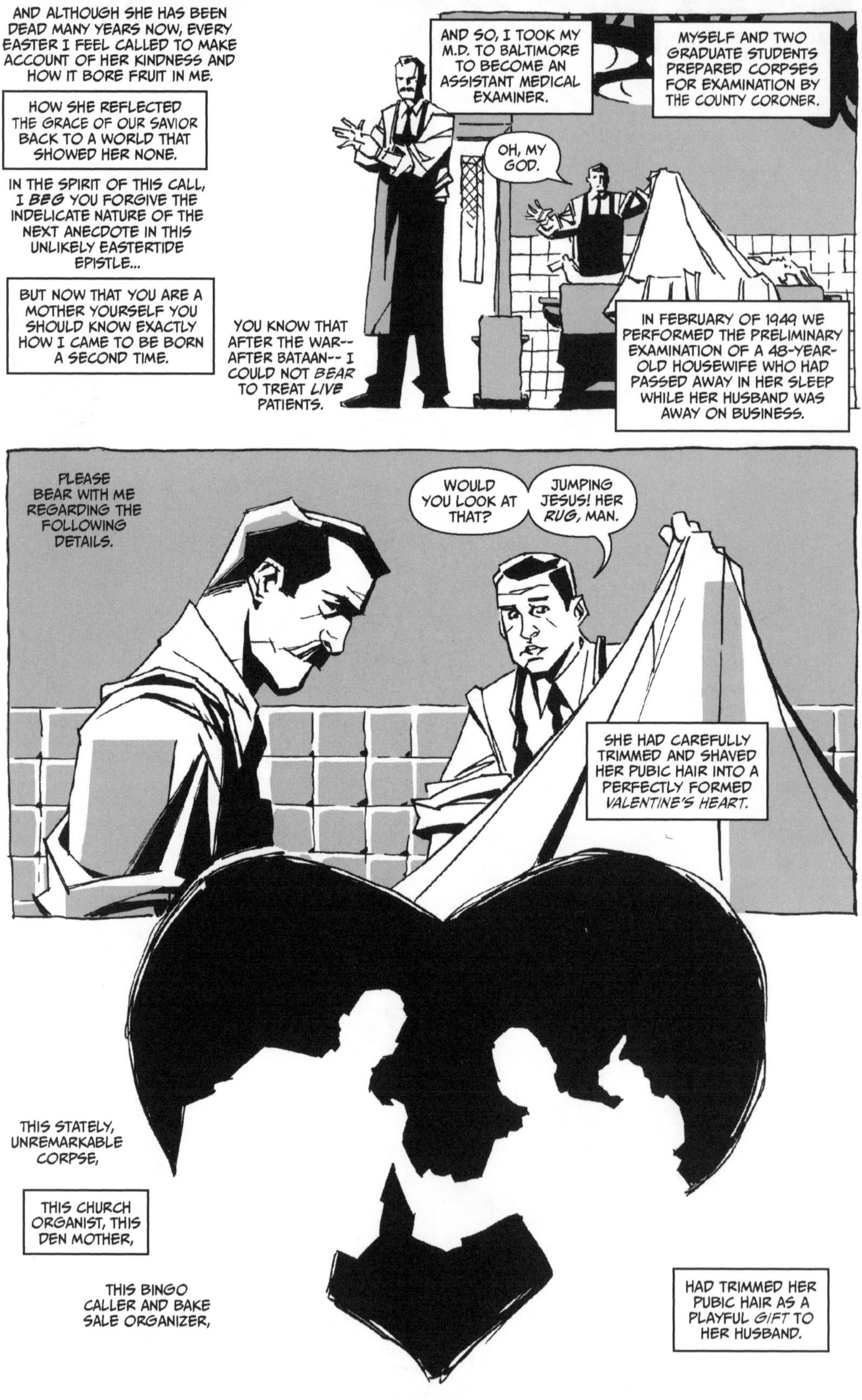
AND ALTHOUGH SHE HAS BEEN DEAD MANY YEARS NOW, EVERY EASTER I FEEL CALLED TO MAKE ACCOUNT OF HER KINDNESS AND HOW IT BORE FRUIT IN ME.
HOW SHE REFLECTED THE GRACE OF OUR SAVIOR BACK TO A WORLD THAT SHOWED HER NONE.
IN THE SPIRIT OF THIS CALL, I *BEG* YOU FORGIVE THE INDELICATE NATURE OF THE NEXT ANECDOTE IN THIS UNLIKELY EASTERTIDE EPISTLE...
BUT NOW THAT YOU ARE A MOTHER YOURSELF YOU SHOULD KNOW EXACTLY HOW I CAME TO BE BORN A SECOND TIME.
YOU KNOW THAT AFTER THE WAR-- AFTER BATAAN-- I COULD NOT *BEAR* TO TREAT *LIVE* PATIENTS.
AND SO, I TOOK MY M.D. TO BALTIMORE TO BECOME AN ASSISTANT MEDICAL EXAMINER.
MYSELF AND TWO GRADUATE STUDENTS PREPARED CORPSES FOR EXAMINATION BY THE COUNTY CORONER.
OH, MY GOD.
IN FEBRUARY OF 1949 WE PERFORMED THE PRELIMINARY EXAMINATION OF A 48-YEAR-OLD HOUSEWIFE WHO HAD PASSED AWAY IN HER SLEEP WHILE HER HUSBAND WAS AWAY ON BUSINESS.
PLEASE BEAR WITH ME REGARDING THE FOLLOWING DETAILS.
WOULD YOU LOOK AT THAT?
JUMPING JESUS! HER *RUG,* MAN.
SHE HAD CAREFULLY TRIMMED AND SHAVED HER PUBIC HAIR INTO A PERFECTLY FORMED *VALENTINE'S HEART.*
THIS STATELY, UNREMARKABLE CORPSE,
THIS CHURCH ORGANIST, THIS DEN MOTHER,
THIS BINGO CALLER AND BAKE SALE ORGANIZER,
HAD TRIMMED HER PUBIC HAIR AS A PLAYFUL *GIFT* TO HER HUSBAND.

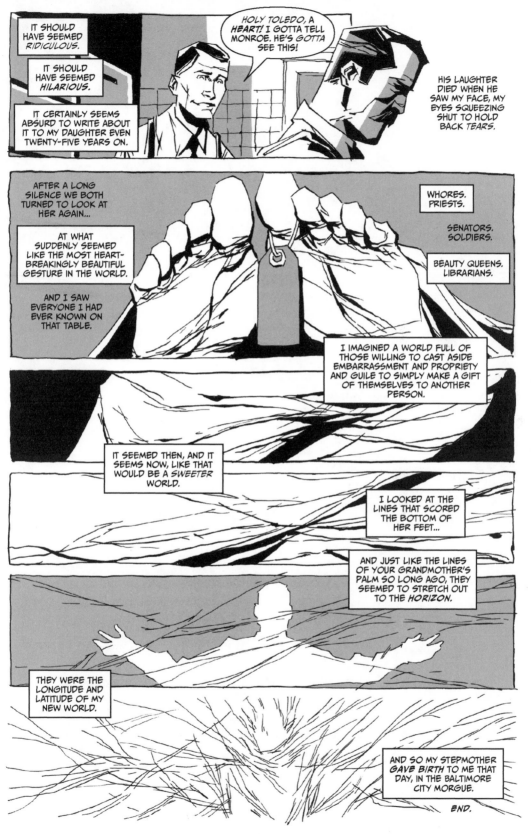

IT SHOULD HAVE SEEMED *RIDICULOUS.*

IT SHOULD HAVE SEEMED *HILARIOUS.*

IT CERTAINLY SEEMS ABSURD TO WRITE ABOUT IT TO MY DAUGHTER EVEN TWENTY-FIVE YEARS ON.

HOLY TOLEDO, A *HEART!* I GOTTA TELL MONROE. HE'S *GOTTA* SEE THIS!

HIS LAUGHTER DIED WHEN HE SAW MY FACE, MY EYES SQUEEZING SHUT TO HOLD BACK *TEARS.*

AFTER A LONG SILENCE WE BOTH TURNED TO LOOK AT HER AGAIN...

AT WHAT SUDDENLY SEEMED LIKE THE MOST HEART-BREAKINGLY BEAUTIFUL GESTURE IN THE WORLD.

AND I SAW EVERYONE I HAD EVER KNOWN ON THAT TABLE.

WHORES. PRIESTS.

SENATORS. SOLDIERS.

BEAUTY QUEENS. LIBRARIANS.

I IMAGINED A WORLD FULL OF THOSE WILLING TO CAST ASIDE EMBARRASSMENT AND PROPRIETY AND GUILE TO SIMPLY MAKE A GIFT OF THEMSELVES TO ANOTHER PERSON.

IT SEEMED THEN, AND IT SEEMS NOW, LIKE THAT WOULD BE A *SWEETER* WORLD.

I LOOKED AT THE LINES THAT SCORED THE BOTTOM OF HER FEET...

AND JUST LIKE THE LINES OF YOUR GRANDMOTHER'S PALM SO LONG AGO, THEY SEEMED TO STRETCH OUT TO THE *HORIZON.*

THEY WERE THE LONGITUDE AND LATITUDE OF MY NEW WORLD.

AND SO MY STEPMOTHER *GAVE BIRTH* TO ME THAT DAY, IN THE BALTIMORE CITY MORGUE.

END.

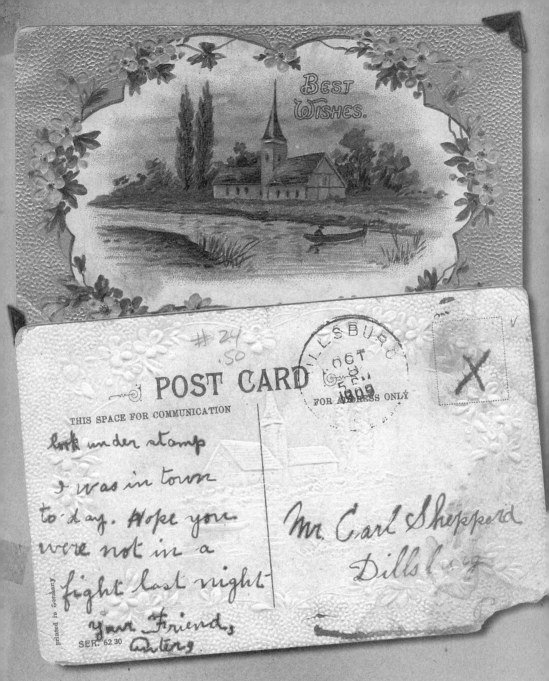

Best Wishes.

POST CARD

THIS SPACE FOR COMMUNICATION

look under stamp
I was in town
to-day. Hope you
were not in a
fight last night

Your Friend,
Winters

SER. 62 30

printed in Germany

#24
.50

HILLSBURG
OCT 8
5 PM
1909

FOR ADDRESS ONLY

Mr. Carl Sheppard
Dillsburg

Believe it or not, I have several postcards like this one. Instructions to check
under the stamp where some cryptic message or symbol can be found. Stuart
and Michael combined the mysterious "X" under the stamp with the ominous,
"I hope you didn't get into a fight last night" to show how a postcard can serve as
an attempted reconciliation.

TIC-TAC-BANG-BANG

STORY BY
STUART MOORE
ILLUSTRATED BY
MICHAEL GAYDOS

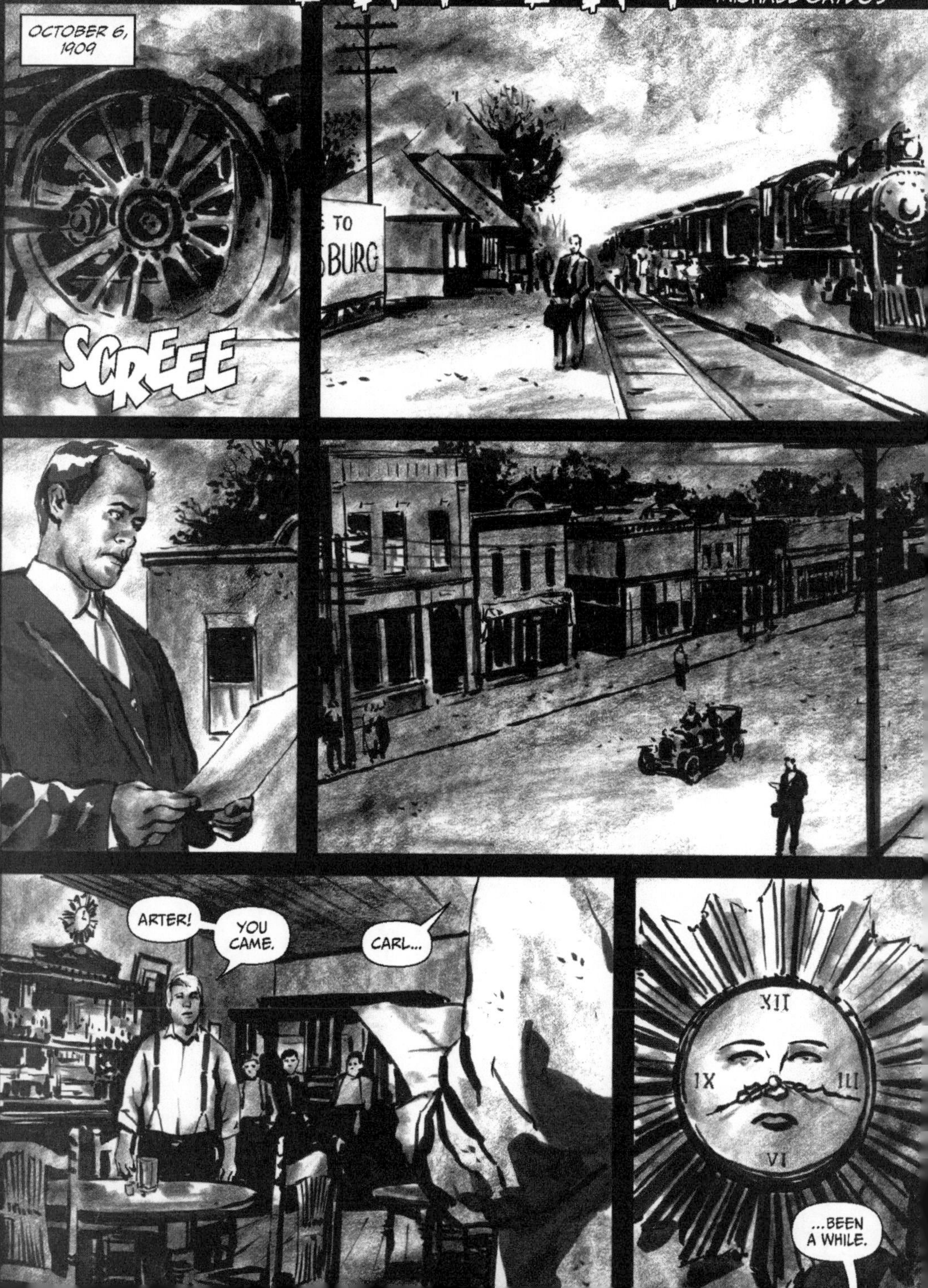
OCTOBER 6, 1909
SCREEE
ARTER!
YOU CAME.
CARL...
XII
IX
III
VI
...BEEN A WHILE.

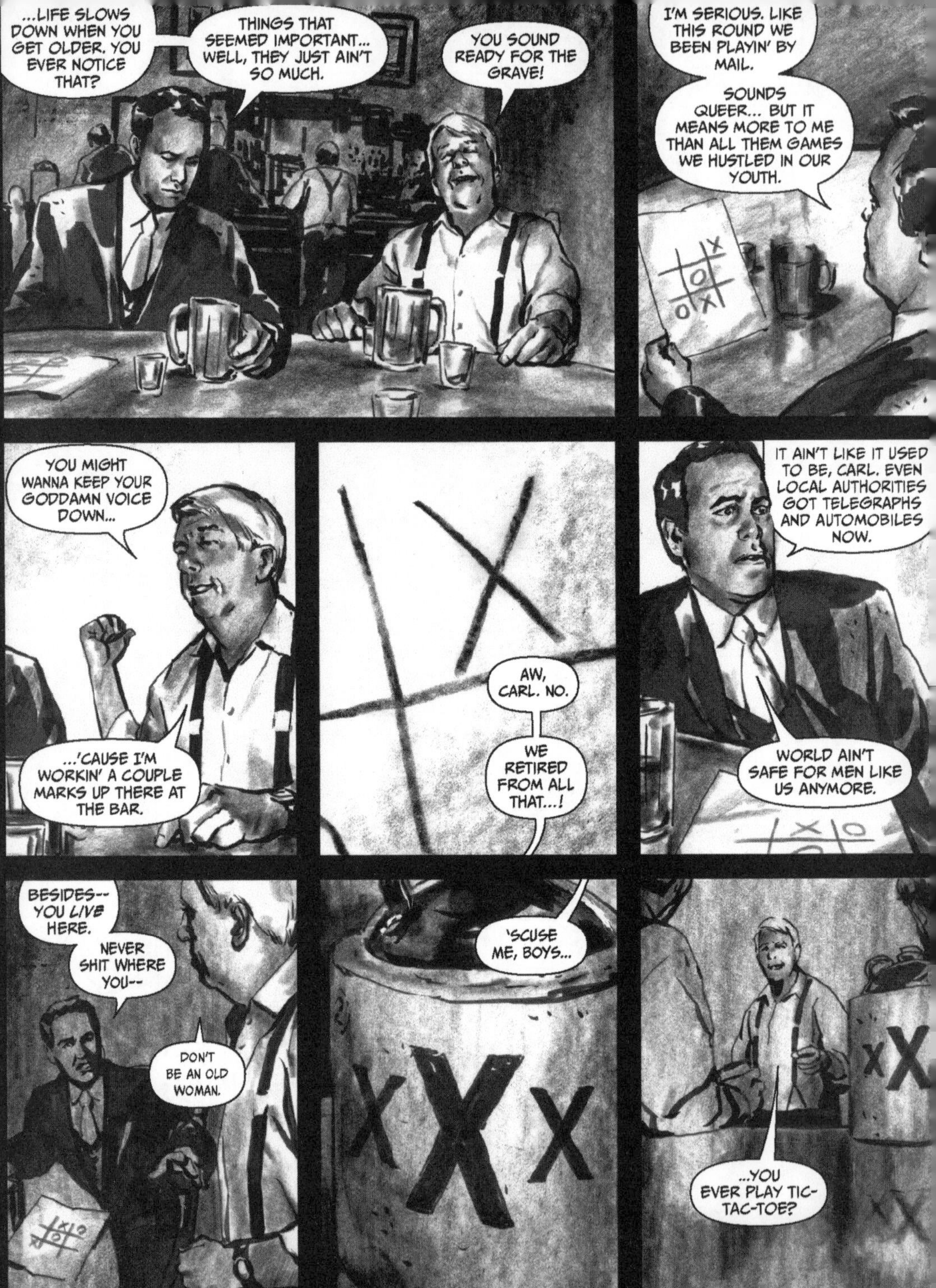
...LIFE SLOWS DOWN WHEN YOU GET OLDER. YOU EVER NOTICE THAT?
THINGS THAT SEEMED IMPORTANT... WELL, THEY JUST AIN'T SO MUCH.
YOU SOUND READY FOR THE GRAVE!
I'M SERIOUS. LIKE THIS ROUND WE BEEN PLAYIN' BY MAIL.
SOUNDS QUEER... BUT IT MEANS MORE TO ME THAN ALL THEM GAMES WE HUSTLED IN OUR YOUTH.
YOU MIGHT WANNA KEEP YOUR GODDAMN VOICE DOWN...
...'CAUSE I'M WORKIN' A COUPLE MARKS UP THERE AT THE BAR.
AW, CARL. NO.
WE RETIRED FROM ALL THAT...!
IT AIN'T LIKE IT USED TO BE, CARL. EVEN LOCAL AUTHORITIES GOT TELEGRAPHS AND AUTOMOBILES NOW.
WORLD AIN'T SAFE FOR MEN LIKE US ANYMORE.
BESIDES-- YOU *LIVE* HERE.
NEVER SHIT WHERE YOU--
DON'T BE AN OLD WOMAN.
'SCUSE ME, BOYS...
XXX
...YOU EVER PLAY TIC-TAC-TOE?

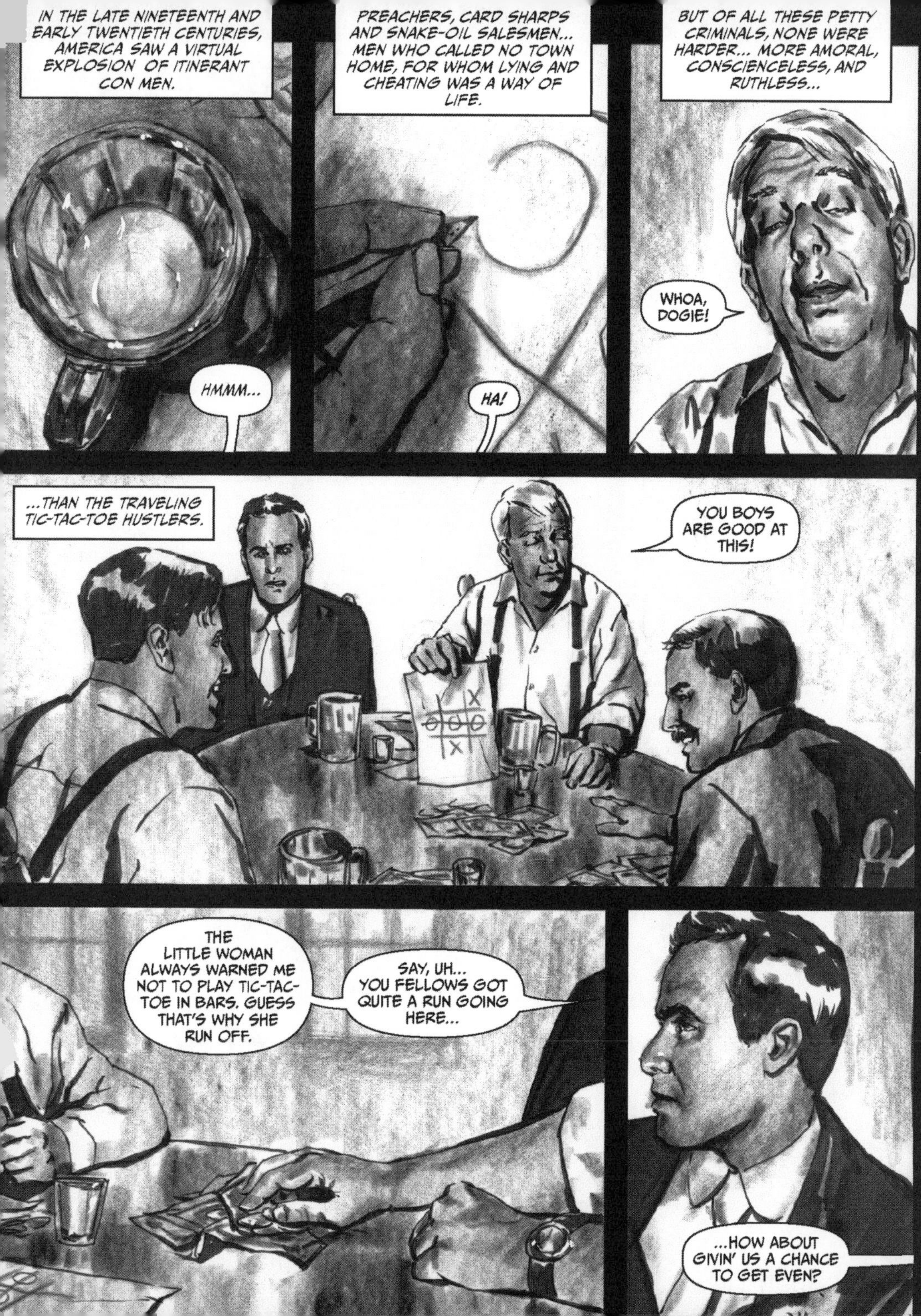
IN THE LATE NINETEENTH AND EARLY TWENTIETH CENTURIES, AMERICA SAW A VIRTUAL EXPLOSION OF ITINERANT CON MEN.
HMMM...
PREACHERS, CARD SHARPS AND SNAKE-OIL SALESMEN... MEN WHO CALLED NO TOWN HOME, FOR WHOM LYING AND CHEATING WAS A WAY OF LIFE.
HA!
BUT OF ALL THESE PETTY CRIMINALS, NONE WERE HARDER... MORE AMORAL, CONSCIENCELESS, AND RUTHLESS...
WHOA, DOGIE!
...THAN THE TRAVELING TIC-TAC-TOE HUSTLERS.
YOU BOYS ARE GOOD AT THIS!
THE LITTLE WOMAN ALWAYS WARNED ME NOT TO PLAY TIC-TAC-TOE IN BARS. GUESS THAT'S WHY SHE RUN OFF.
SAY, UH... YOU FELLOWS GOT QUITE A RUN GOING HERE...
...HOW ABOUT GIVIN' US A CHANCE TO GET EVEN?

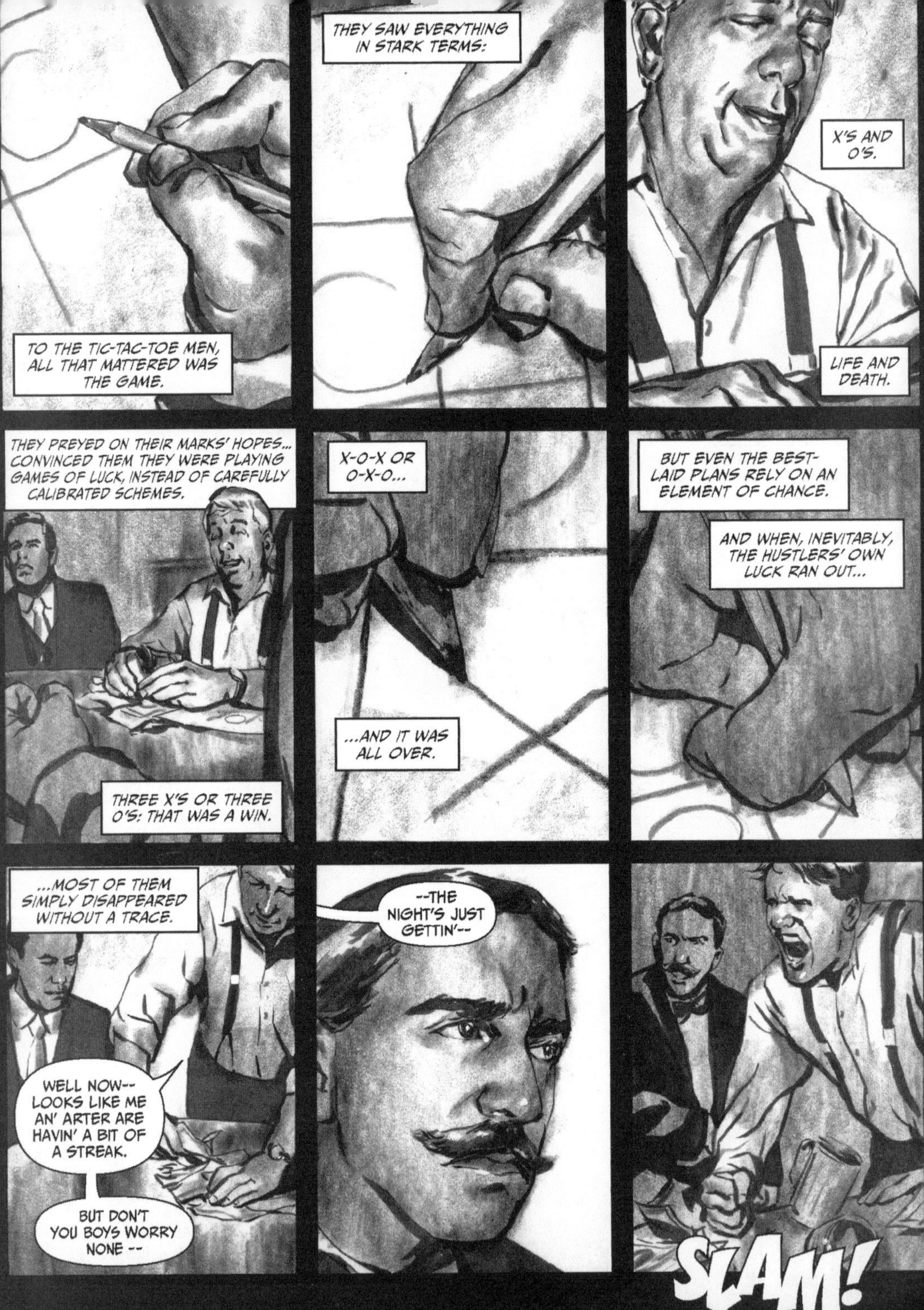
TO THE TIC-TAC-TOE MEN, ALL THAT MATTERED WAS THE GAME.
THEY SAW EVERYTHING IN STARK TERMS:
X'S AND O'S.
LIFE AND DEATH.
THEY PREYED ON THEIR MARKS' HOPES... CONVINCED THEM THEY WERE PLAYING GAMES OF LUCK, INSTEAD OF CAREFULLY CALIBRATED SCHEMES.
THREE X'S OR THREE O'S: THAT WAS A WIN.
X-O-X OR O-X-O...
...AND IT WAS ALL OVER.
BUT EVEN THE BEST-LAID PLANS RELY ON AN ELEMENT OF CHANCE.
AND WHEN, INEVITABLY, THE HUSTLERS' OWN LUCK RAN OUT...
...MOST OF THEM SIMPLY DISAPPEARED WITHOUT A TRACE.
WELL NOW-- LOOKS LIKE ME AN' ARTER ARE HAVIN' A BIT OF A STREAK.
BUT DON'T YOU BOYS WORRY NONE --
--THE NIGHT'S JUST GETTIN'--
SLAM!

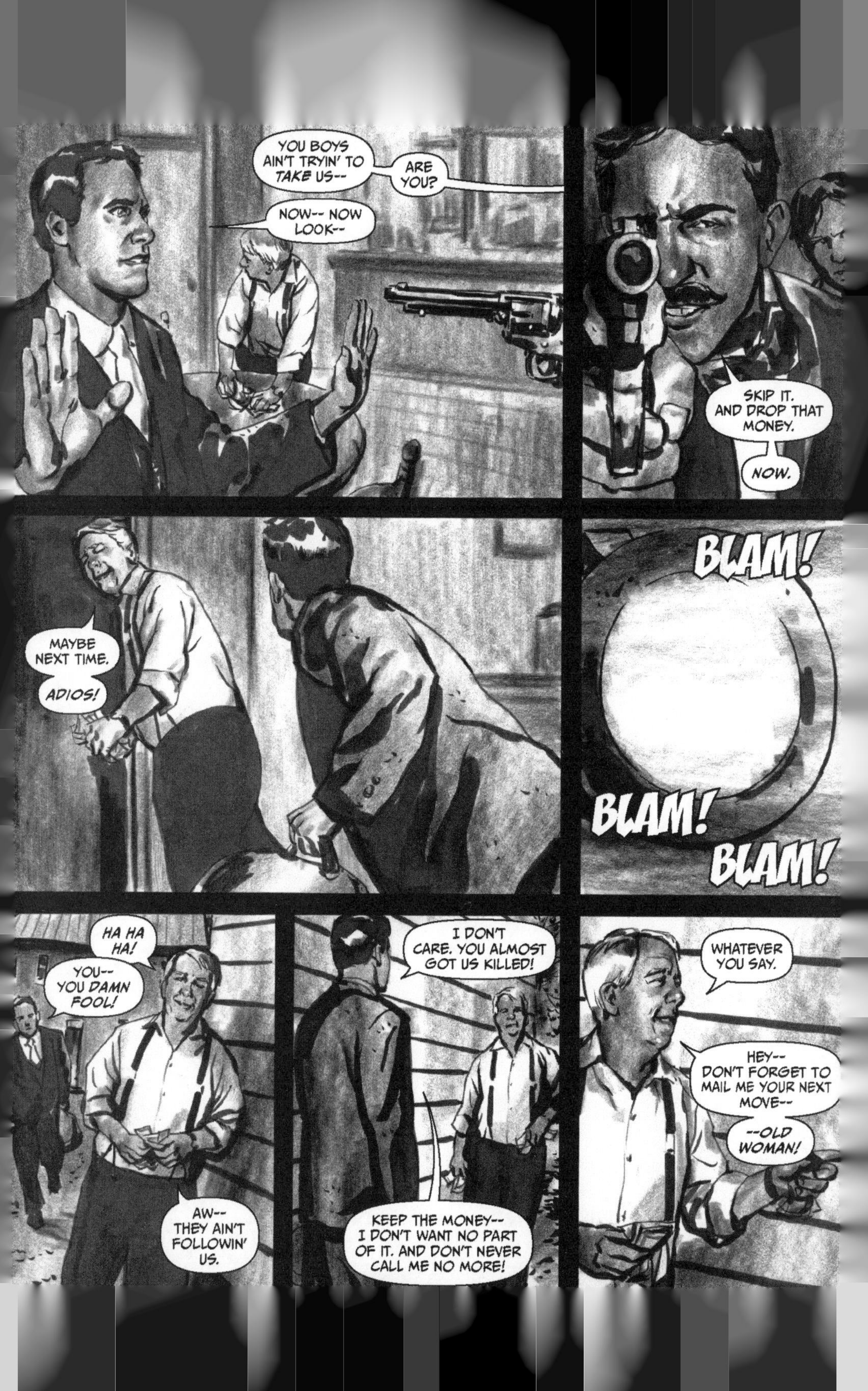
YOU BOYS AIN'T TRYIN' TO TAKE US--
ARE YOU?
NOW-- NOW LOOK--
SKIP IT. AND DROP THAT MONEY.
NOW.
MAYBE NEXT TIME.
ADIOS!
BLAM!
BLAM!
BLAM!
HA HA HA!
YOU-- YOU DAMN FOOL!
AW-- THEY AIN'T FOLLOWIN' US.
I DON'T CARE. YOU ALMOST GOT US KILLED!
KEEP THE MONEY-- I DON'T WANT NO PART OF IT. AND DON'T NEVER CALL ME NO MORE!
WHATEVER YOU SAY.
HEY-- DON'T FORGET TO MAIL ME YOUR NEXT MOVE--
--OLD WOMAN!

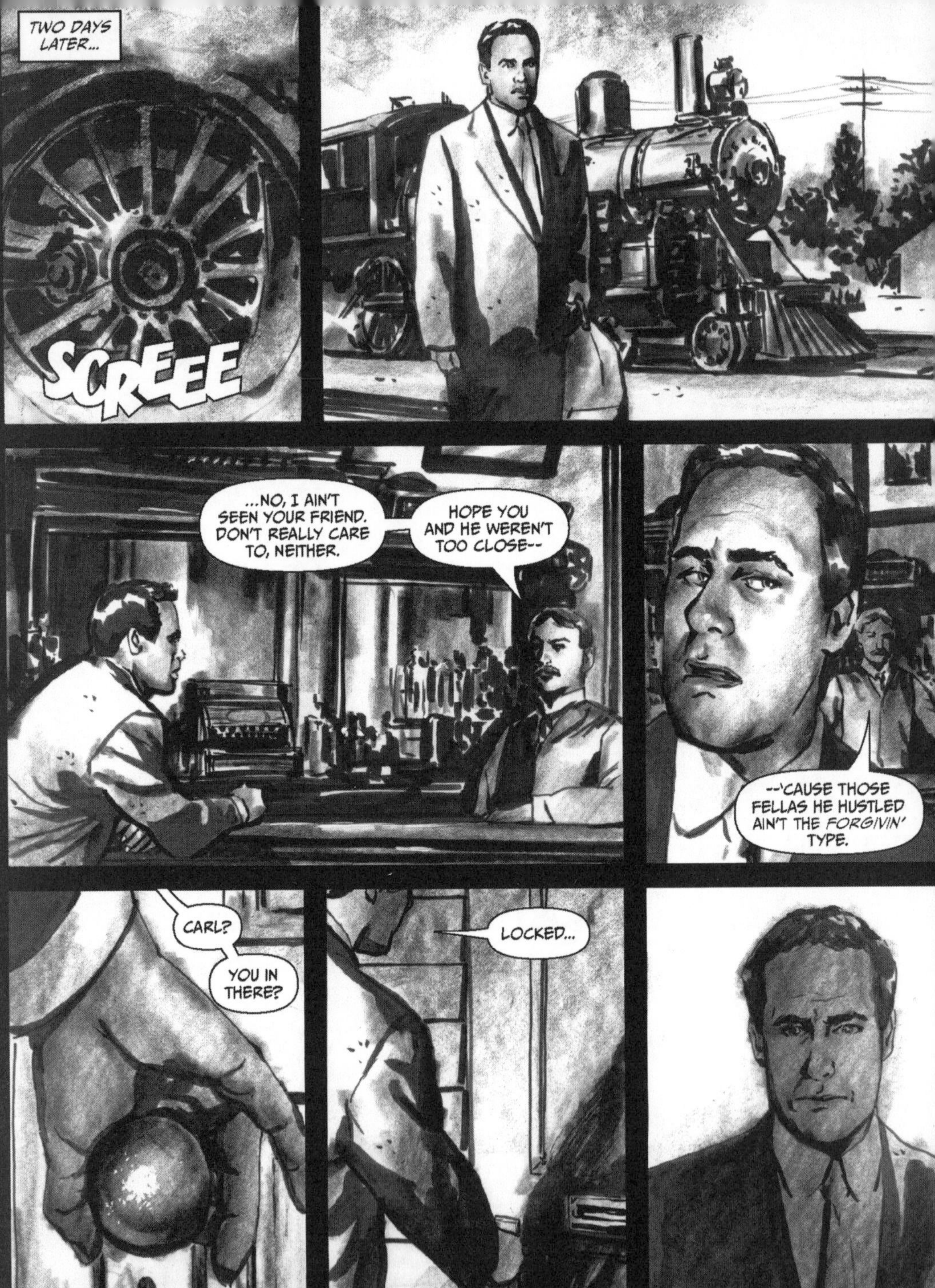
TWO DAYS LATER...
SCREEE
...NO, I AIN'T SEEN YOUR FRIEND. DON'T REALLY CARE TO, NEITHER.
HOPE YOU AND HE WEREN'T TOO CLOSE--
--'CAUSE THOSE FELLAS HE HUSTLED AIN'T THE *FORGIVIN'* TYPE.
CARL?
YOU IN THERE?
LOCKED...

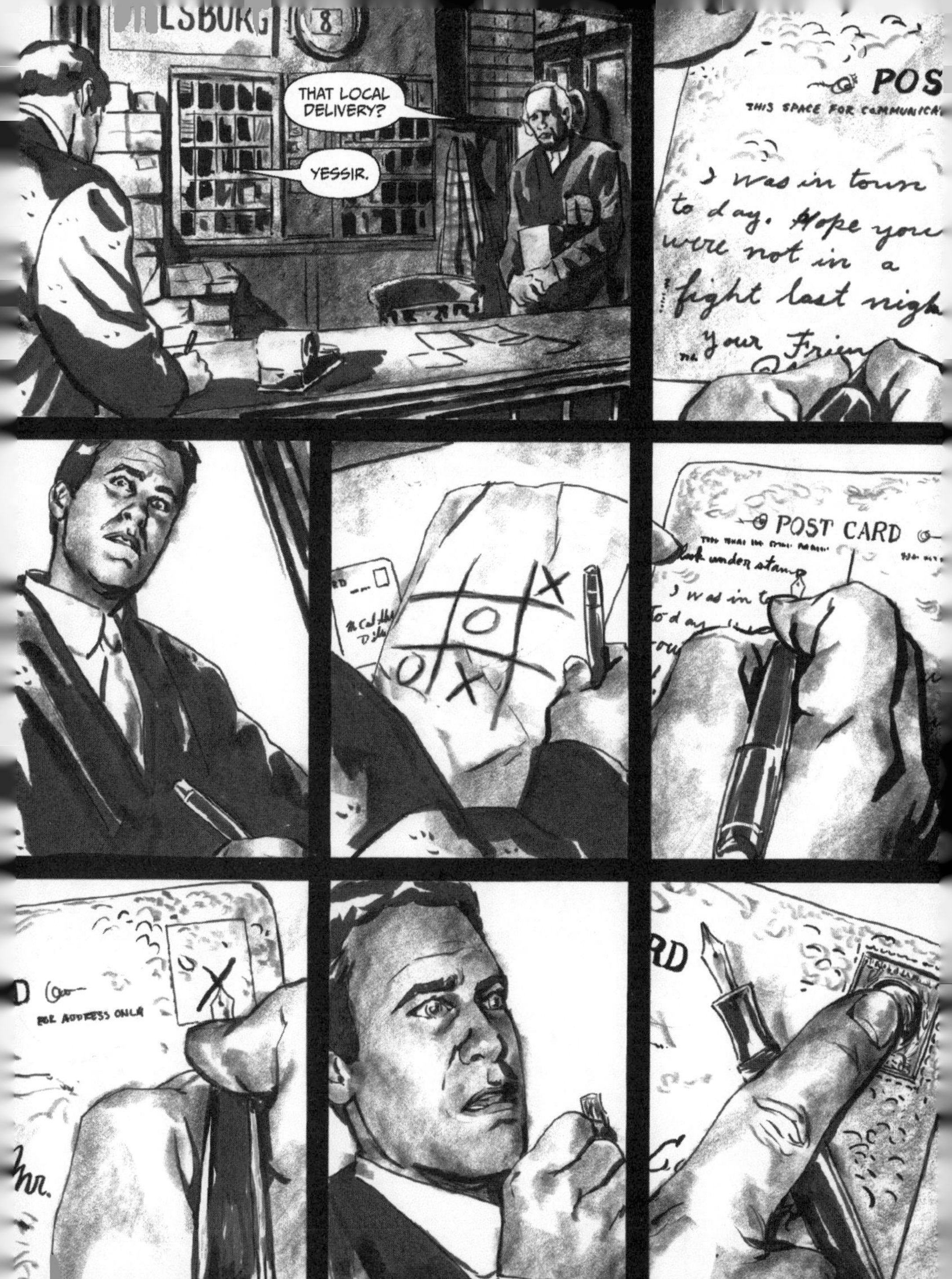
THAT LOCAL DELIVERY?
YESSIR.
8
THIS SPACE FOR COMMUNICA
I was in town
to day. Hope you
were not in a
fight last nigh
Your Frien
POST CARD
Look under stamp
I was in t
FOR ADDRESS ONLY
Mr.

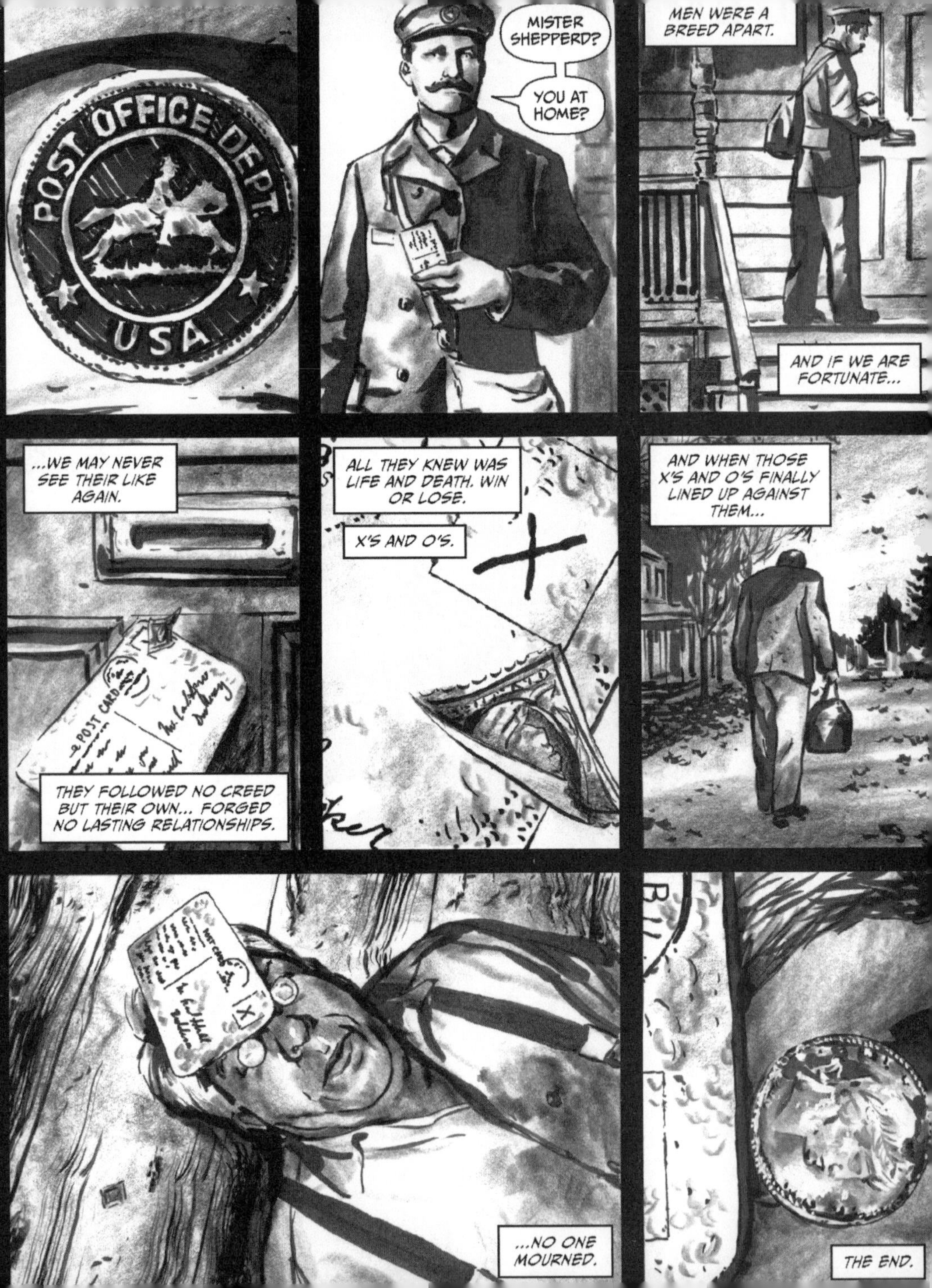
POST OFFICE DEPT.
USA
MISTER SHEPPERD?
YOU AT HOME?
MEN WERE A BREED APART.
AND IF WE ARE FORTUNATE...
...WE MAY NEVER SEE THEIR LIKE AGAIN.
POST CARD
THEY FOLLOWED NO CREED BUT THEIR OWN... FORGED NO LASTING RELATIONSHIPS.
ALL THEY KNEW WAS LIFE AND DEATH. WIN OR LOSE.
X'S AND O'S.
AND WHEN THOSE X'S AND O'S FINALLY LINED UP AGAINST THEM...
...NO ONE MOURNED.
THE END.

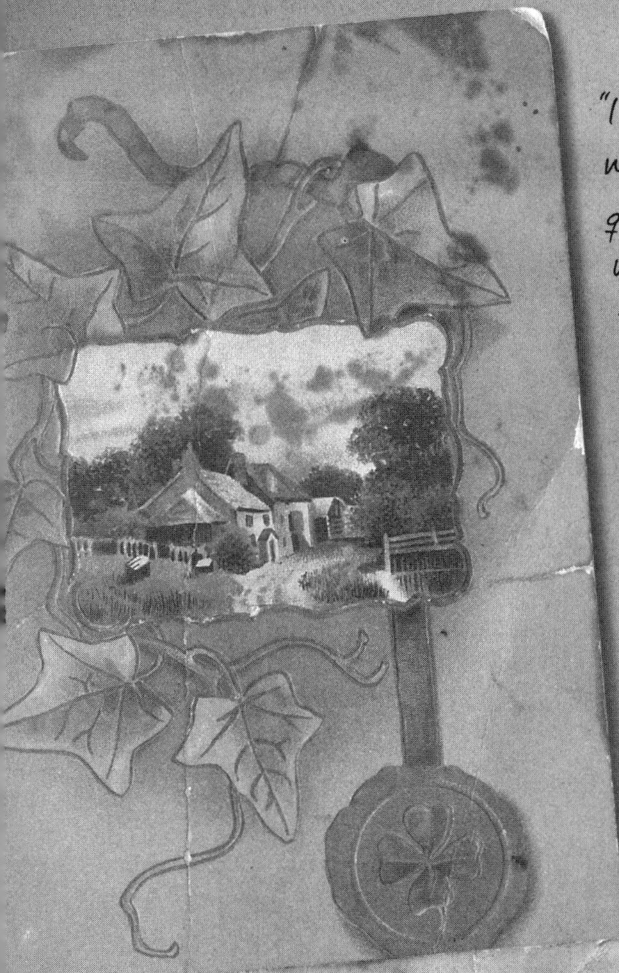

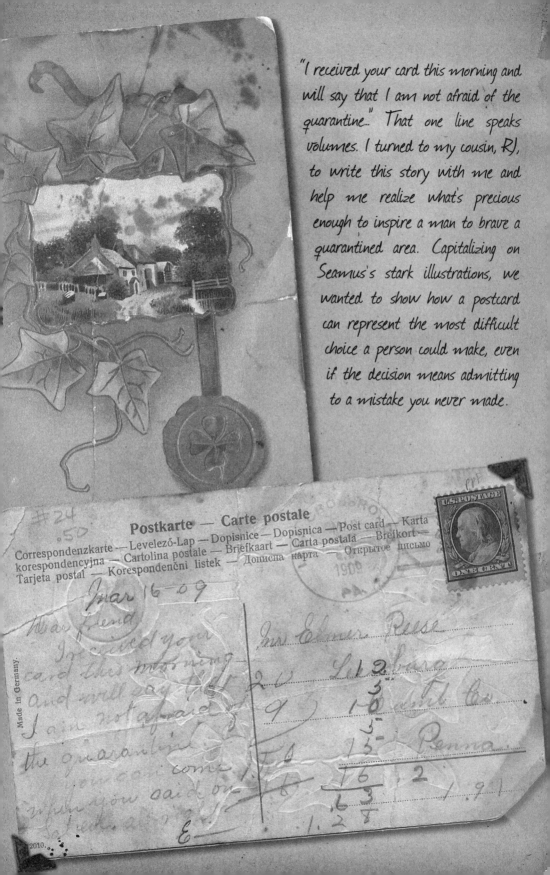

"I received your card this morning and will say that I am not afraid of the quarantine..." That one line speaks volumes. I turned to my cousin, RJ, to write this story with me and help me realize what's precious enough to inspire a man to brave a quarantined area. Capitalizing on Seamus's stark illustrations, we wanted to show how a postcard can represent the most difficult choice a person could make, even if the decision means admitting to a mistake you never made.

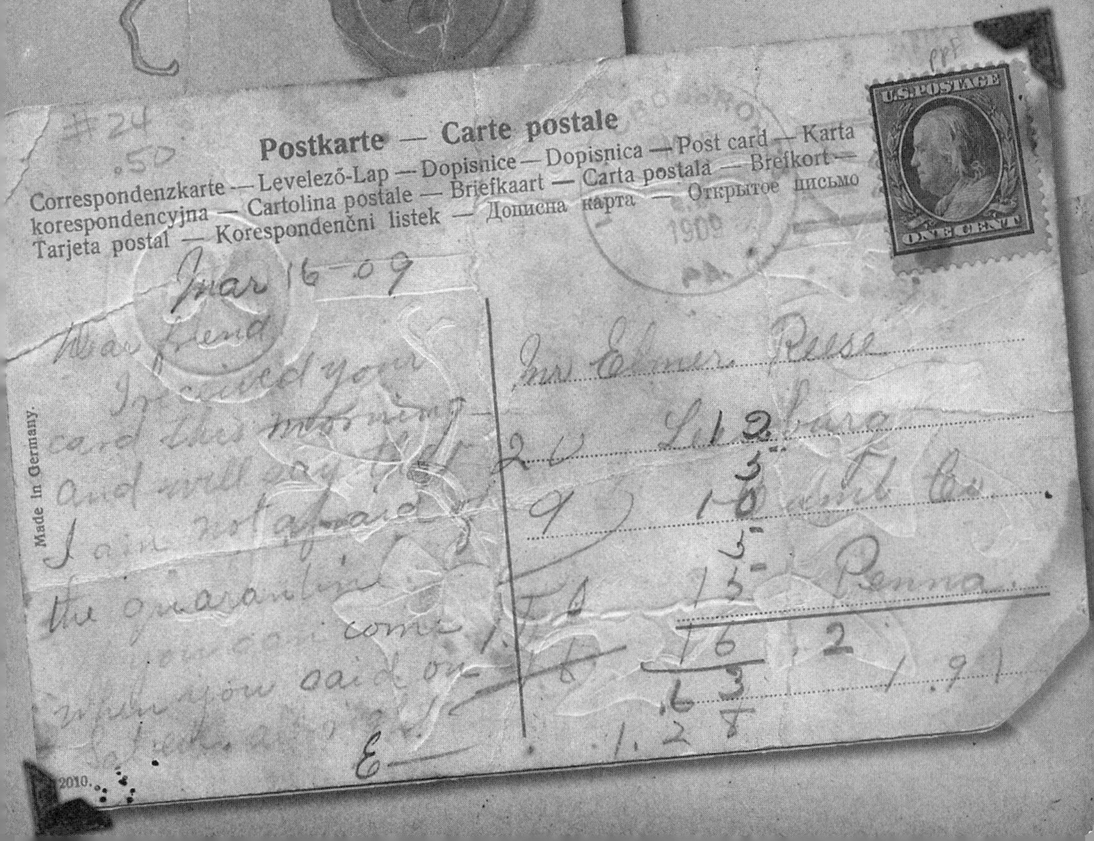
Postkarte — Carte postale
Correspondenzkarte — Levelező-Lap — Dopisnice — Dopisnica — Post card — Karta korespondencyjna — Cartolina postale — Briefkaart — Carta postala — Brefkort — Tarjeta postal — Korespondenčni listek — Дописна карта — Открытое письмо
U.S. POSTAGE
ONE CENT
1909
PA.
Made in Germany.
2010.

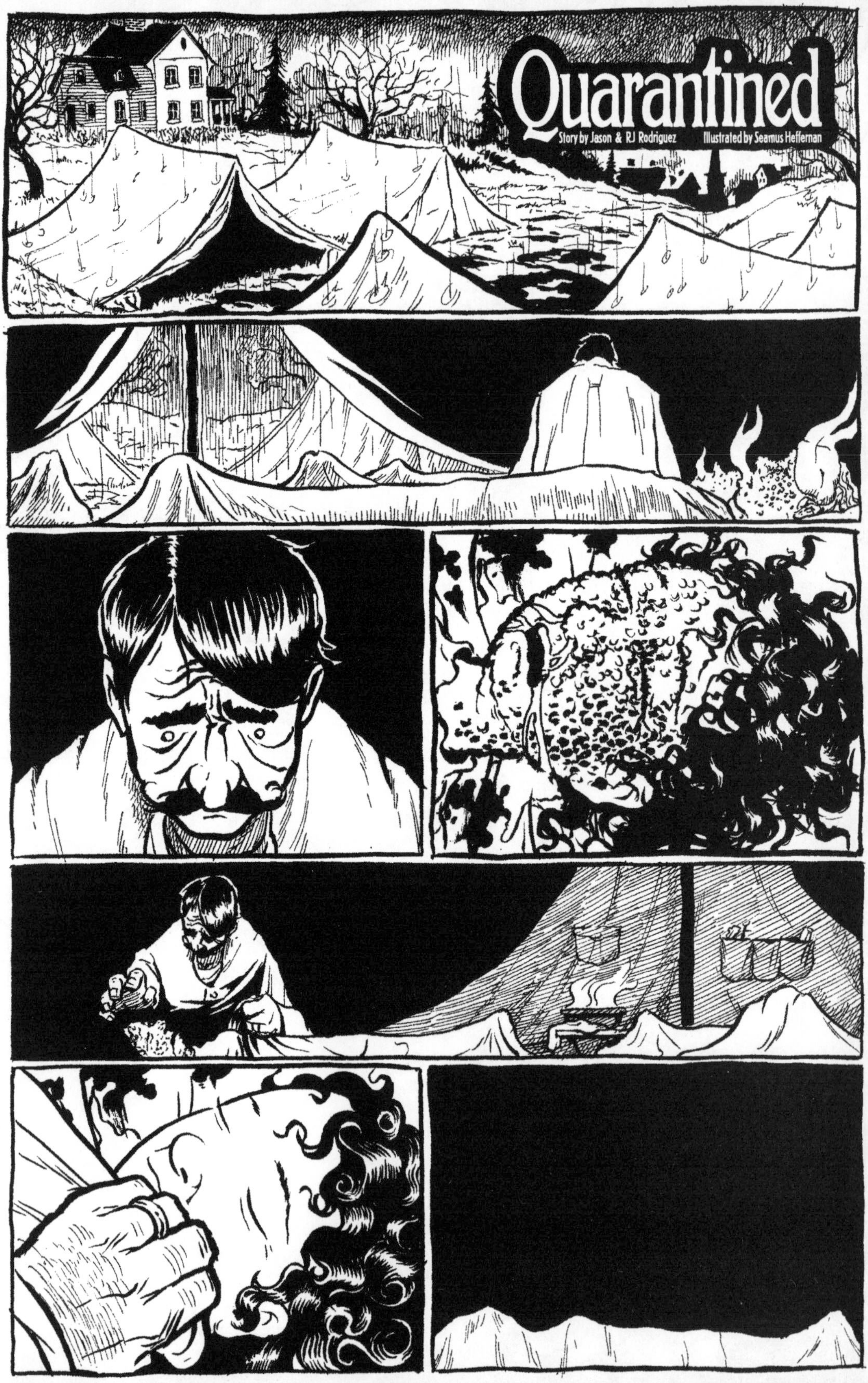
Quarantined
Story by Jason & RJ Rodriguez
Illustrated by Seamus Heffernan

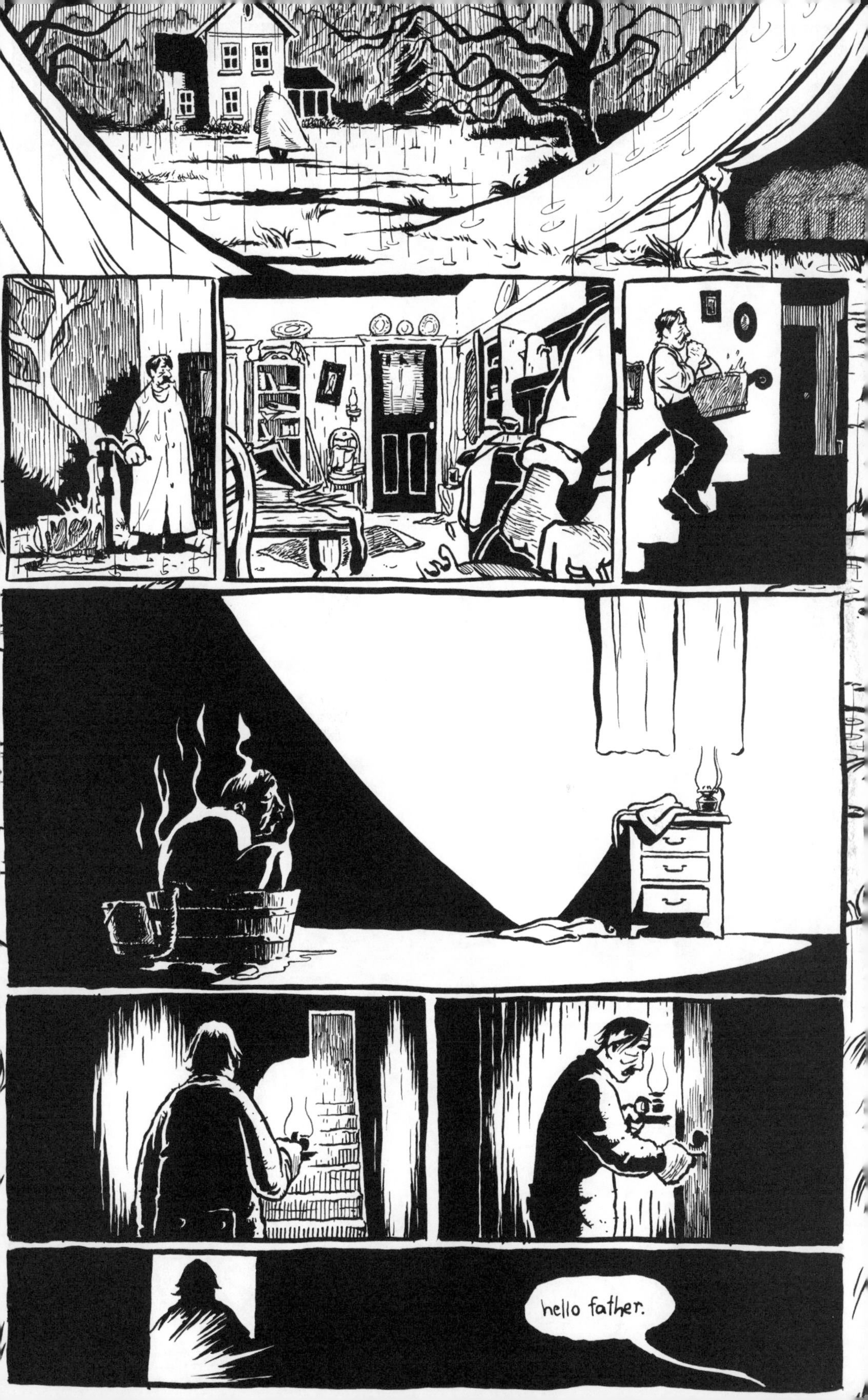
hello father.

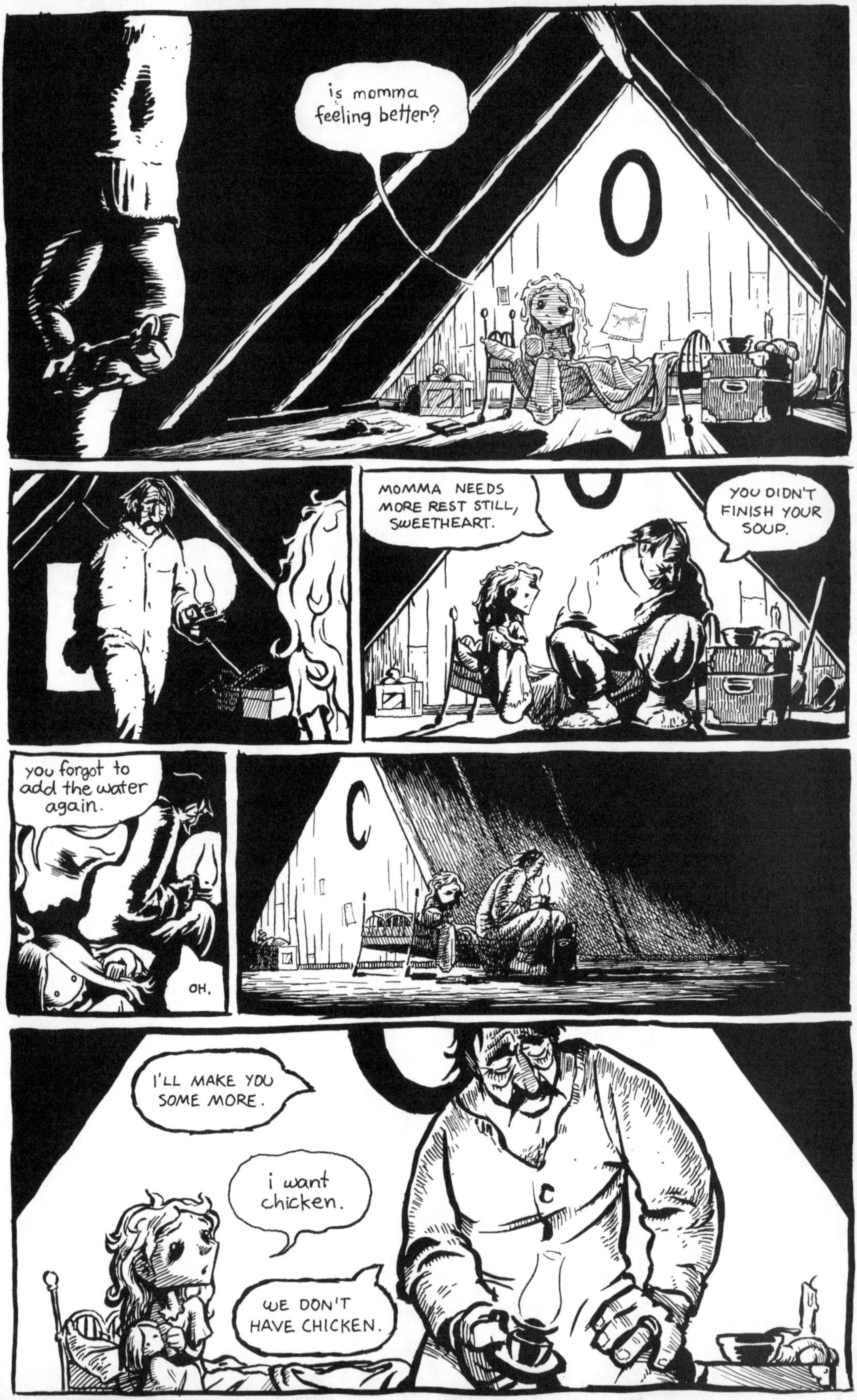
is momma feeling better?
MOMMA NEEDS MORE REST STILL, SWEETHEART.
YOU DIDN'T FINISH YOUR SOUP.
you forgot to add the water again.
OH.
I'LL MAKE YOU SOME MORE.
i want chicken.
WE DON'T HAVE CHICKEN.

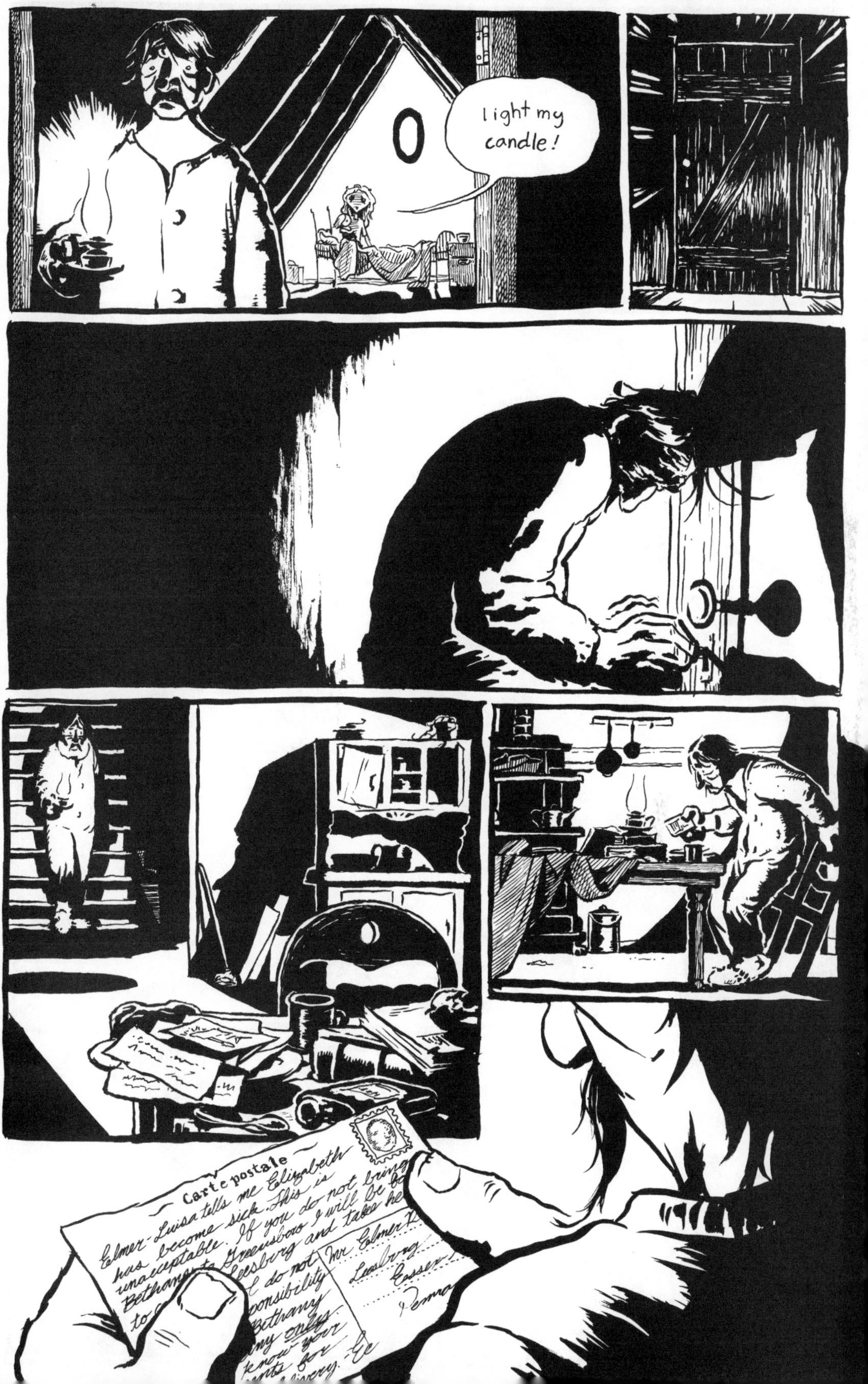
light my candle!
Carte postale
Elmer- Luisa tells me Elizabeth
has become sick. This is
unacceptable. If you do not bring
Bethany to Greensboro I will be
Leesburg and take
I do not
sponsibility
Bethany
my only
know your
ents for
livery. -Ee
Mr Elmer
Leesburg
Essex

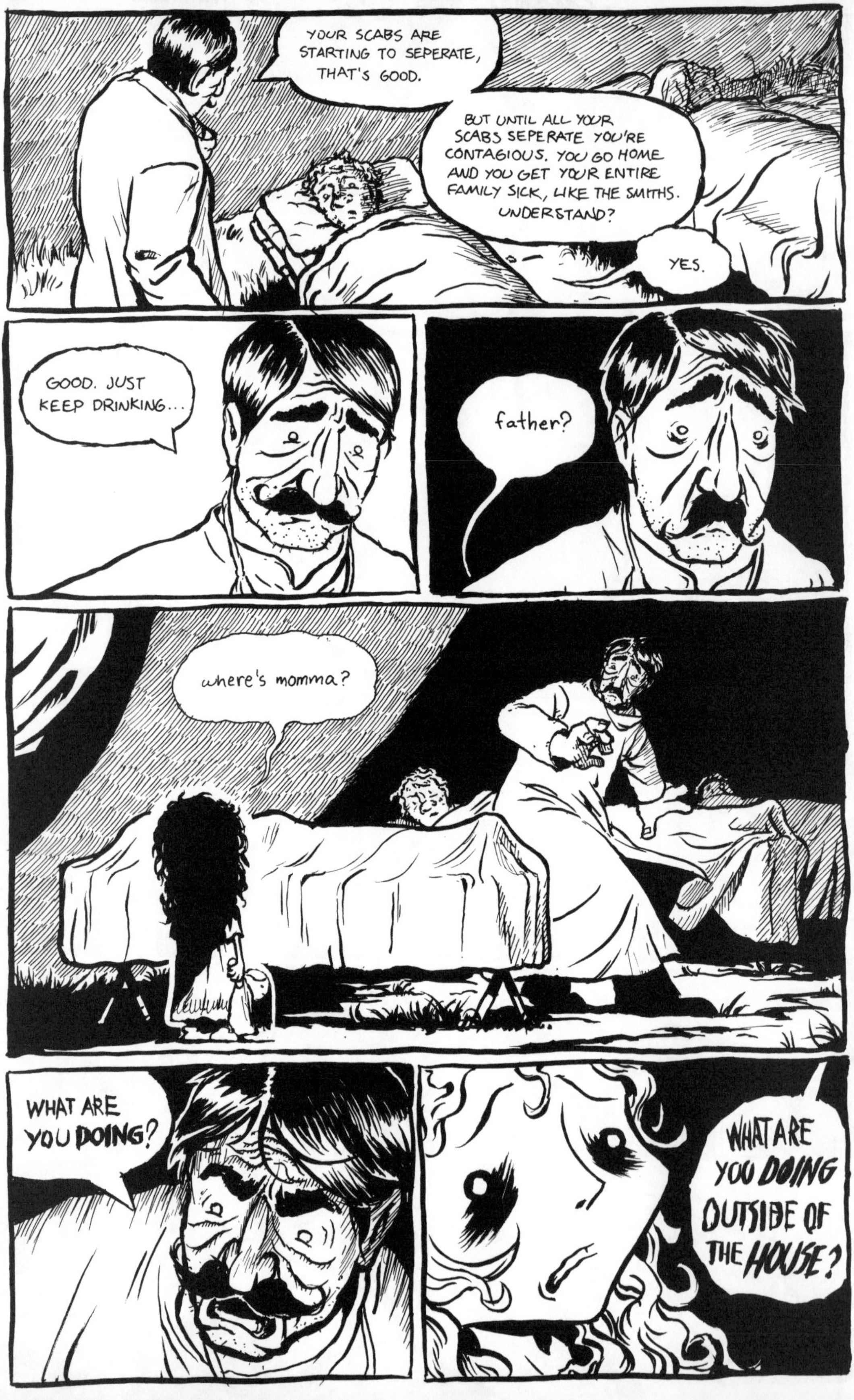
YOUR SCABS ARE STARTING TO SEPERATE, THAT'S GOOD.
BUT UNTIL ALL YOUR SCABS SEPERATE YOU'RE CONTAGIOUS. YOU GO HOME AND YOU GET YOUR ENTIRE FAMILY SICK, LIKE THE SMITHS. UNDERSTAND?
YES.
GOOD. JUST KEEP DRINKING...
father?
where's momma?
WHAT ARE YOU DOING?
WHAT ARE YOU DOING OUTSIDE OF THE HOUSE?

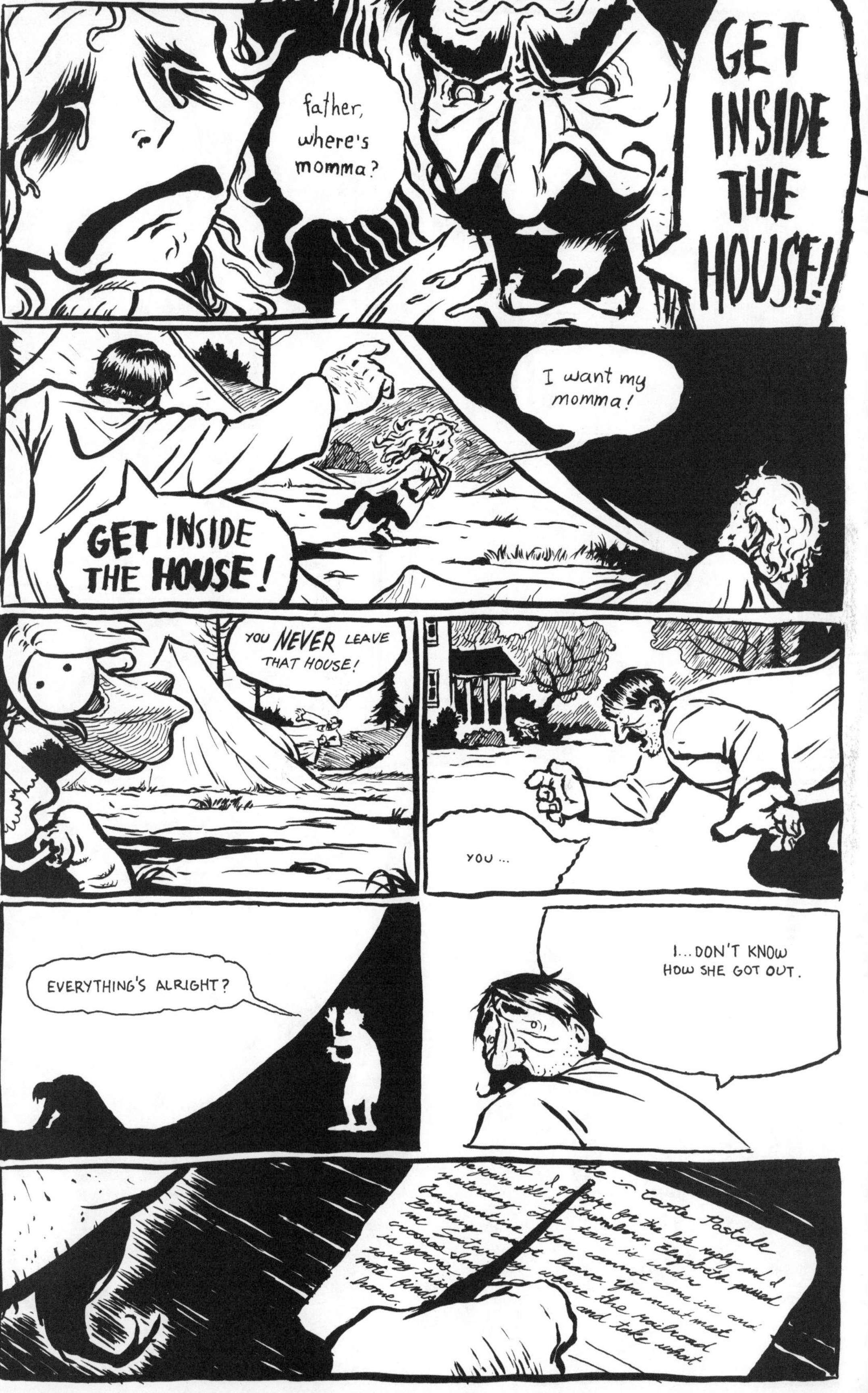

father, where's momma?
GET INSIDE THE HOUSE!
I want my momma!
GET INSIDE THE HOUSE!
YOU NEVER LEAVE THAT HOUSE!
YOU ...
EVERYTHING'S ALRIGHT?
I... DON'T KNOW HOW SHE GOT OUT.
Castle Postale
for the late reply and I
yesterday.
Elizabeth passed
town is under
Quarantine
you cannot come in and
leave. You must meet
where the railroad
and take what
is yours.
home.

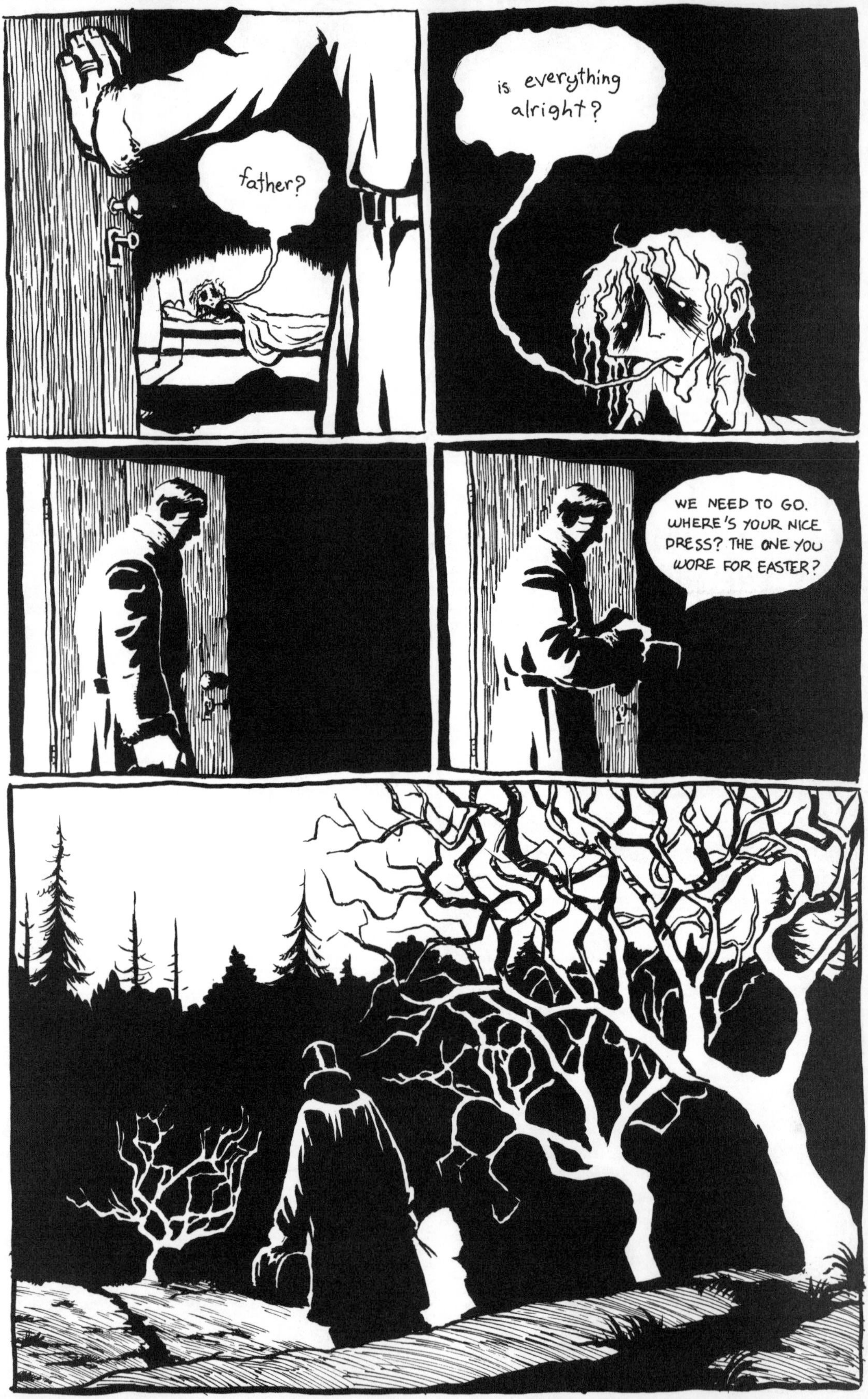
father?
is everything alright?
WE NEED TO GO. WHERE'S YOUR NICE DRESS? THE ONE YOU WORE FOR EASTER?

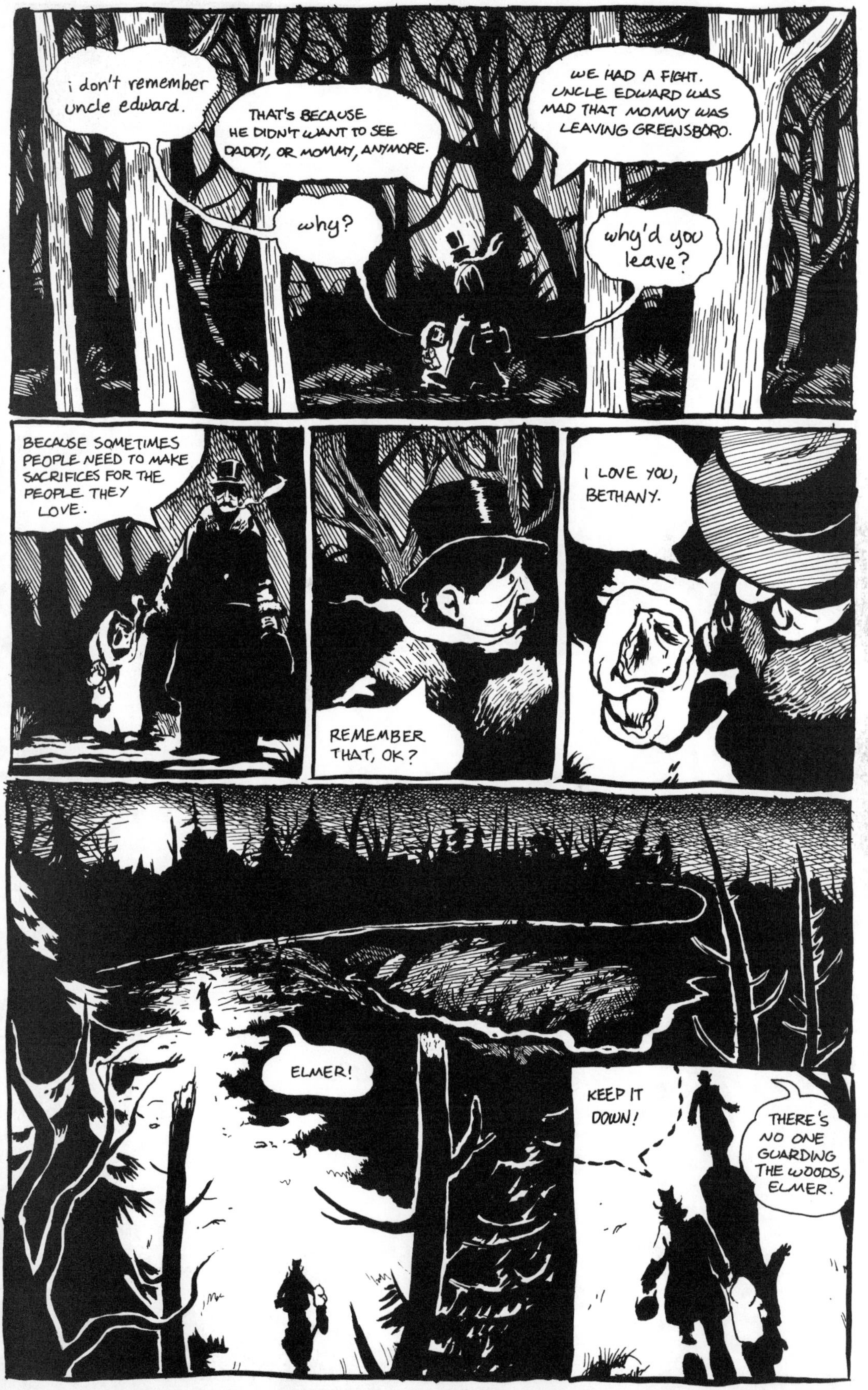
i don't remember uncle edward.
THAT'S BECAUSE HE DIDN'T WANT TO SEE DADDY, OR MOMMY, ANYMORE.
why?
WE HAD A FIGHT. UNCLE EDWARD WAS MAD THAT MOMMY WAS LEAVING GREENSBORO.
why'd you leave?
BECAUSE SOMETIMES PEOPLE NEED TO MAKE SACRIFICES FOR THE PEOPLE THEY LOVE.
REMEMBER THAT, OK?
I LOVE YOU, BETHANY.
ELMER!
KEEP IT DOWN!
THERE'S NO ONE GUARDING THE WOODS, ELMER.

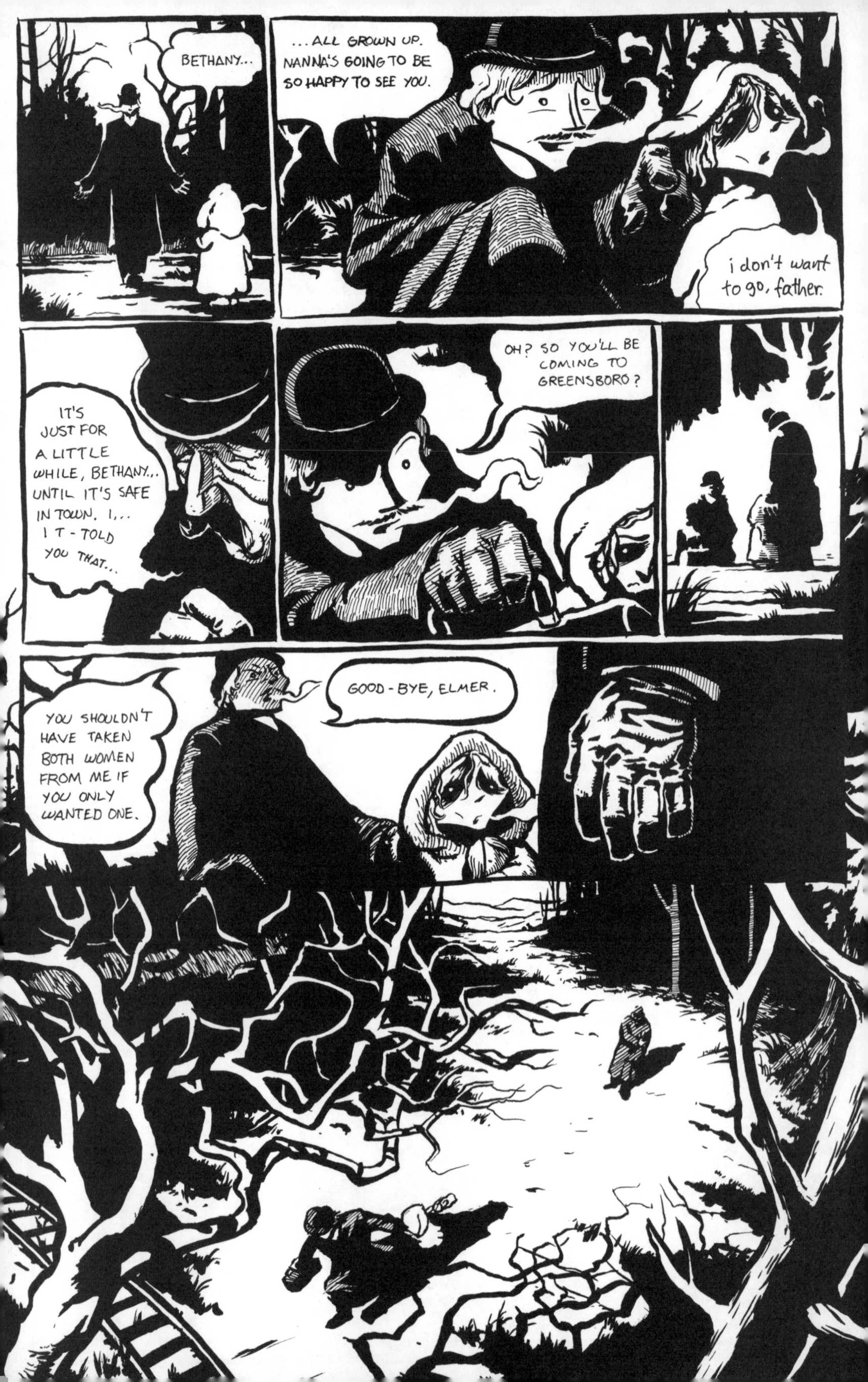

BETHANY...
...ALL GROWN UP. NANNA'S GOING TO BE SO HAPPY TO SEE YOU.
i don't want to go, father.
IT'S JUST FOR A LITTLE WHILE, BETHANY... UNTIL IT'S SAFE IN TOWN. I,.. I T-TOLD YOU THAT...
OH? SO YOU'LL BE COMING TO GREENSBORO?
YOU SHOULDN'T HAVE TAKEN BOTH WOMEN FROM ME IF YOU ONLY WANTED ONE.
GOOD-BYE, ELMER.

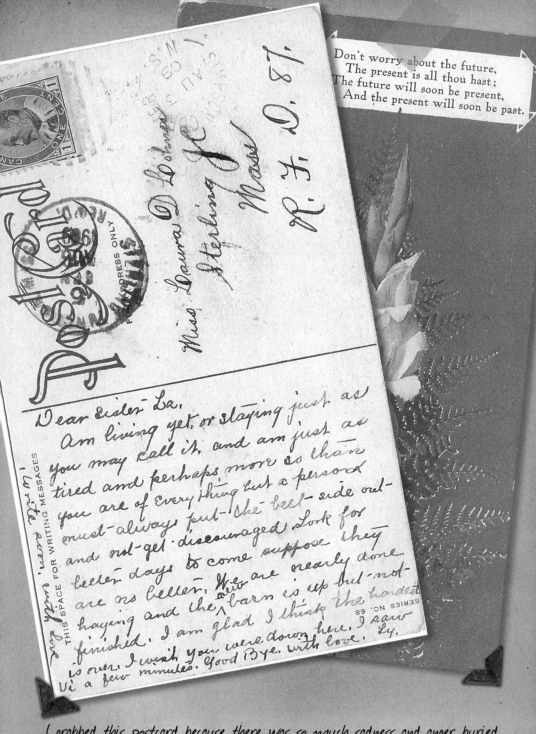

Miss Laura D. Lohnes
Sterling
Mass
R. F. D. 87.

Don't worry about the future,
The present is all thou hast;
The future will soon be present,
And the present will soon be past.

Dear sister La,
Am living yet, or staying just as
you may call it, and am just as
tired and perhaps more so than
you are of every thing but a person
must always put the best side out-
and not get discouraged Look for
better days to come suppose they
are no better, We are nearly done
haying and the barn is up but not-
finished. I am glad I think the hardest
is over, I wish you were down here, I saw
Vi a few minutes. Good Bye, with love, Ly.

THIS SPACE FOR WRITING MESSAGES

SERIES NO. 68

I grabbed this postcard because there was so much sadness and anger buried
inside the message. I saw it as a cry for help from an individual too proud to
come out and ask for it. I passed it on to Antony and Noel, expecting a tale of
a woman giving up on herself. Instead they show how a postcard can represent
hope in the form of little rebellions.

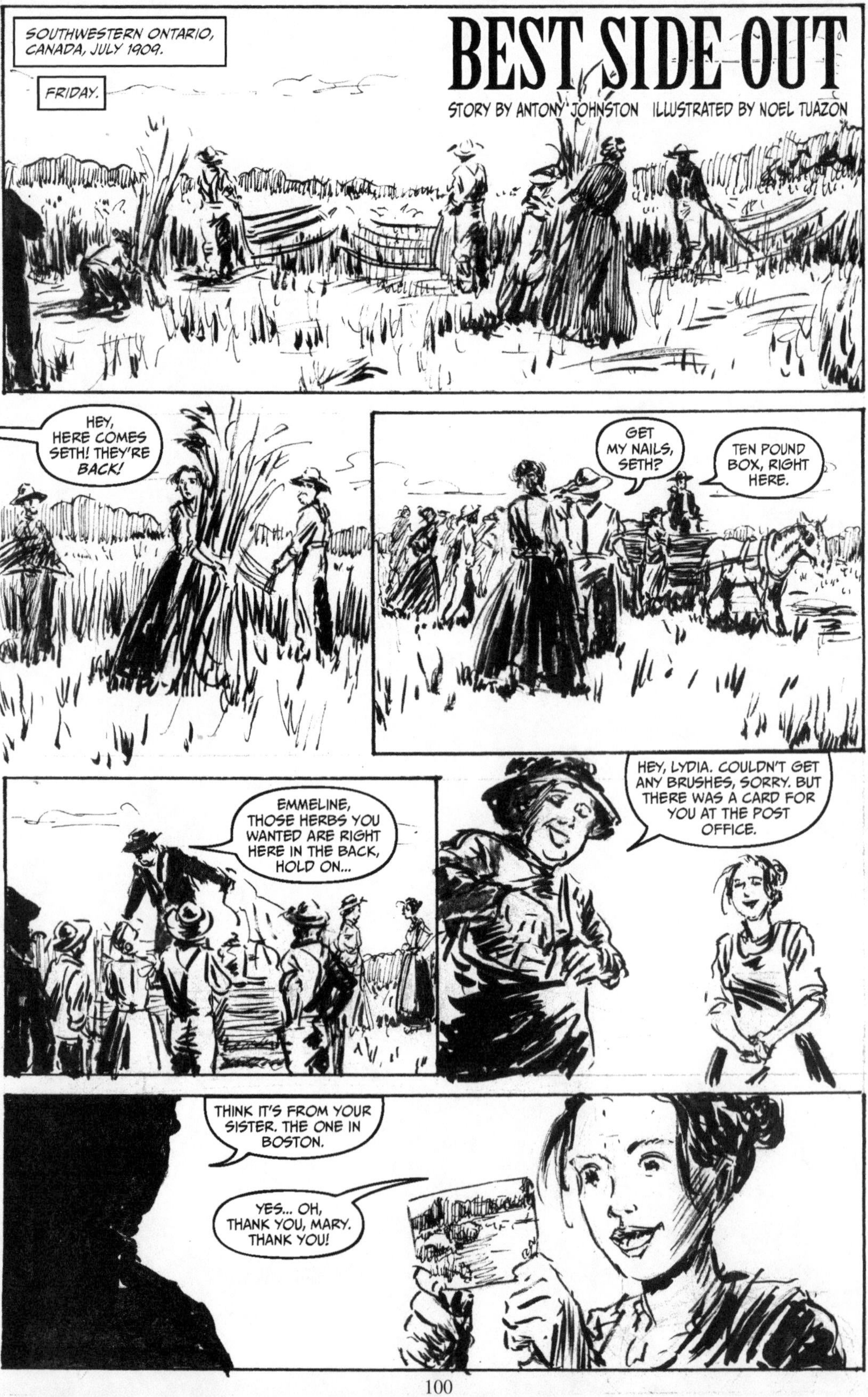
SOUTHWESTERN ONTARIO, CANADA, JULY 1909.
FRIDAY.
BEST SIDE OUT
STORY BY ANTONY JOHNSTON ILLUSTRATED BY NOEL TUAZON
HEY, HERE COMES SETH! THEY'RE BACK!
GET MY NAILS, SETH?
TEN POUND BOX, RIGHT HERE.
EMMELINE, THOSE HERBS YOU WANTED ARE RIGHT HERE IN THE BACK, HOLD ON...
HEY, LYDIA. COULDN'T GET ANY BRUSHES, SORRY. BUT THERE WAS A CARD FOR YOU AT THE POST OFFICE.
THINK IT'S FROM YOUR SISTER. THE ONE IN BOSTON.
YES... OH, THANK YOU, MARY. THANK YOU!

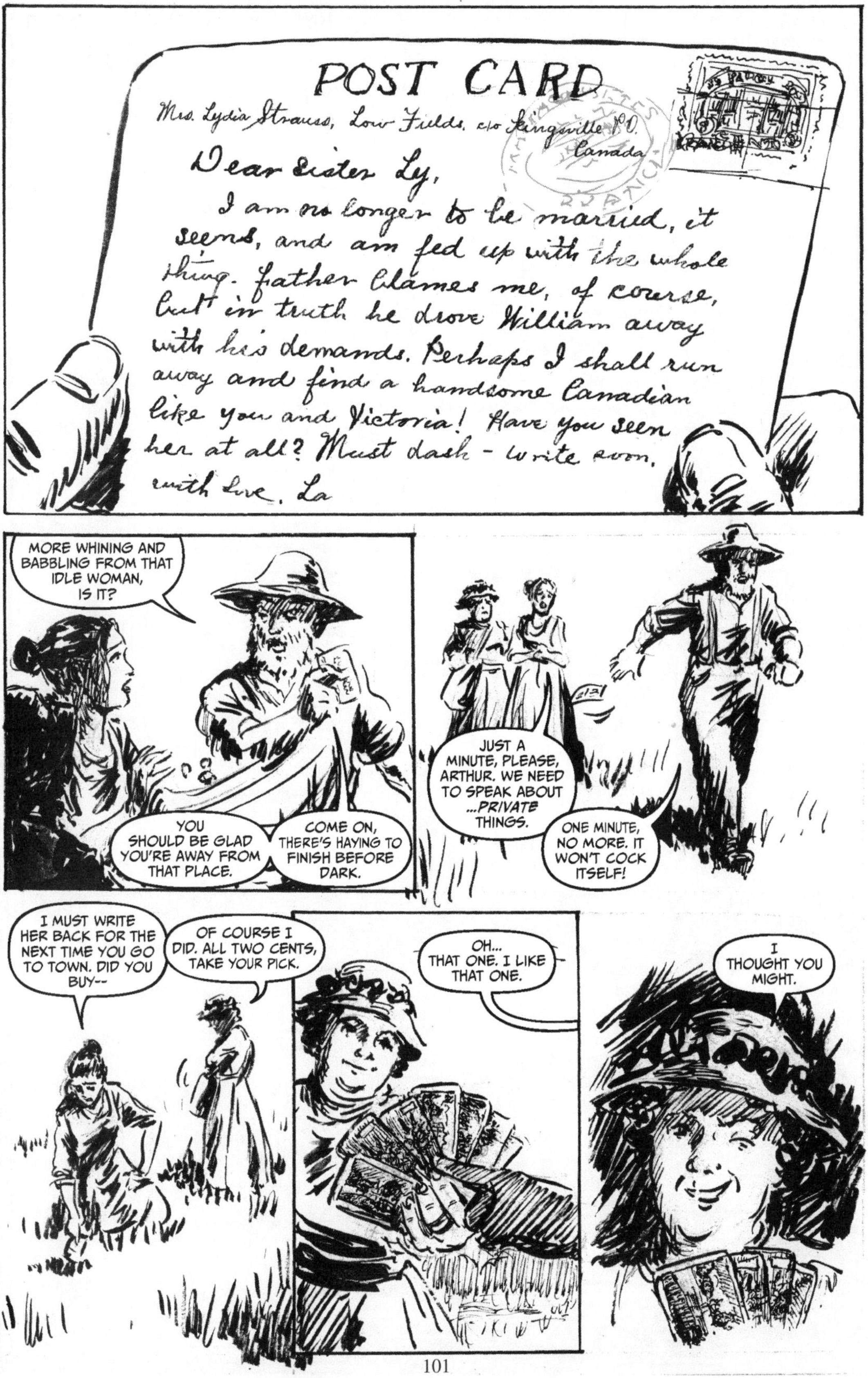
POST CARD
Mrs. Lydia Strauss, Low Fields. c/o Kingsville P.O.
Canada
Dear Sister Ly,
I am no longer to be married, it seems, and am fed up with the whole thing. Father blames me, of course, but in truth he drove William away with his demands. Perhaps I shall run away and find a handsome Canadian like you and Victoria! Have you seen her at all? Must dash - write soon.
With love, La
MORE WHINING AND BABBLING FROM THAT IDLE WOMAN, IS IT?
YOU SHOULD BE GLAD YOU'RE AWAY FROM THAT PLACE.
COME ON, THERE'S HAYING TO FINISH BEFORE DARK.
JUST A MINUTE, PLEASE, ARTHUR. WE NEED TO SPEAK ABOUT ...PRIVATE THINGS.
ONE MINUTE, NO MORE. IT WON'T COCK ITSELF!
I MUST WRITE HER BACK FOR THE NEXT TIME YOU GO TO TOWN. DID YOU BUY--
OF COURSE I DID. ALL TWO CENTS, TAKE YOUR PICK.
OH... THAT ONE. I LIKE THAT ONE.
I THOUGHT YOU MIGHT.

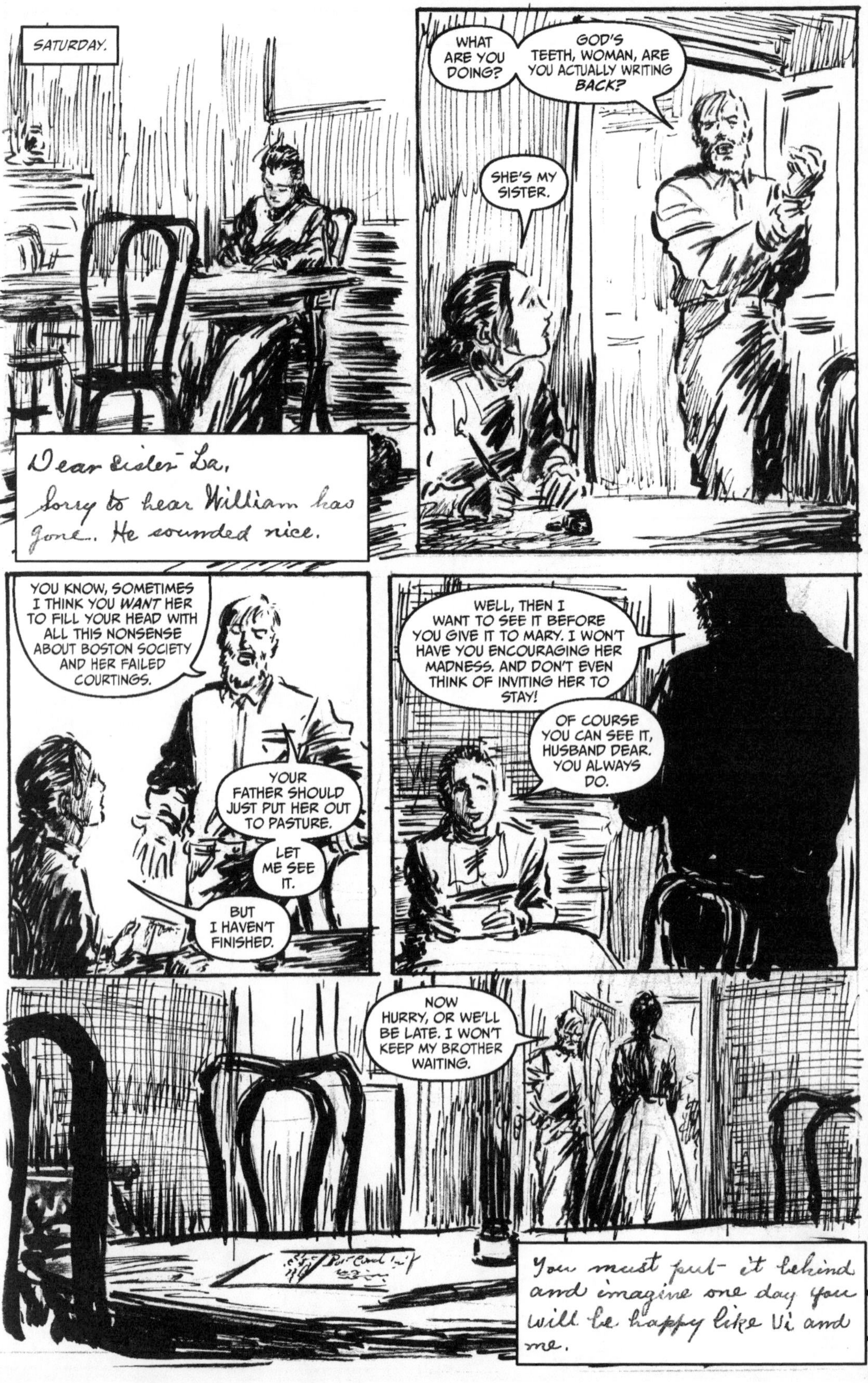
SATURDAY.
Dear sister La,
Sorry to hear William has gone.. He sounded nice.
WHAT ARE YOU DOING?
GOD'S TEETH, WOMAN, ARE YOU ACTUALLY WRITING BACK?
SHE'S MY SISTER.
YOU KNOW, SOMETIMES I THINK YOU WANT HER TO FILL YOUR HEAD WITH ALL THIS NONSENSE ABOUT BOSTON SOCIETY AND HER FAILED COURTINGS.
YOUR FATHER SHOULD JUST PUT HER OUT TO PASTURE.
LET ME SEE IT.
BUT I HAVEN'T FINISHED.
WELL, THEN I WANT TO SEE IT BEFORE YOU GIVE IT TO MARY. I WON'T HAVE YOU ENCOURAGING HER MADNESS. AND DON'T EVEN THINK OF INVITING HER TO STAY!
OF COURSE YOU CAN SEE IT, HUSBAND DEAR. YOU ALWAYS DO.
NOW HURRY, OR WE'LL BE LATE. I WON'T KEEP MY BROTHER WAITING.
You must put it behind and imagine one day you will be happy like Vi and me.

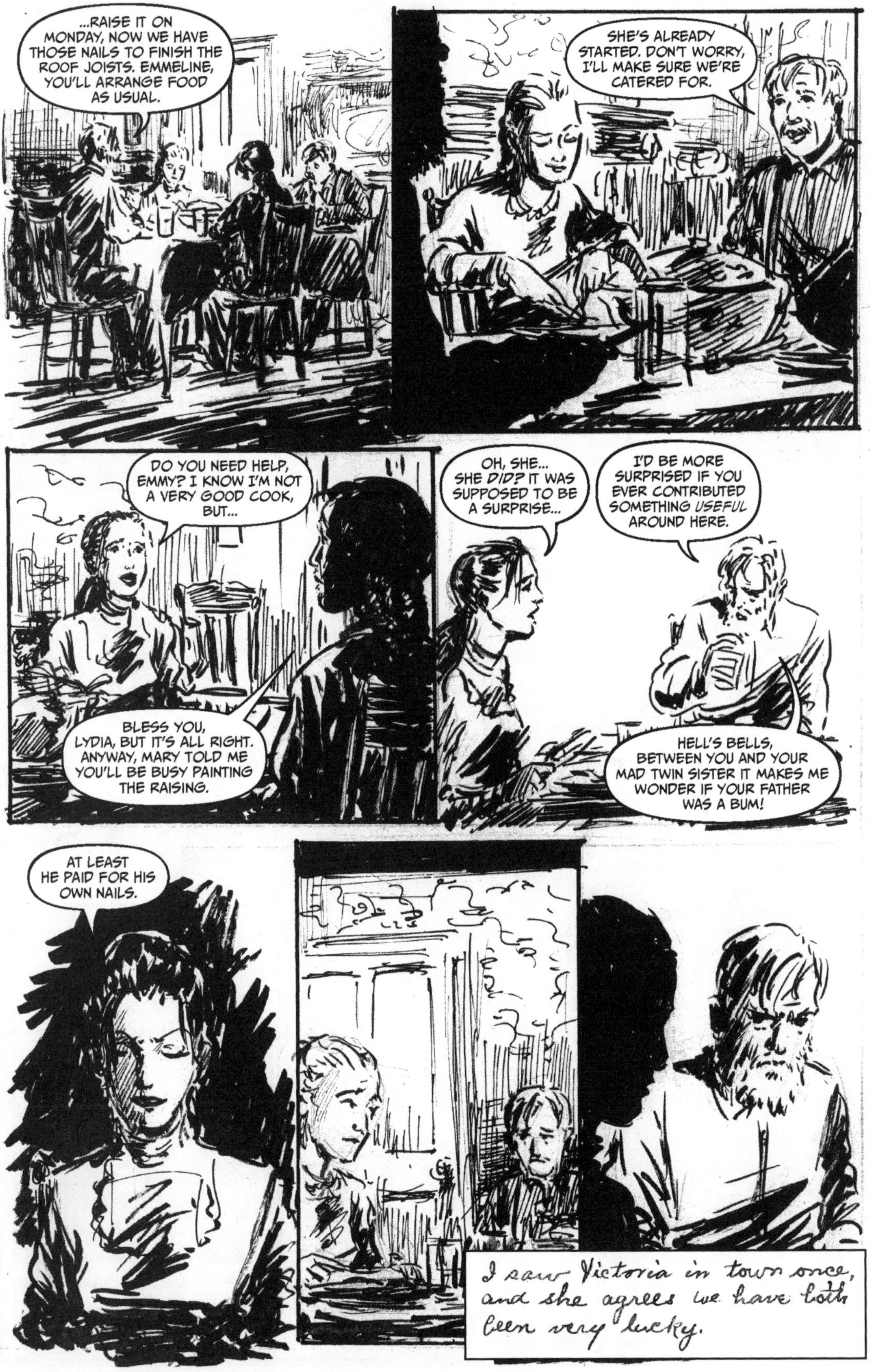
...RAISE IT ON MONDAY, NOW WE HAVE THOSE NAILS TO FINISH THE ROOF JOISTS. EMMELINE, YOU'LL ARRANGE FOOD AS USUAL.
SHE'S ALREADY STARTED. DON'T WORRY, I'LL MAKE SURE WE'RE CATERED FOR.
DO YOU NEED HELP, EMMY? I KNOW I'M NOT A VERY GOOD COOK, BUT...
BLESS YOU, LYDIA, BUT IT'S ALL RIGHT. ANYWAY, MARY TOLD ME YOU'LL BE BUSY PAINTING THE RAISING.
OH, SHE... SHE *DID?* IT WAS SUPPOSED TO BE A SURPRISE...
I'D BE MORE SURPRISED IF YOU EVER CONTRIBUTED SOMETHING *USEFUL* AROUND HERE.
HELL'S BELLS, BETWEEN YOU AND YOUR MAD TWIN SISTER IT MAKES ME WONDER IF YOUR FATHER WAS A BUM!
AT LEAST HE PAID FOR HIS OWN NAILS.
I saw Victoria in town once, and she agrees we have both been very lucky.

SUNDAY.

...AND JESUS ANSWERED AND SAID UNTO THEM, FOR THE HARDNESS OF YOUR HEART HE WROTE YOU THIS PRECEPT. BUT FROM THE BEGINNING OF CREATION GOD MADE THEM MALE AND FEMALE.

"FOR THIS CAUSE SHALL A MAN LEAVE HIS FATHER AND MOTHER, AND CLEAVE TO HIS WIFE.

"AND THEY TWAIN SHALL BE ONE FLESH: SO THEN THEY ARE NO MORE TWAIN, BUT ONE FLESH.

"WHAT THEREFORE GOD HATH JOINED TOGETHER, LET NO MAN PUT ASUNDER."

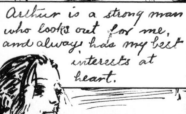

Arthur is a strong man who looks out for me, and always has my best interests at heart.

I hope you are lucky enough to find someone like him who will look after you, dear sister.

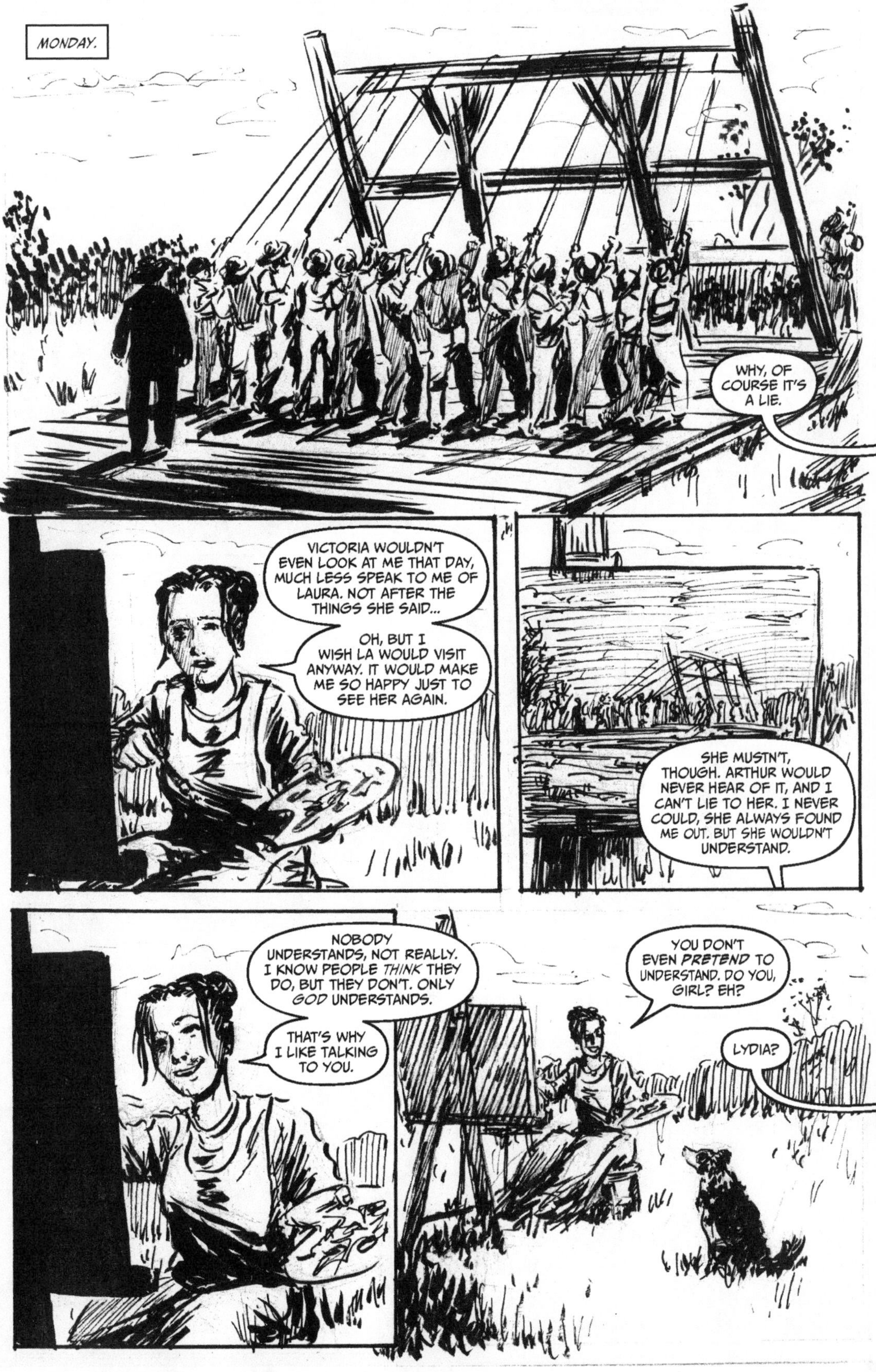
MONDAY.
WHY, OF COURSE IT'S A LIE.
VICTORIA WOULDN'T EVEN LOOK AT ME THAT DAY, MUCH LESS SPEAK TO ME OF LAURA. NOT AFTER THE THINGS SHE SAID...
OH, BUT I WISH LA WOULD VISIT ANYWAY. IT WOULD MAKE ME SO HAPPY JUST TO SEE HER AGAIN.
SHE MUSTN'T, THOUGH. ARTHUR WOULD NEVER HEAR OF IT, AND I CAN'T LIE TO HER. I NEVER COULD, SHE ALWAYS FOUND ME OUT. BUT SHE WOULDN'T UNDERSTAND.
NOBODY UNDERSTANDS, NOT REALLY. I KNOW PEOPLE *THINK* THEY DO, BUT THEY DON'T. ONLY *GOD* UNDERSTANDS.
THAT'S WHY I LIKE TALKING TO YOU.
YOU DON'T EVEN *PRETEND* TO UNDERSTAND. DO YOU, GIRL? EH?
LYDIA?

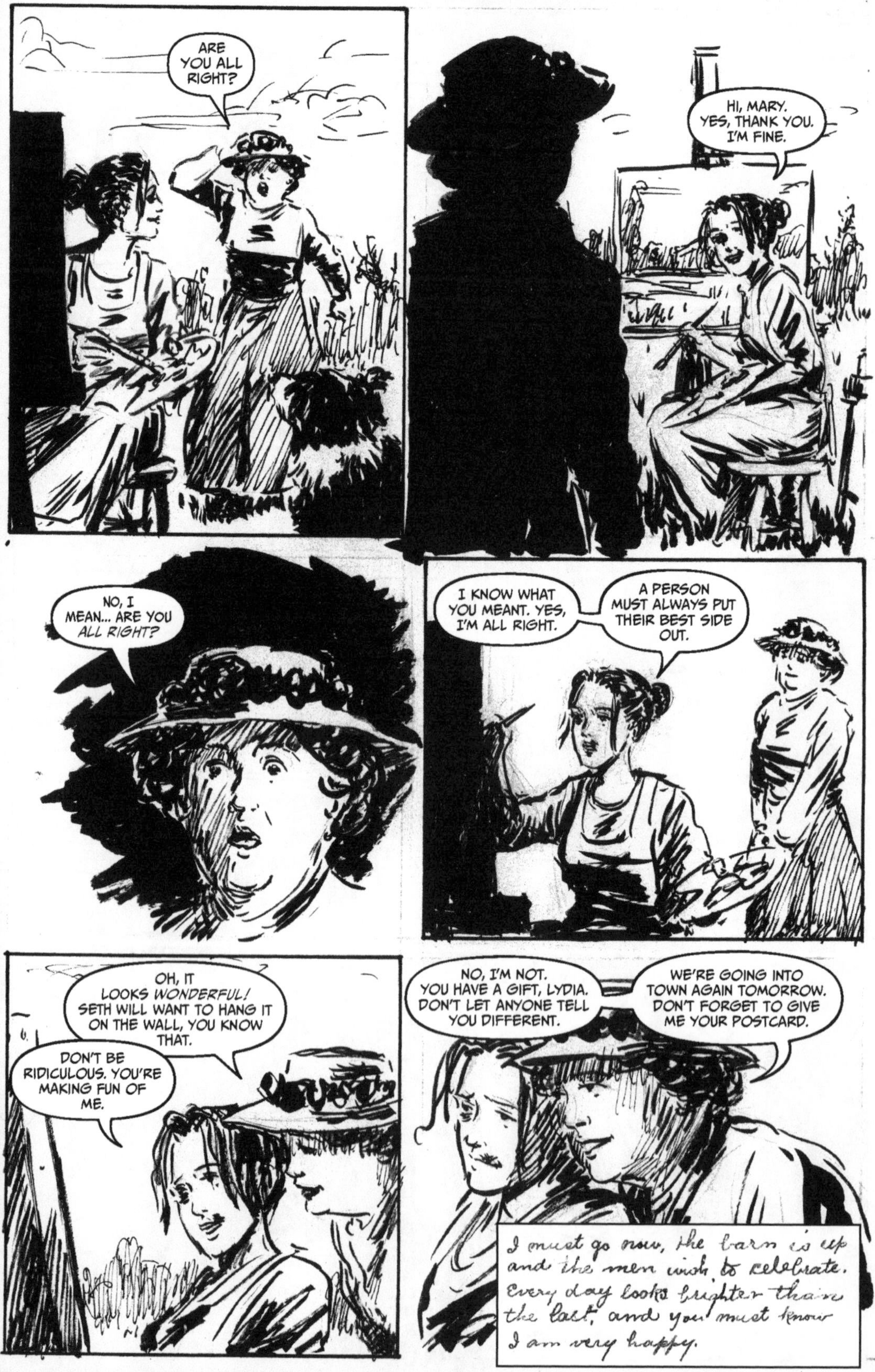
ARE YOU ALL RIGHT?
HI, MARY. YES, THANK YOU. I'M FINE.
NO, I MEAN... ARE YOU *ALL RIGHT?*
I KNOW WHAT YOU MEANT. YES, I'M ALL RIGHT.
A PERSON MUST ALWAYS PUT THEIR BEST SIDE OUT.
OH, IT LOOKS *WONDERFUL!* SETH WILL WANT TO HANG IT ON THE WALL, YOU KNOW THAT.
DON'T BE RIDICULOUS. YOU'RE MAKING FUN OF ME.
NO, I'M NOT. YOU HAVE A GIFT, LYDIA. DON'T LET ANYONE TELL YOU DIFFERENT.
WE'RE GOING INTO TOWN AGAIN TOMORROW. DON'T FORGET TO GIVE ME YOUR POSTCARD.
I must go now, the barn is up and the men wish to celebrate. Every day looks brighter than the last, and you must know I am very happy.

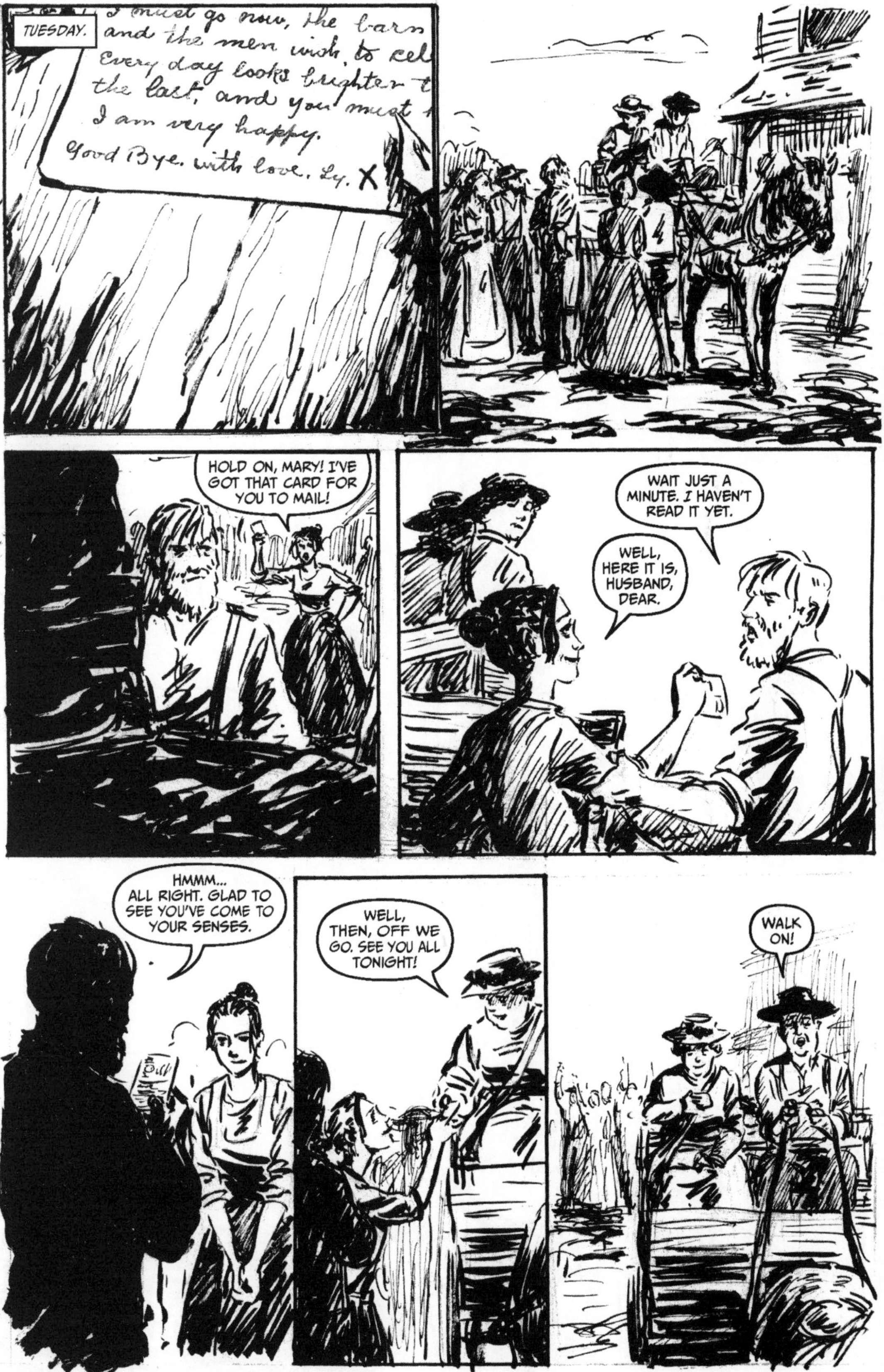
TUESDAY.
I must go now, the barn
and the men wish to cel
Every day looks brighter t
the last, and you must
I am very happy.
Good Bye. with love. Ly. X
HOLD ON, MARY! I'VE GOT THAT CARD FOR YOU TO MAIL!
WAIT JUST A MINUTE. I HAVEN'T READ IT YET.
WELL, HERE IT IS, HUSBAND, DEAR.
HMMM... ALL RIGHT. GLAD TO SEE YOU'VE COME TO YOUR SENSES.
WELL, THEN, OFF WE GO. SEE YOU ALL TONIGHT!
WALK ON!

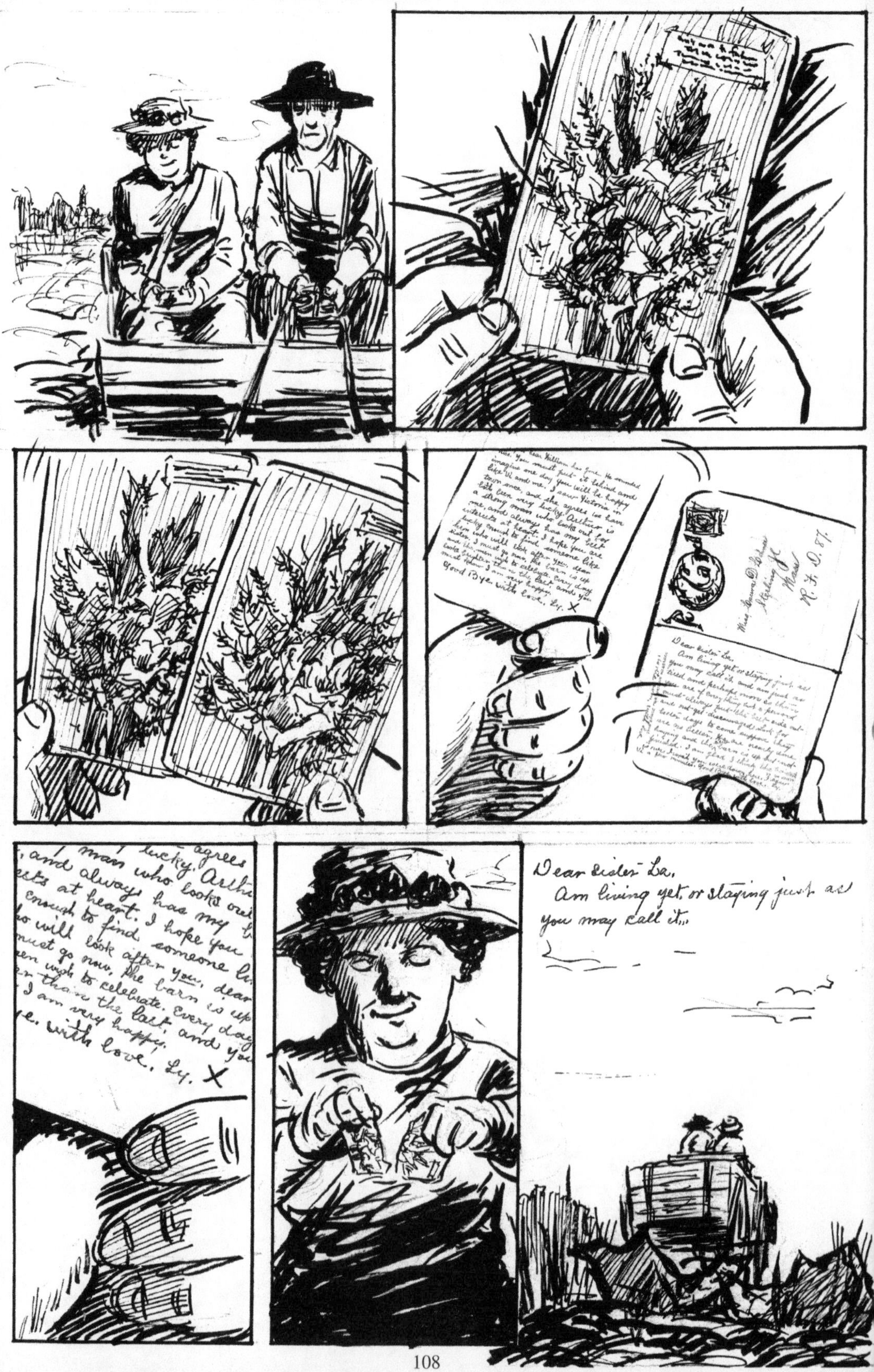
Dear sister La.
Am living yet, or staying just as you may call it...

A JOLLY XMAS

Had I all the Wishes in
The World to give,
I'd give them all to you

152

POST CARD

CORRESPONDENCE ADDRESS

BERMUDIAN
JAN
8
1919
PA.

Mrs Earl James
Dillsburg
York Co

"Butchered last week,
now we have fresh meat." I love that line — it has
such a turn-of-the-century Americana feel to it. Neil and Jake latched
onto that line, too, and crafted a story that shows how postcards can inspire people
to recognize one's own needs and offer help to others.

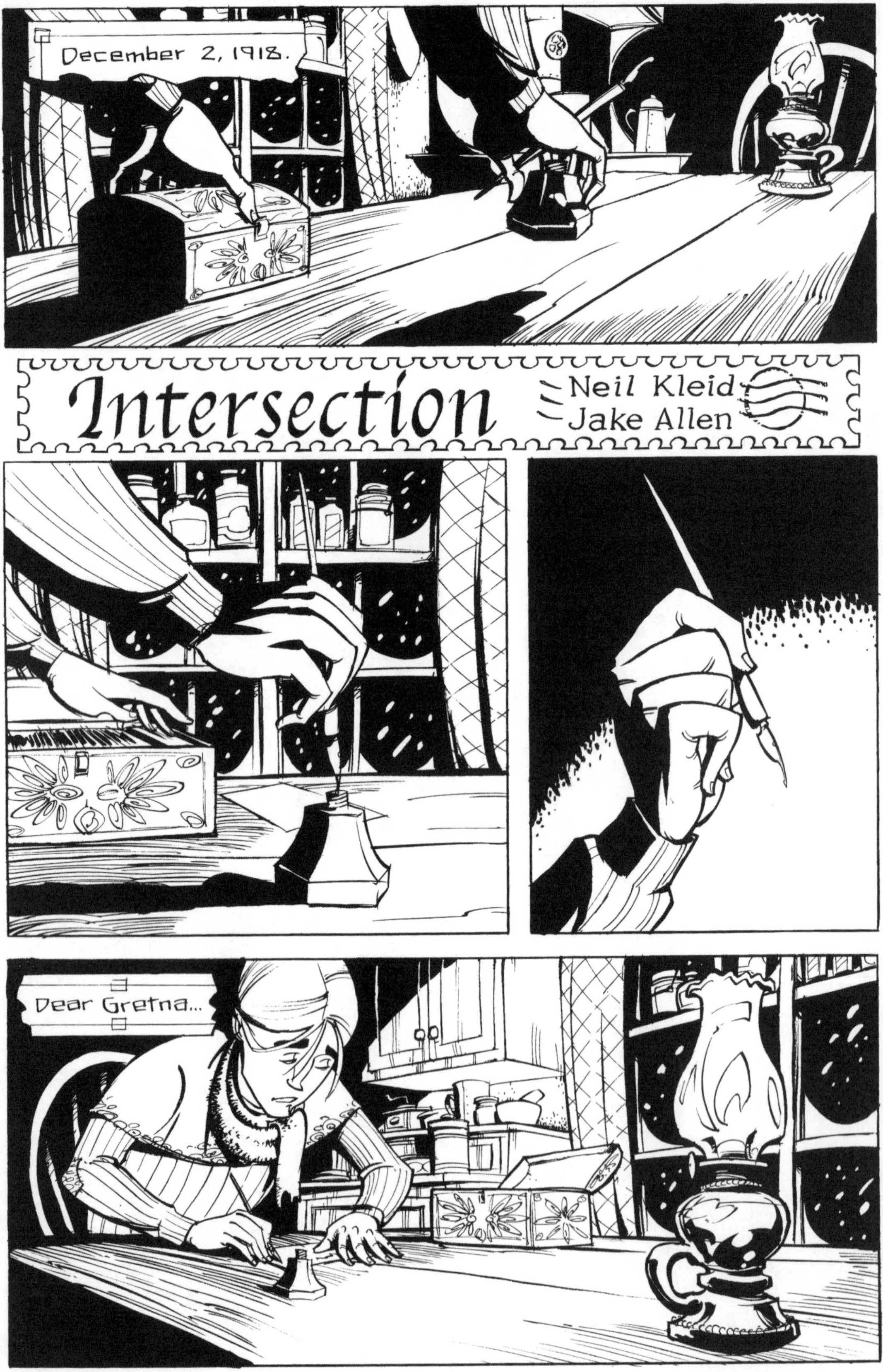
December 2, 1918.
Intersection
Neil Kleid
Jake Allen
Dear Gretna...

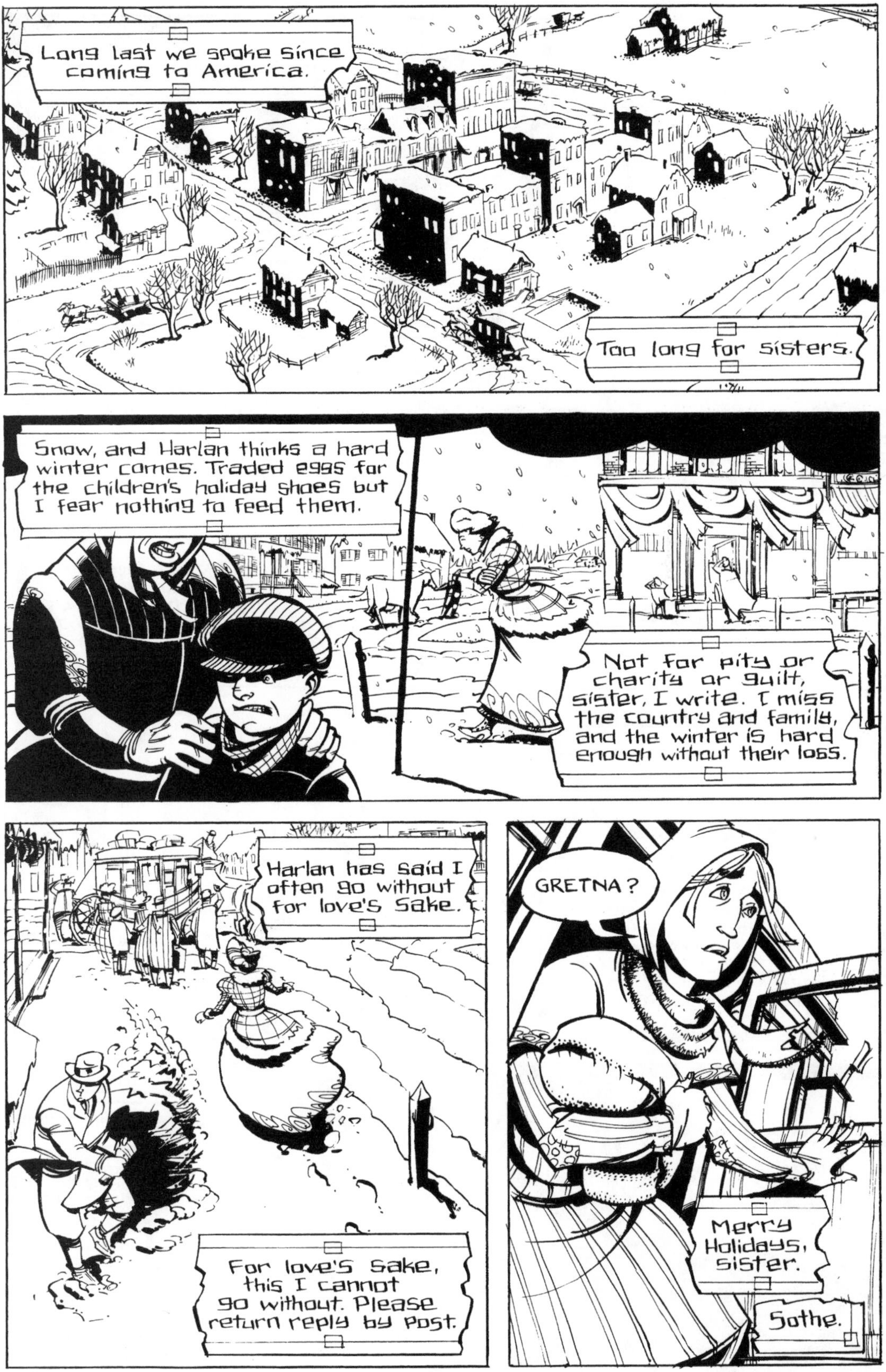
Long last we spoke since coming to America.
Too long for sisters.
Snow, and Harlan thinks a hard winter comes. Traded eggs for the children's holiday shoes but I fear nothing to feed them.
Not for pity or charity or guilt, sister, I write. I miss the country and family, and the winter is hard enough without their loss.
Harlan has said I often go without for love's sake.
For love's sake, this I cannot go without. Please return reply by post.
GRETNA?
Merry Holidays, sister.
Sothe.

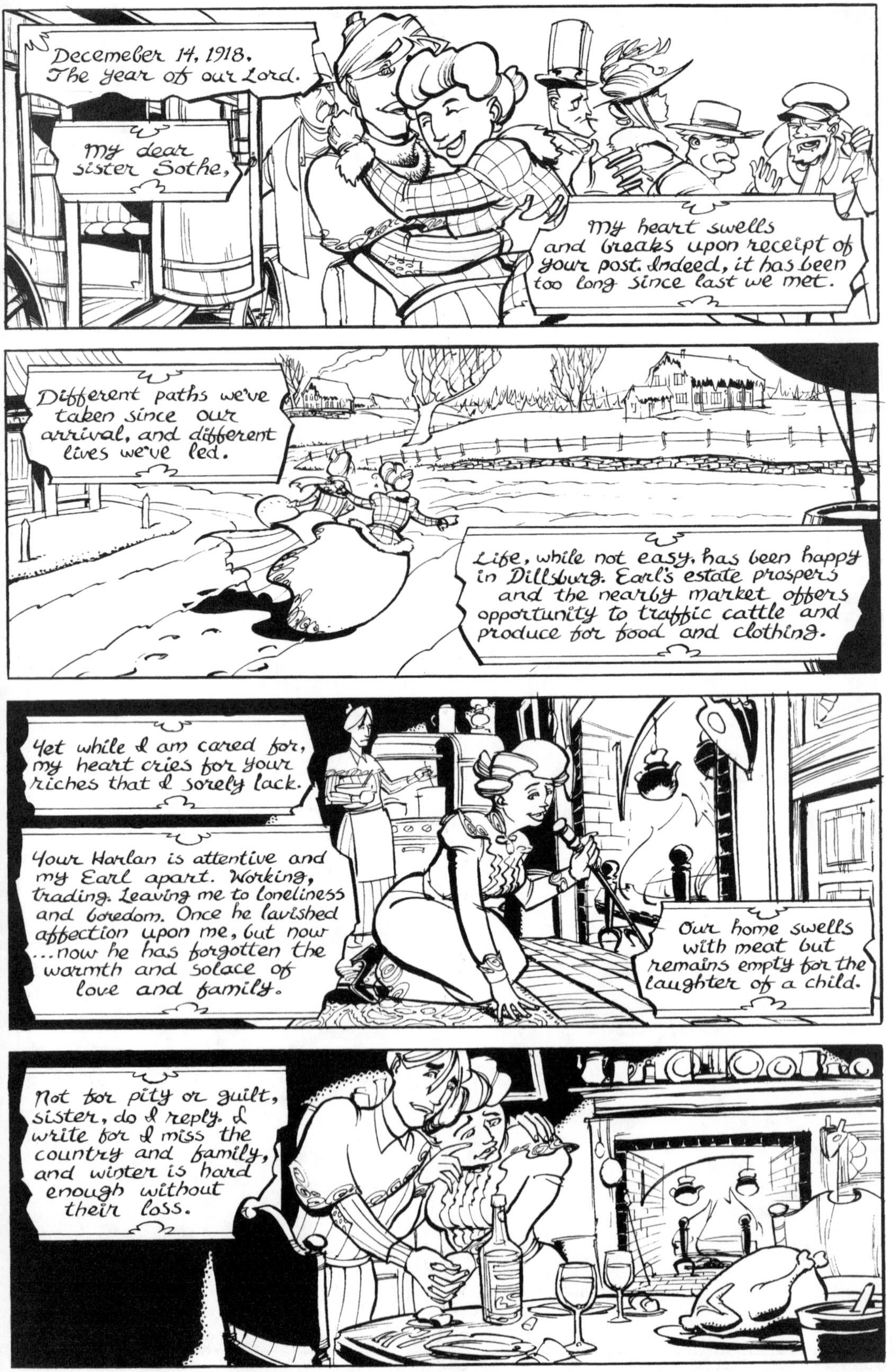

Decemeber 14, 1918. The year of our Lord.
My dear sister Sothe,
My heart swells and breaks upon receipt of your post. Indeed, it has been too long since last we met.
Different paths we've taken since our arrival, and different lives we've led.
Life, while not easy, has been happy in Dillsburg. Earl's estate prospers and the nearby market offers opportunity to traffic cattle and produce for food and clothing.
Yet while I am cared for, my heart cries for your riches that I sorely lack.
Your Harlan is attentive and my Earl apart. Working, trading. Leaving me to loneliness and boredom. Once he lavished affection upon me, but now ...now he has forgotten the warmth and solace of love and family.
Our home swells with meat but remains empty for the laughter of a child.
Not for pity or guilt, sister, do I reply. I write for I miss the country and family, and winter is hard enough without their loss.

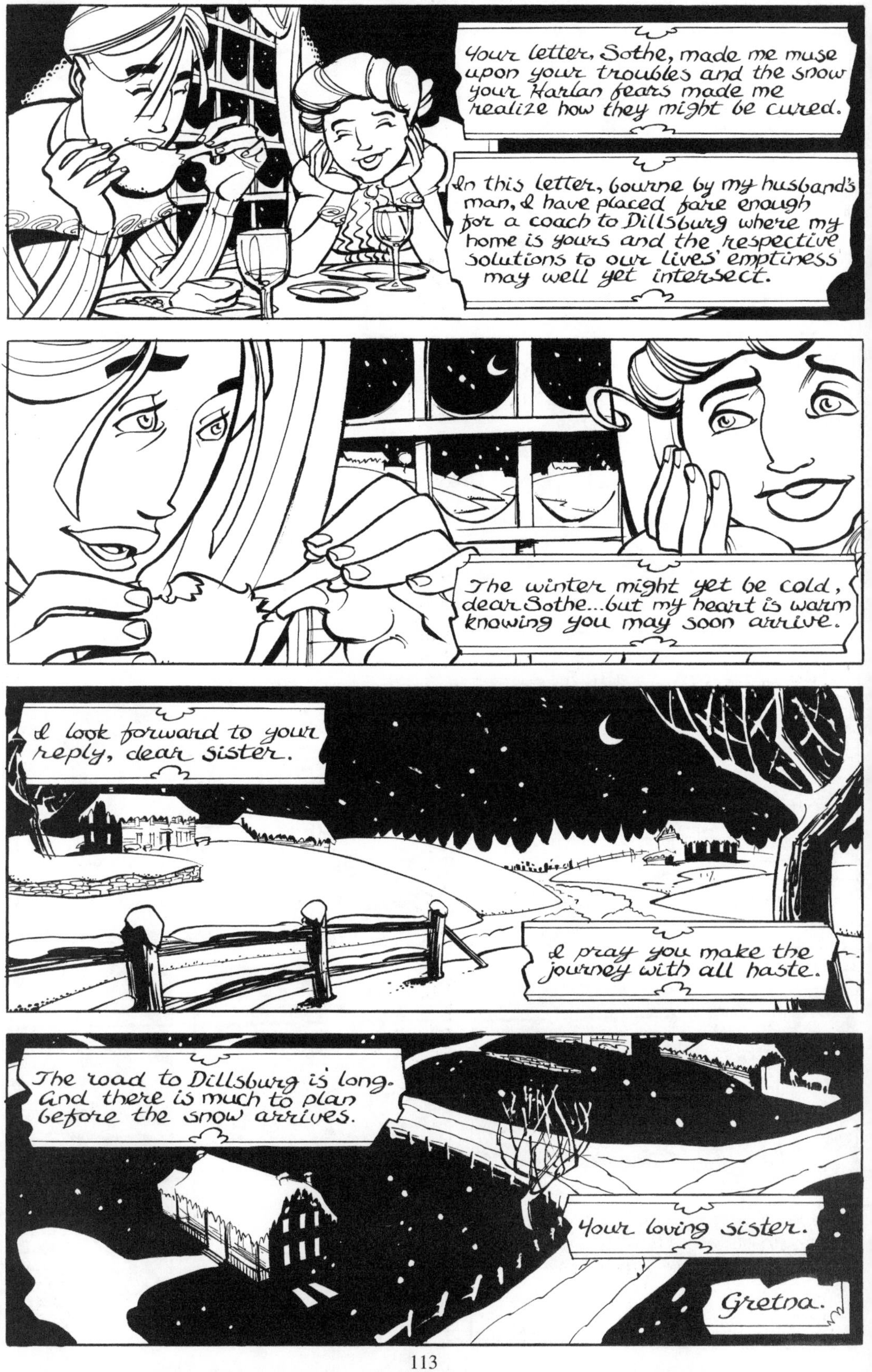
Your letter, Sothe, made me muse upon your troubles and the snow your Harlan fears made me realize how they might be cured.
In this letter, bourne by my husband's man, I have placed fare enough for a coach to Dillsburg where my home is yours and the respective solutions to our lives' emptiness may well yet intersect.
The winter might yet be cold, dear Sothe...but my heart is warm knowing you may soon arrive.
I look forward to your reply, dear sister.
I pray you make the journey with all haste.
The road to Dillsburg is long. And there is much to plan before the snow arrives.
Your loving sister.
Gretna.

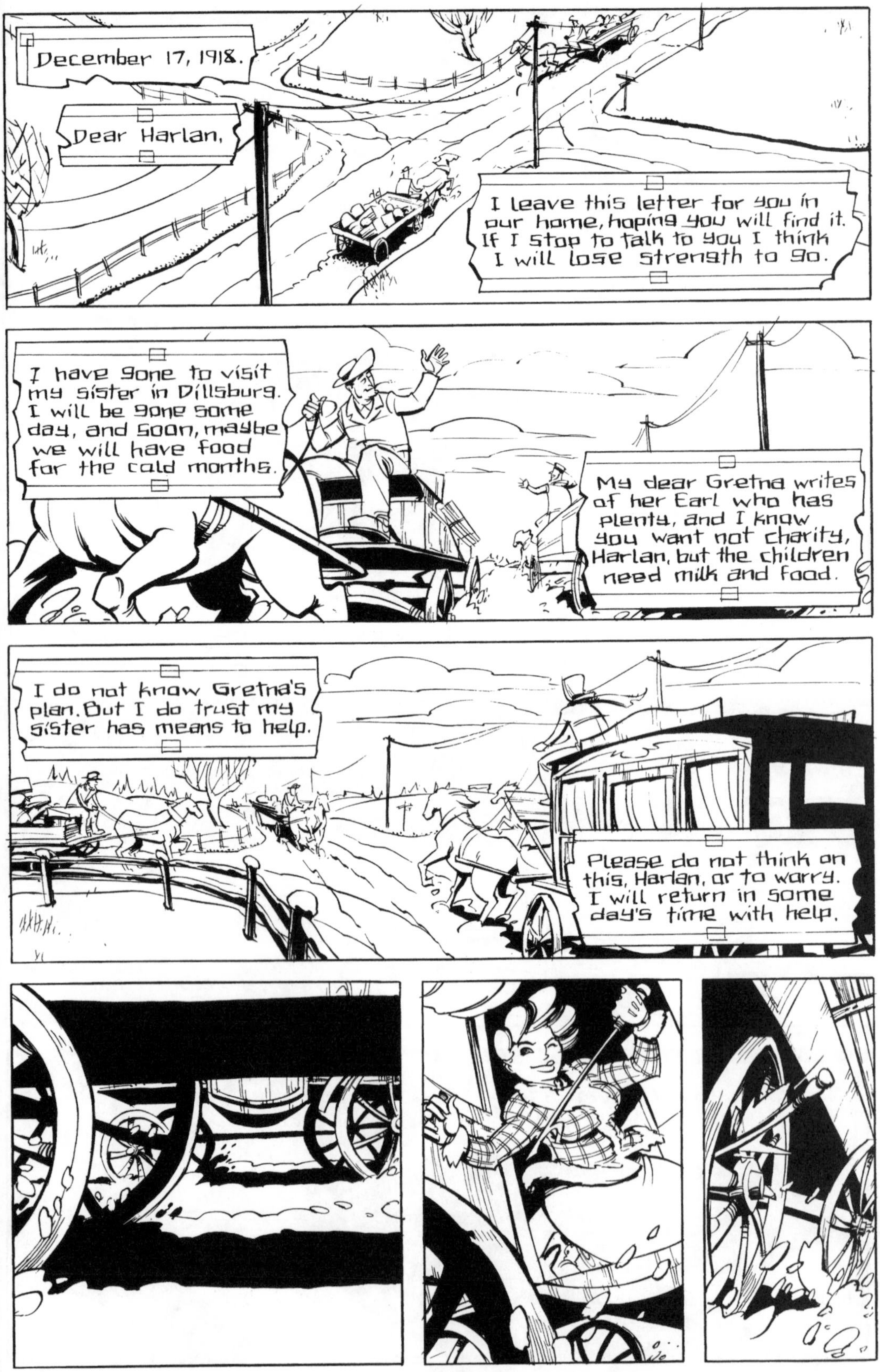
December 17, 1918.
Dear Harlan,
I leave this letter for you in our home, hoping you will find it. If I stop to talk to you I think I will lose strength to go.
I have gone to visit my sister in Dillsburg. I will be gone some day, and soon, maybe we will have food for the cold months.
My dear Gretna writes of her Earl who has plenty, and I know you want not charity, Harlan, but the children need milk and food.
I do not know Gretna's plan. But I do trust my sister has means to help.
Please do not think on this, Harlan, or to worry. I will return in some day's time with help.

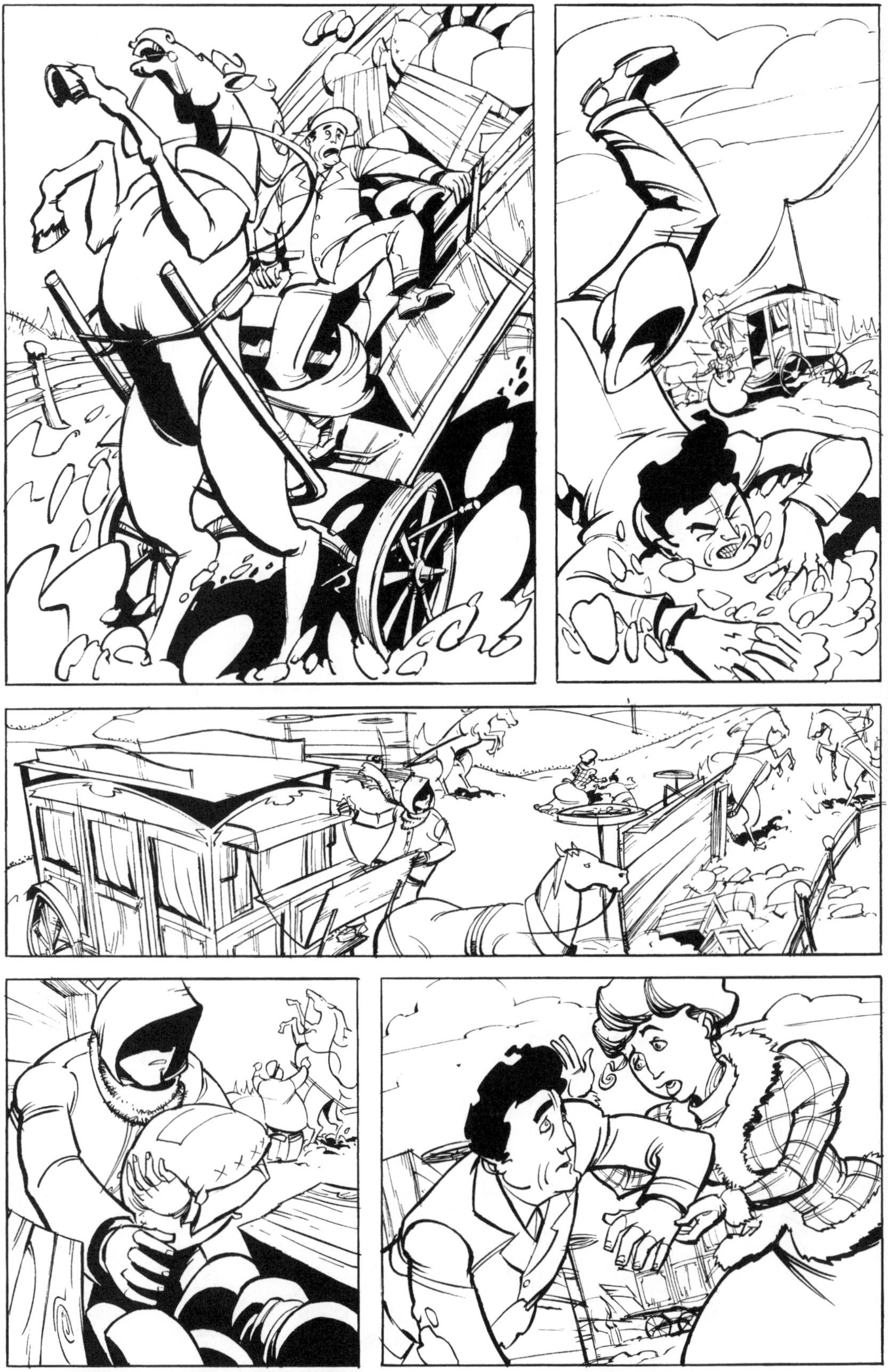

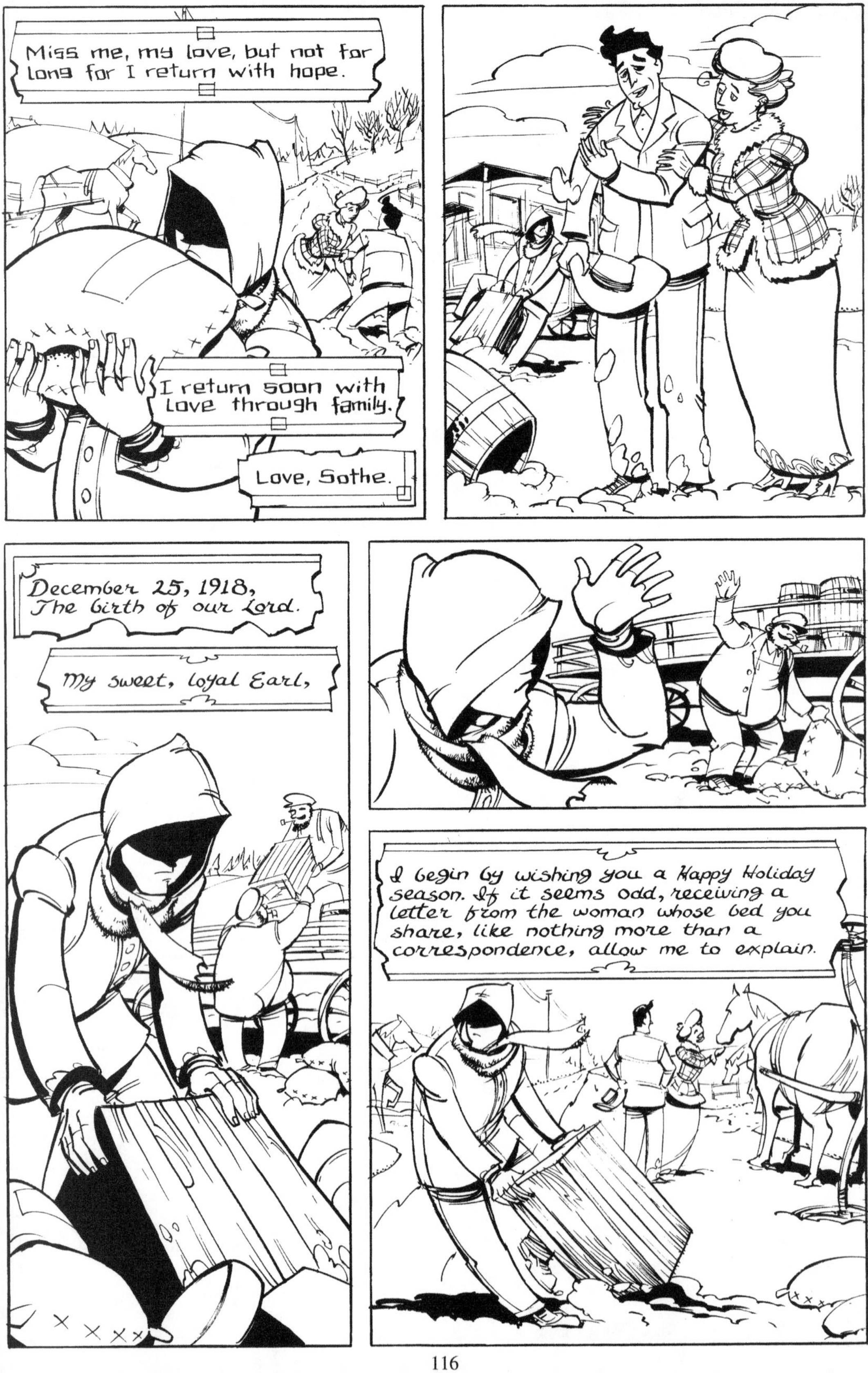
Miss me, my love, but not for long for I return with hope.
I return soon with love through family.
Love, Sothe.
December 25, 1918, The birth of our Lord.
My sweet, loyal Earl,
I begin by wishing you a Happy Holiday season. If it seems odd, receiving a letter from the woman whose bed you share, like nothing more than a correspondence, allow me to explain.

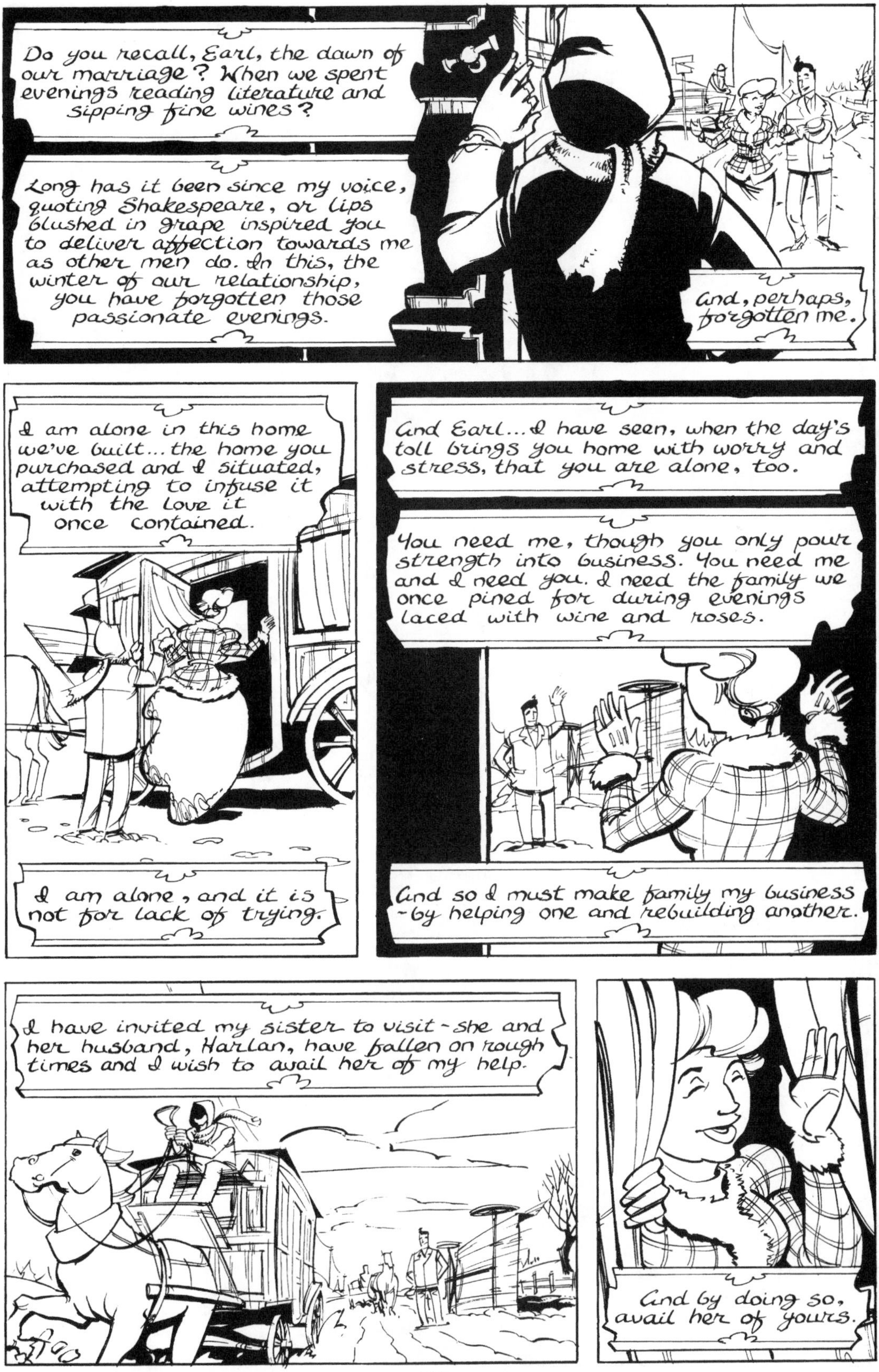
Do you recall, Earl, the dawn of our marriage? When we spent evenings reading literature and sipping fine wines?
Long has it been since my voice, quoting Shakespeare, or lips blushed in grape inspired you to deliver affection towards me as other men do. In this, the winter of our relationship, you have forgotten those passionate evenings.
And, perhaps, forgotten me.
I am alone in this home we've built... the home you purchased and I situated, attempting to infuse it with the love it once contained.
I am alone, and it is not for lack of trying.
And Earl... I have seen, when the day's toll brings you home with worry and stress, that you are alone, too.
You need me, though you only pour strength into business. You need me and I need you. I need the family we once pined for during evenings laced with wine and roses.
And so I must make family my business - by helping one and rebuilding another.
I have invited my sister to visit - she and her husband, Harlan, have fallen on rough times and I wish to avail her of my help.
And by doing so, avail her of yours.

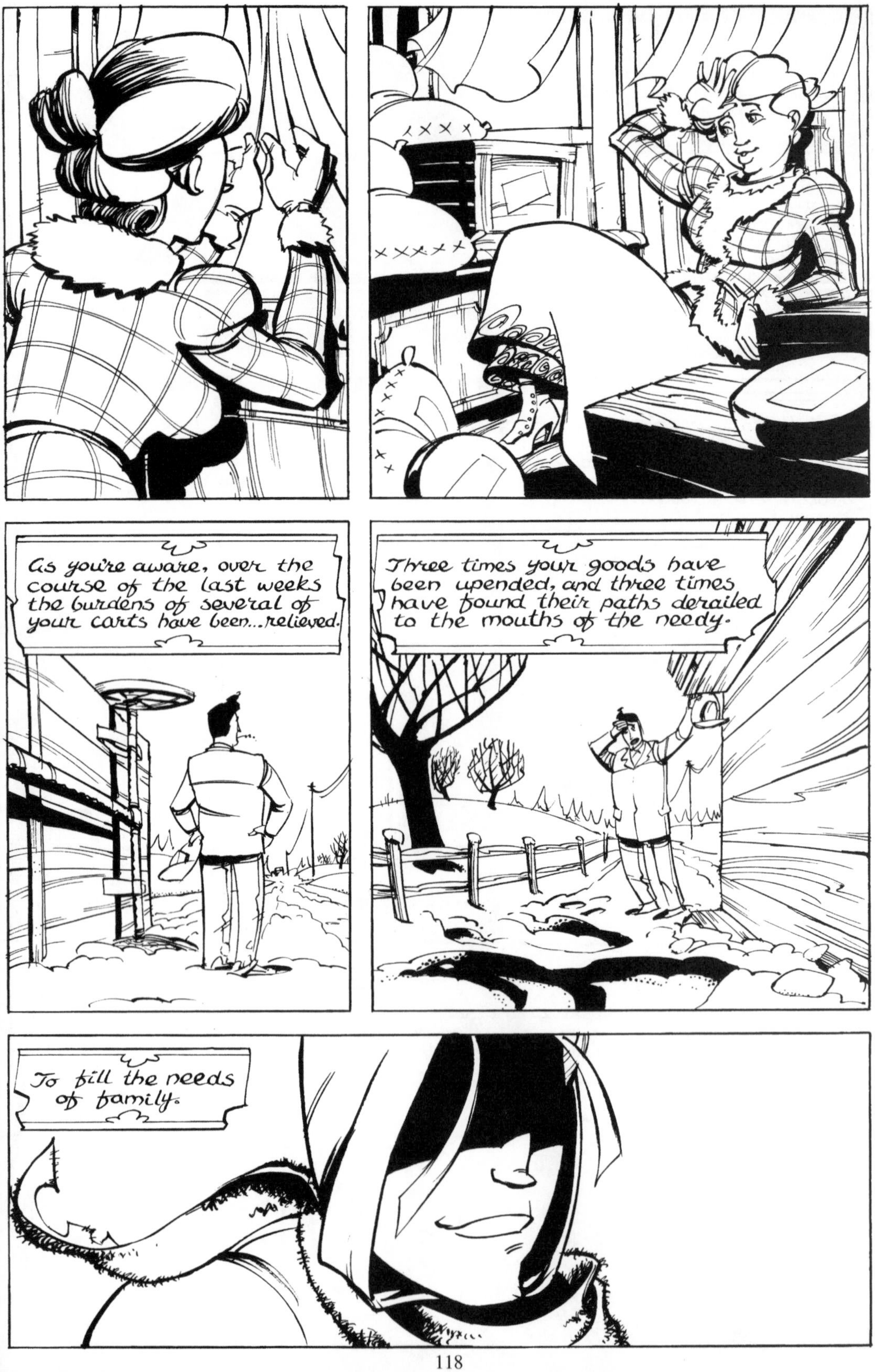
As you're aware, over the course of the last weeks the burdens of several of your carts have been... relieved.
Three times your goods have been upended, and three times have found their paths derailed to the mouths of the needy.
To fill the needs of family.

By now, dearest Earl, I am sure you have discovered these losses were no accident.

Your reaction will be anger...the word 'Betrayal' may cross your mind.

Remember, sweet Earl, who was betrayed first. Whispers of love and sweet vows to cherish and hold were cast aside for your devotion to goods and produce.

Our larders are plentiful, Earl. You have always provided. Now let me open your eyes and help provide what you are sorely lacking.

My actions seek merely your attentions. Let me provide you with that which you've long since betrayed yourself... and in turn... provide me the service of your attention once more.

Let us give each other the greatest gift we can this Holiday season: Family and Love.

My fondest wishes to you, my husband, this winter.

Your loving wife, Gretna.

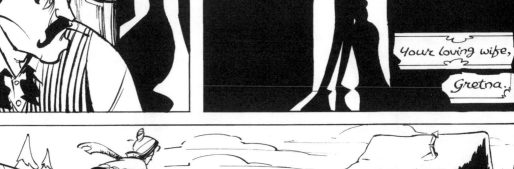

119

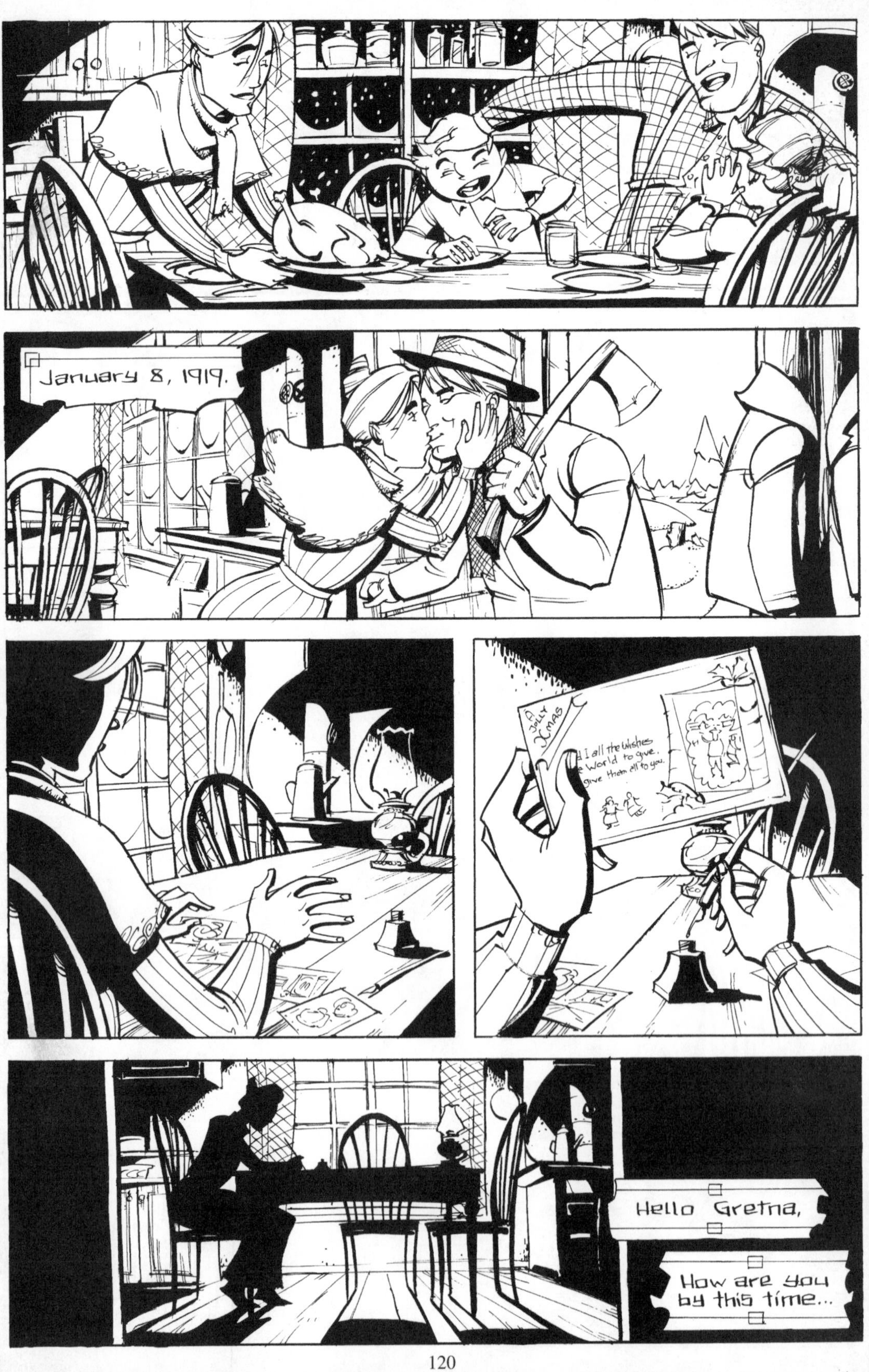
January 8, 1919.
JOLLY XMAS
Hello Gretna,
How are you by this time...

BROADWAY LOOKING WEST FROM SUSQUEHANNA STREET,
MAUCH CHUNK, PA.

A million people can look at this card and come up with a million different stories. When you send a card like this to a comic creator, you never know what you'll get back. Robert, Brendon, and Brian looked at this card and saw caped crimefighters and radio plays. They saw how a postcard can cause a hero to spring into action and save the day.

2.25

Hello Annie —
did you know
who you waved
to this morning
Margaret —

34664—PUBLISHED BY TOSH'S DEPARTMENT STORE,
MAUCH CHUNK, PA. MADE IN U.S.A.

COMMERCIALCHROME

Post Card

U.S. POSTAGE
1 CENT 1

Mrs. George Albright
Perkasie
Pa

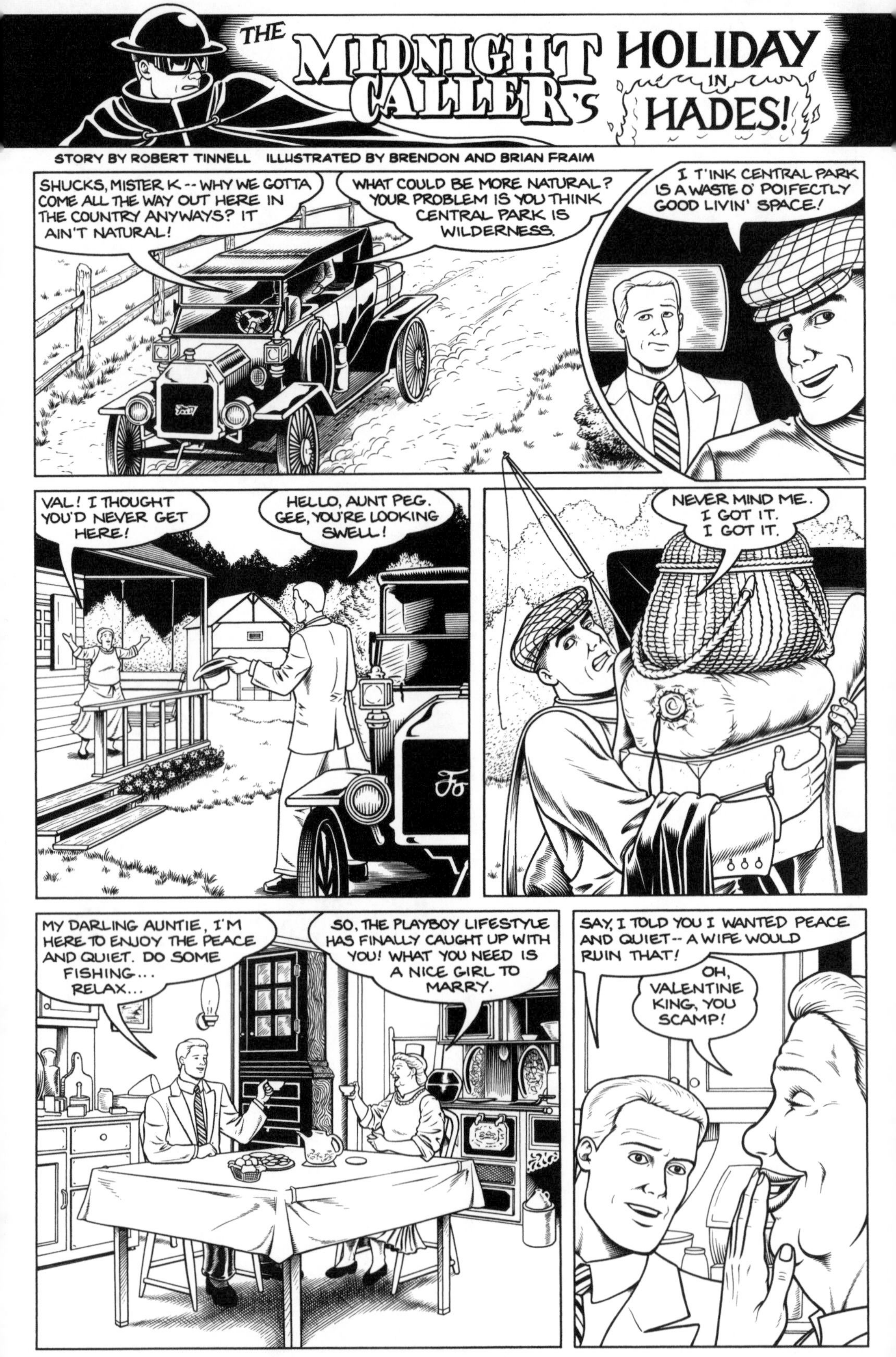
THE MIDNIGHT CALLER'S HOLIDAY IN HADES!
STORY BY ROBERT TINNELL ILLUSTRATED BY BRENDON AND BRIAN FRAIM
SHUCKS, MISTER K -- WHY WE GOTTA COME ALL THE WAY OUT HERE IN THE COUNTRY ANYWAYS? IT AIN'T NATURAL!
WHAT COULD BE MORE NATURAL? YOUR PROBLEM IS YOU THINK CENTRAL PARK IS WILDERNESS.
I T'INK CENTRAL PARK IS A WASTE O' POIFECTLY GOOD LIVIN' SPACE!
VAL! I THOUGHT YOU'D NEVER GET HERE!
HELLO, AUNT PEG. GEE, YOU'RE LOOKING SWELL!
NEVER MIND ME. I GOT IT. I GOT IT.
MY DARLING AUNTIE, I'M HERE TO ENJOY THE PEACE AND QUIET. DO SOME FISHING... RELAX...
SO, THE PLAYBOY LIFESTYLE HAS FINALLY CAUGHT UP WITH YOU! WHAT YOU NEED IS A NICE GIRL TO MARRY.
SAY, I TOLD YOU I WANTED PEACE AND QUIET-- A WIFE WOULD RUIN THAT!
OH, VALENTINE KING, YOU SCAMP!

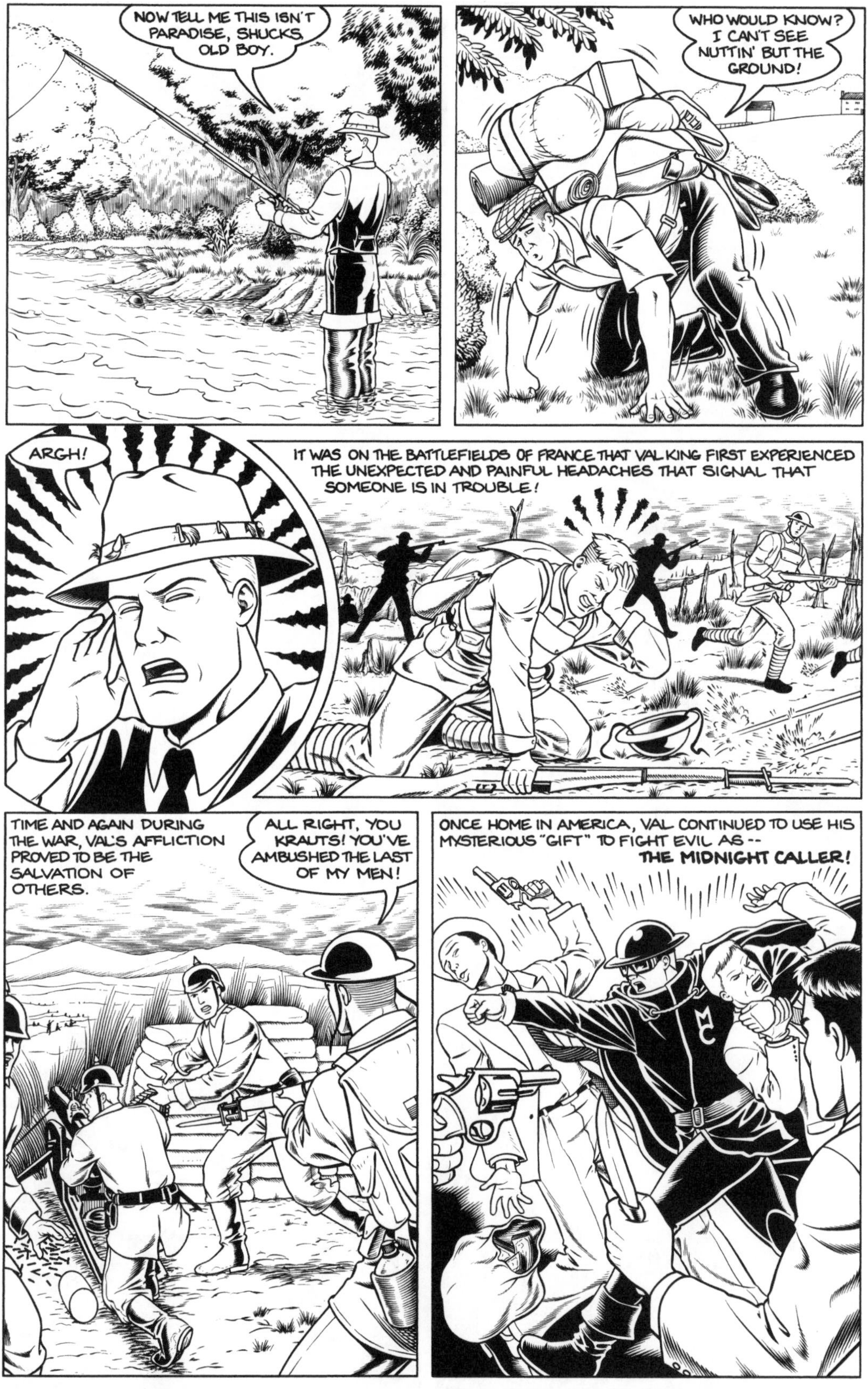
NOW TELL ME THIS ISN'T PARADISE, SHUCKS, OLD BOY.
WHO WOULD KNOW? I CAN'T SEE NUTTIN' BUT THE GROUND!
ARGH!
IT WAS ON THE BATTLEFIELDS OF FRANCE THAT VAL KING FIRST EXPERIENCED THE UNEXPECTED AND PAINFUL HEADACHES THAT SIGNAL THAT SOMEONE IS IN TROUBLE!
TIME AND AGAIN DURING THE WAR, VAL'S AFFLICTION PROVED TO BE THE SALVATION OF OTHERS.
ALL RIGHT, YOU KRAUTS! YOU'VE AMBUSHED THE LAST OF MY MEN!
ONCE HOME IN AMERICA, VAL CONTINUED TO USE HIS MYSTERIOUS "GIFT" TO FIGHT EVIL AS --
THE MIDNIGHT CALLER!

IN THE PRESENT. FAITHFUL SHUCKS HELPS HIS BOSS TO THE RIVERBANK.

ONE OF YOUR HEADACHES? OUT HERE? I DON'T GET IT, MISTER K. NOT UNLESS THERE'S A CRIMINAL COW ON THE PREMISES.

SOMEONE'S IN TROUBLE, AND THE MIDNIGHT CALLER HAS TO FIND OUT WHO -- AND WHY!

I CAN FEEL IT -- DOWN THERE -- ON THAT SIDE STREET. DANGER.

DUTCH CAVERNS

PRIDE of PENNSYLVANIA

WALL PAPER
Window shades
PAINTS OILS VARNISHES
PAPERHANGING
AND
DECORATING

WALL PAPER
Window shades
PAINTS OILS VARNISHES
PAPERHANGING
AND
DECORATING

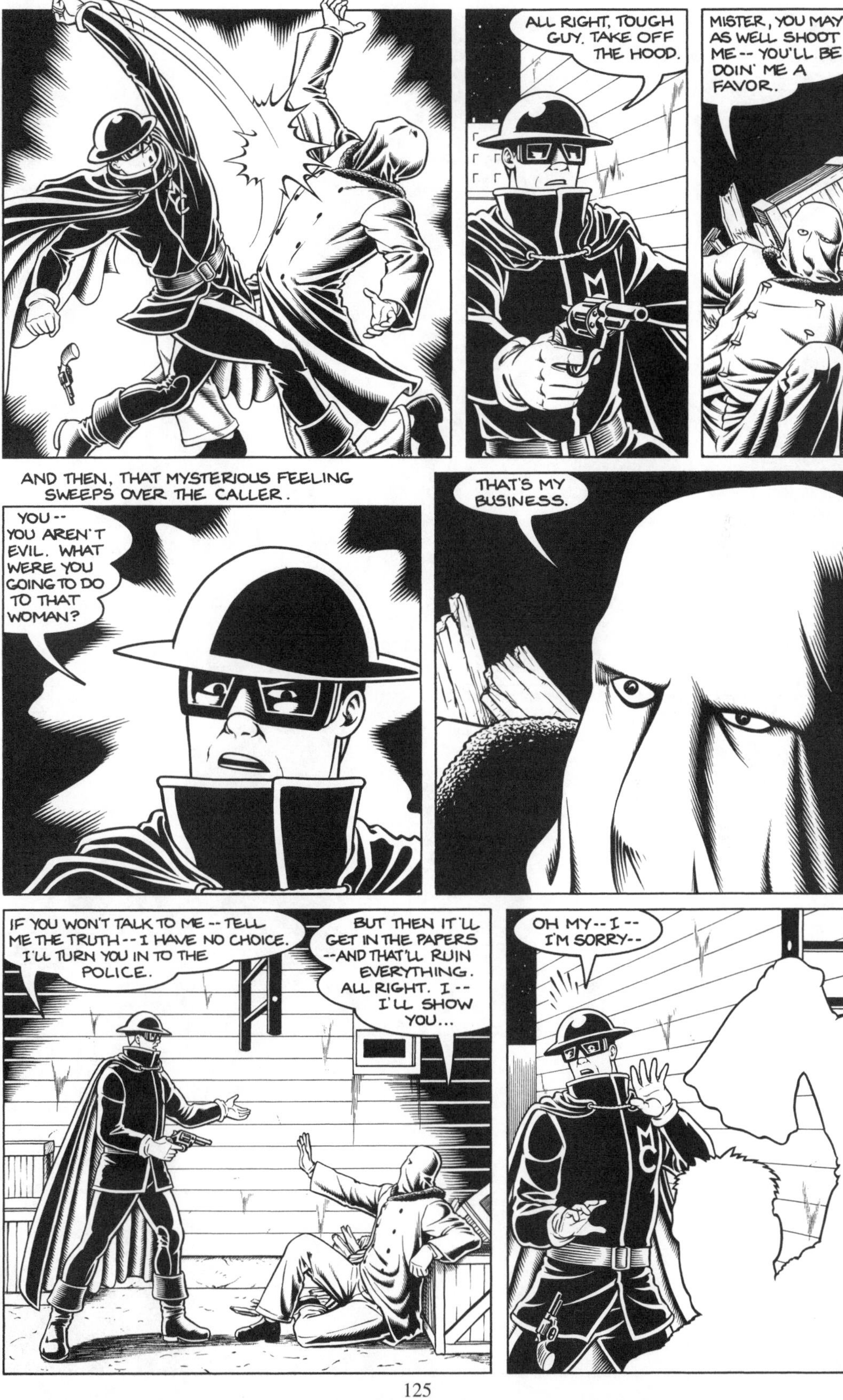
ALL RIGHT, TOUGH GUY. TAKE OFF THE HOOD.
MISTER, YOU MAY AS WELL SHOOT ME -- YOU'LL BE DOIN' ME A FAVOR.
AND THEN, THAT MYSTERIOUS FEELING SWEEPS OVER THE CALLER.
YOU -- YOU AREN'T EVIL. WHAT WERE YOU GOING TO DO TO THAT WOMAN?
THAT'S MY BUSINESS.
IF YOU WON'T TALK TO ME -- TELL ME THE TRUTH -- I HAVE NO CHOICE. I'LL TURN YOU IN TO THE POLICE.
BUT THEN IT'LL GET IN THE PAPERS -- AND THAT'LL RUIN EVERYTHING. ALL RIGHT. I -- I'LL SHOW YOU...
OH MY -- I -- I'M SORRY--

SURE YOU ARE . WHO WOULDN'T BE, LOOKING AT MY MUG?

THE MUSTARD GAS, I SUPPOSE.

YEAH. LOUSY WAR. MIND IF I PUT MY HOOD BACK ON?

OF COURSE NOT. BUT WHAT HAS ALL THIS TO DO WITH THAT WOMAN?

HER? SHE'S ONLY MY STEP-SISTER.

EGAD, MAN. WHY WOULD YOU TRY TO KILL YOUR OWN STEP-SISTER?

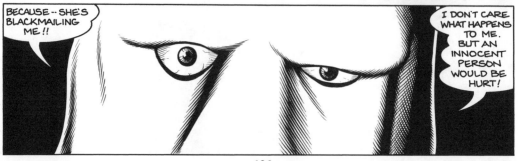

BECAUSE -- SHE'S BLACKMAILING ME!!

I DON'T CARE WHAT HAPPENS TO ME. BUT AN INNOCENT PERSON WOULD BE HURT!

126

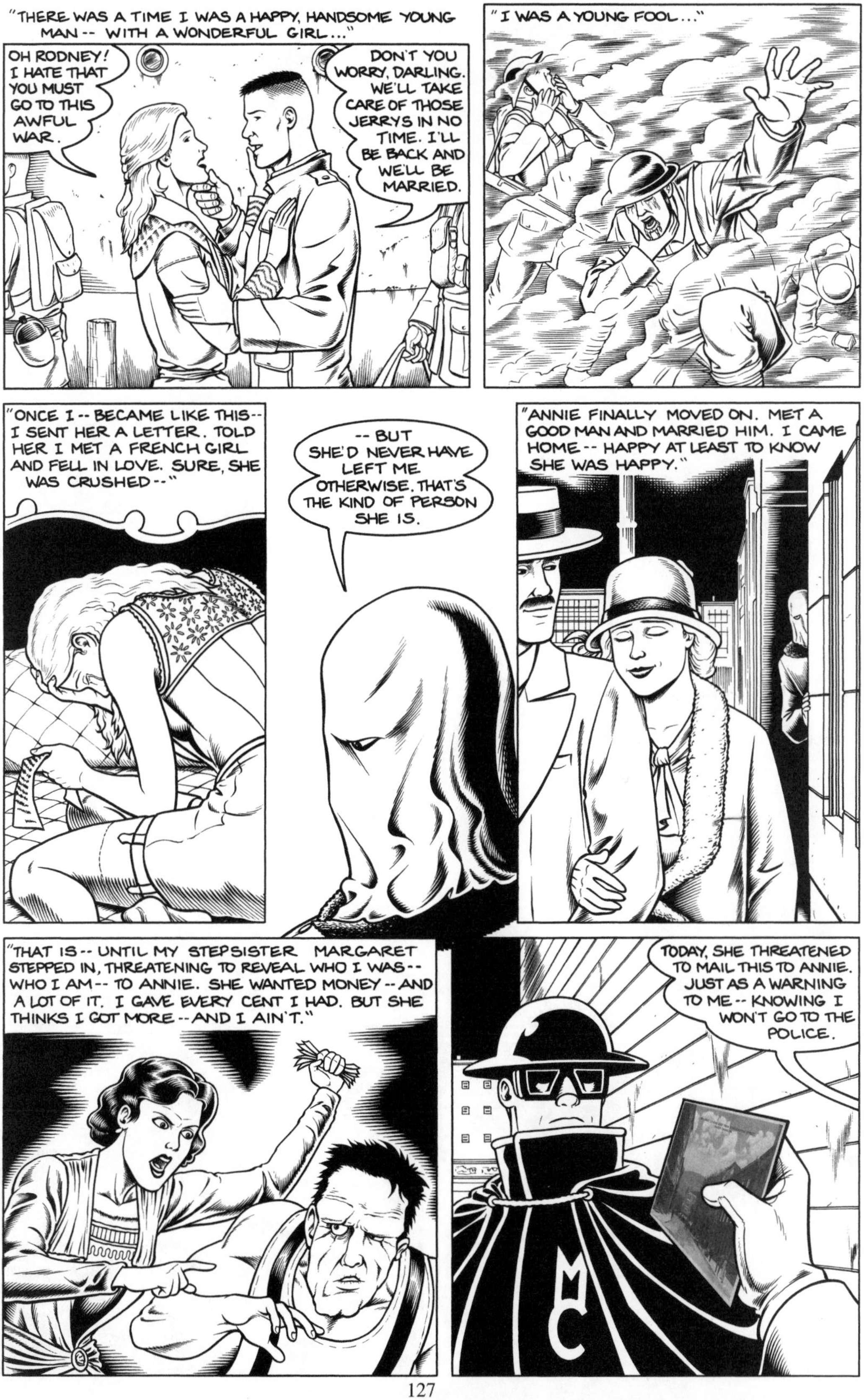
"THERE WAS A TIME I WAS A HAPPY, HANDSOME YOUNG MAN -- WITH A WONDERFUL GIRL..."
OH RODNEY! I HATE THAT YOU MUST GO TO THIS AWFUL WAR.
DON'T YOU WORRY, DARLING. WE'LL TAKE CARE OF THOSE JERRYS IN NO TIME. I'LL BE BACK AND WE'LL BE MARRIED.
"I WAS A YOUNG FOOL..."
"ONCE I -- BECAME LIKE THIS -- I SENT HER A LETTER. TOLD HER I MET A FRENCH GIRL AND FELL IN LOVE. SURE, SHE WAS CRUSHED --"
-- BUT SHE'D NEVER HAVE LEFT ME OTHERWISE. THAT'S THE KIND OF PERSON SHE IS.
"ANNIE FINALLY MOVED ON. MET A GOOD MAN AND MARRIED HIM. I CAME HOME -- HAPPY AT LEAST TO KNOW SHE WAS HAPPY."
"THAT IS -- UNTIL MY STEPSISTER MARGARET STEPPED IN, THREATENING TO REVEAL WHO I WAS -- WHO I AM -- TO ANNIE. SHE WANTED MONEY -- AND A LOT OF IT. I GAVE EVERY CENT I HAD. BUT SHE THINKS I GOT MORE -- AND I AIN'T."
TODAY, SHE THREATENED TO MAIL THIS TO ANNIE. JUST AS A WARNING TO ME -- KNOWING I WON'T GO TO THE POLICE.
MC

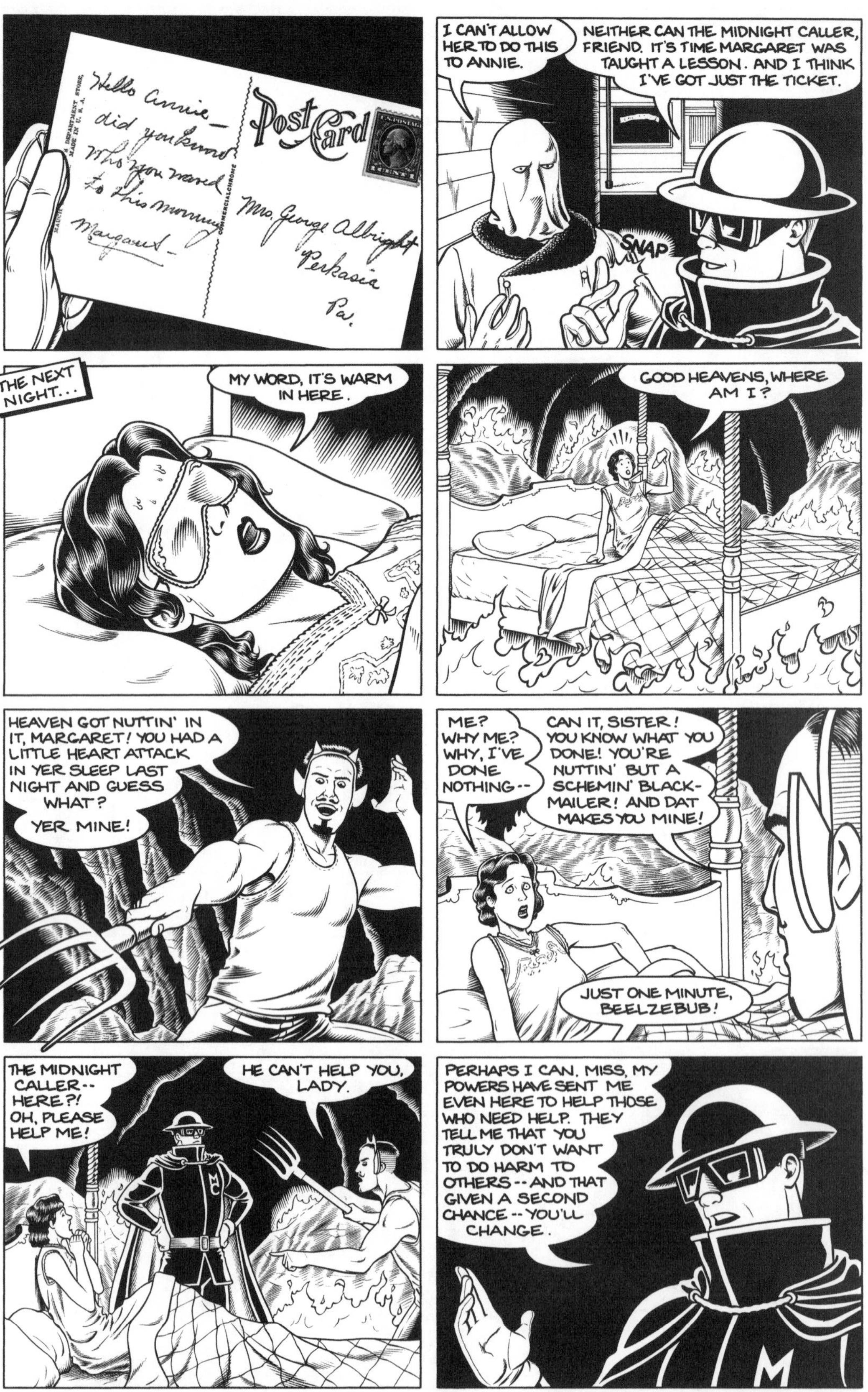
Hello Annie_
did you know
Who you waved
to this morning
Margaret_
Post Card
Mrs. George Albright
Perkasia
Pa.
I CAN'T ALLOW HER TO DO THIS TO ANNIE.
NEITHER CAN THE MIDNIGHT CALLER, FRIEND. IT'S TIME MARGARET WAS TAUGHT A LESSON. AND I THINK I'VE GOT JUST THE TICKET.
SNAP
THE NEXT NIGHT...
MY WORD, IT'S WARM IN HERE.
GOOD HEAVENS, WHERE AM I?
HEAVEN GOT NUTTIN' IN IT, MARGARET! YOU HAD A LITTLE HEART ATTACK IN YER SLEEP LAST NIGHT AND GUESS WHAT?
YER MINE!
ME? WHY ME? WHY, I'VE DONE NOTHING--
CAN IT, SISTER! YOU KNOW WHAT YOU DONE! YOU'RE NUTTIN' BUT A SCHEMIN' BLACK-MAILER! AND DAT MAKES YOU MINE!
JUST ONE MINUTE, BEELZEBUB!
THE MIDNIGHT CALLER-- HERE?! OH, PLEASE HELP ME!
HE CAN'T HELP YOU, LADY.
PERHAPS I CAN, MISS, MY POWERS HAVE SENT ME EVEN HERE TO HELP THOSE WHO NEED HELP. THEY TELL ME THAT YOU TRULY DON'T WANT TO DO HARM TO OTHERS -- AND THAT GIVEN A SECOND CHANCE -- YOU'LL CHANGE.

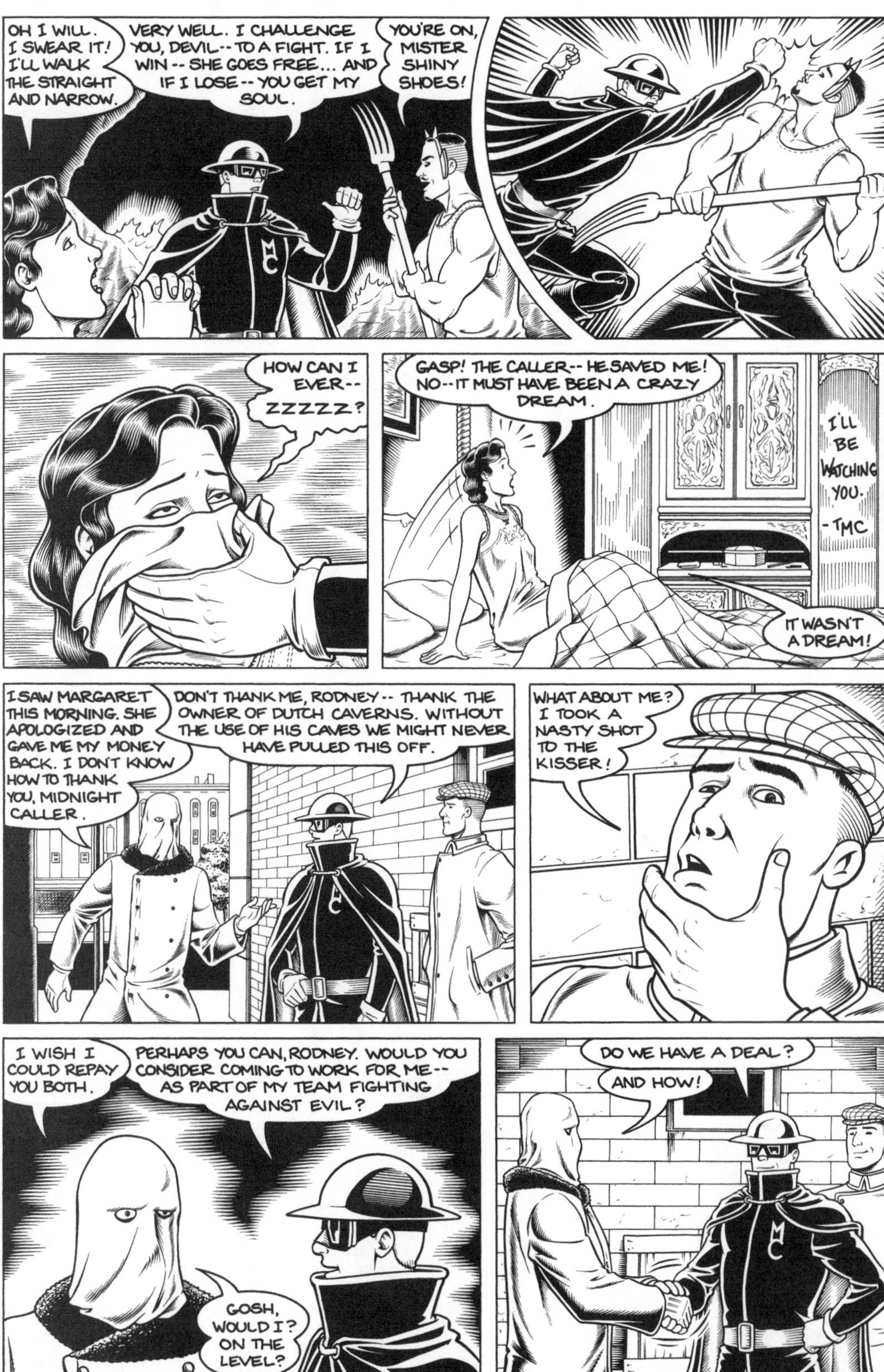
OH I WILL. I SWEAR IT! I'LL WALK THE STRAIGHT AND NARROW.
VERY WELL. I CHALLENGE YOU, DEVIL-- TO A FIGHT. IF I WIN -- SHE GOES FREE... AND IF I LOSE -- YOU GET MY SOUL.
YOU'RE ON, MISTER SHINY SHOES!
HOW CAN I EVER-- ZZZZZ?
GASP! THE CALLER-- HE SAVED ME! NO-- IT MUST HAVE BEEN A CRAZY DREAM.
I'LL BE WATCHING YOU. -TMC
IT WASN'T A DREAM!
I SAW MARGARET THIS MORNING. SHE APOLOGIZED AND GAVE ME MY MONEY BACK. I DON'T KNOW HOW TO THANK YOU, MIDNIGHT CALLER.
DON'T THANK ME, RODNEY -- THANK THE OWNER OF DUTCH CAVERNS. WITHOUT THE USE OF HIS CAVES WE MIGHT NEVER HAVE PULLED THIS OFF.
WHAT ABOUT ME? I TOOK A NASTY SHOT TO THE KISSER!
I WISH I COULD REPAY YOU BOTH.
PERHAPS YOU CAN, RODNEY. WOULD YOU CONSIDER COMING TO WORK FOR ME-- AS PART OF MY TEAM FIGHTING AGAINST EVIL?
GOSH, WOULD I? ON THE LEVEL?
DO WE HAVE A DEAL?
AND HOW!
WHAT'S THIS? A NEW RECRUIT IS JOINING THE MIDNIGHT CALLER IN HIS NEVER-ENDING EFFORT TO DEFEAT THE FORCES OF DARKNESS? JOIN US AGAIN NEXT TIME FOR-- THE MIDNIGHT CALLER!

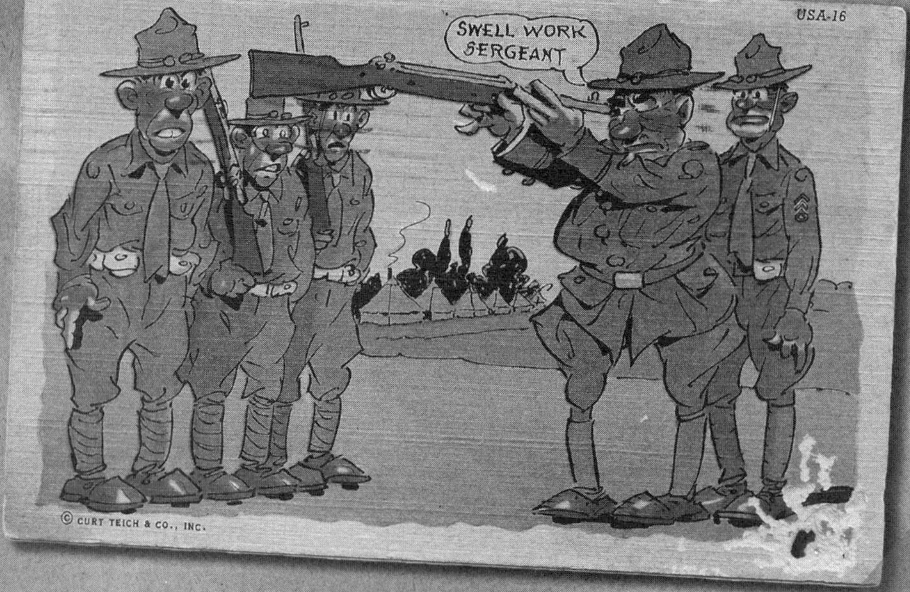
USA-16
SWELL WORK SERGEANT
© CURT TEICH & CO., INC.

This was my first postcard. The one that started it all. So naturally I have a special attachment to it. To me, this card represents the last time the greatest nations truly came together to fight evil. It also represents my grandfather, a decorated war hero whom I never met but who played a prominent role in the stories my mom told. I gave this card to Rick and Rob and waited on pins and needles to see what they would do with it. Their story shows us how a postcard can contain hope and ideals.

It can be the writings of a hero before he becomes one.

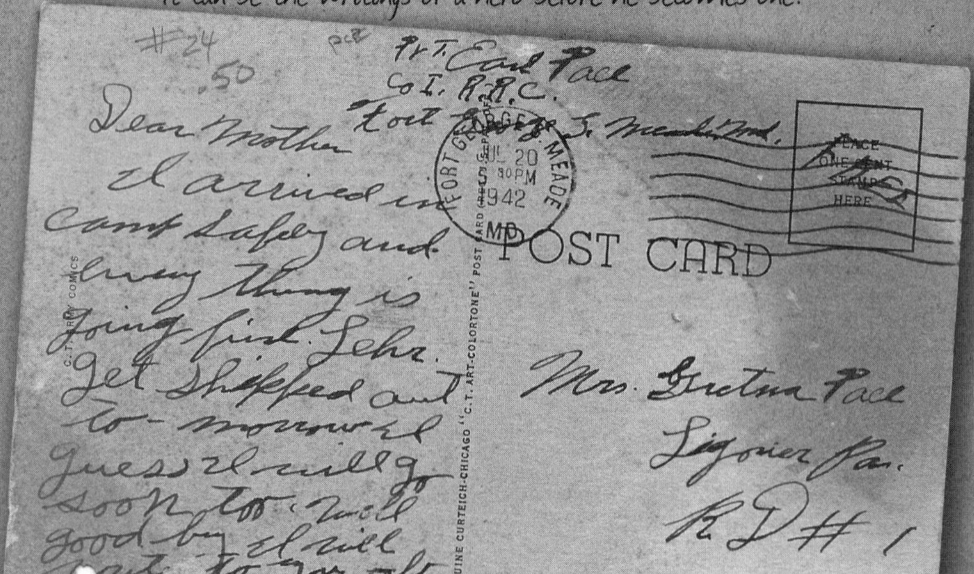
#24
.50
Pvt. Earl Pace
Co. I. R.R.C.
Fort George G. Meade Md.

Dear Mother
I arrived in
camp safely and
every thing is
going fine. Lehr.
Get shipped out
to-morrow I
guess I will go
soon too. Well
good by I will
write to you after
your son Earl.

FORT GEORGE G. MEADE MD
JUL 20 5 30PM 1942

PLACE ONE CENT STAMP HERE

POST CARD

Mrs. Gretna Pace
Ligonier Pa.
R.D. #1

C.T. ... COMICS
GENUINE CURTEICH-CHICAGO "C.T. ART-COLORTONE" POST CARD

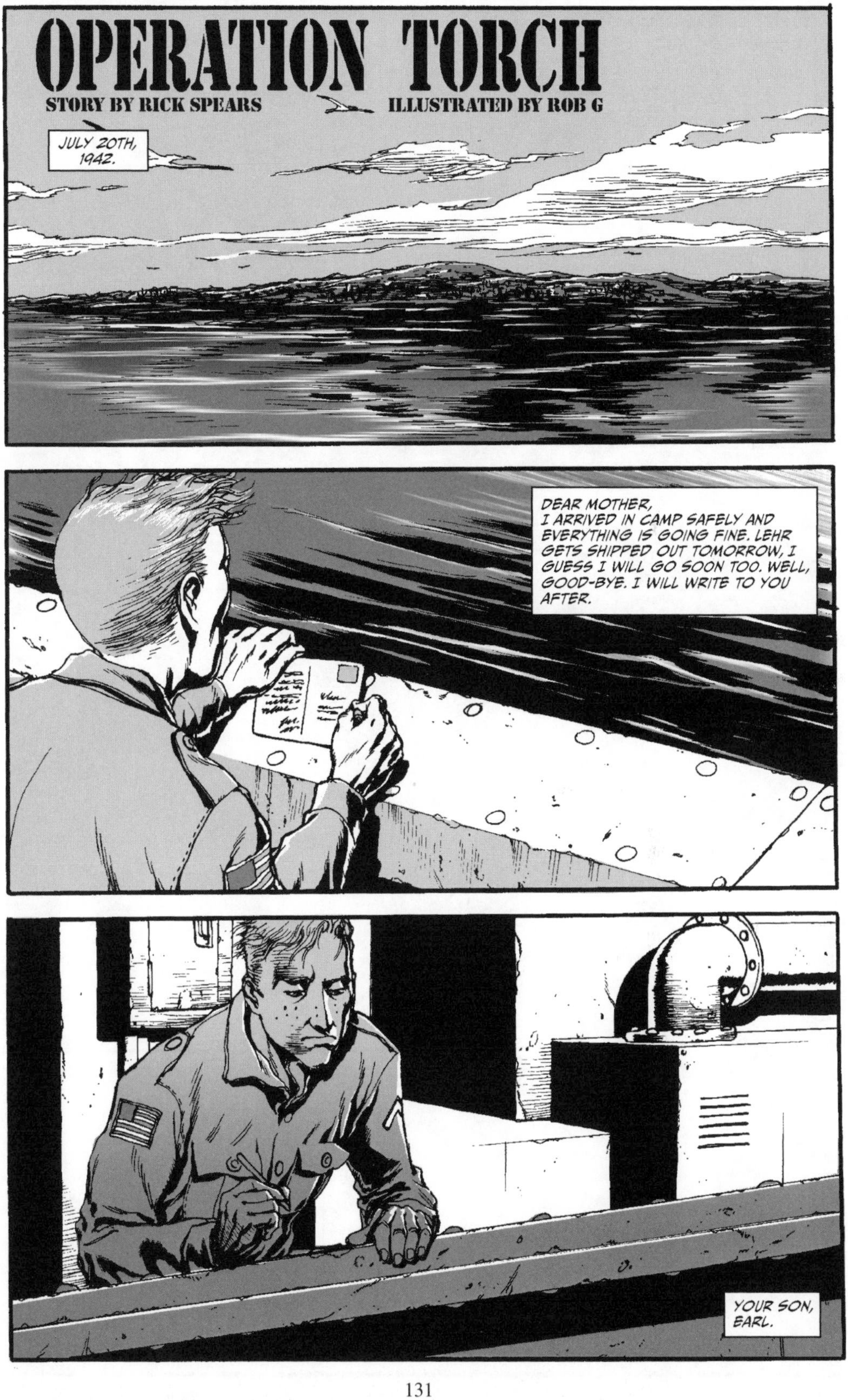
OPERATION TORCH
STORY BY RICK SPEARS
ILLUSTRATED BY ROB G
JULY 20TH, 1942.
DEAR MOTHER,
I ARRIVED IN CAMP SAFELY AND EVERYTHING IS GOING FINE. LEHR GETS SHIPPED OUT TOMORROW, I GUESS I WILL GO SOON TOO. WELL, GOOD-BYE. I WILL WRITE TO YOU AFTER.
YOUR SON, EARL.

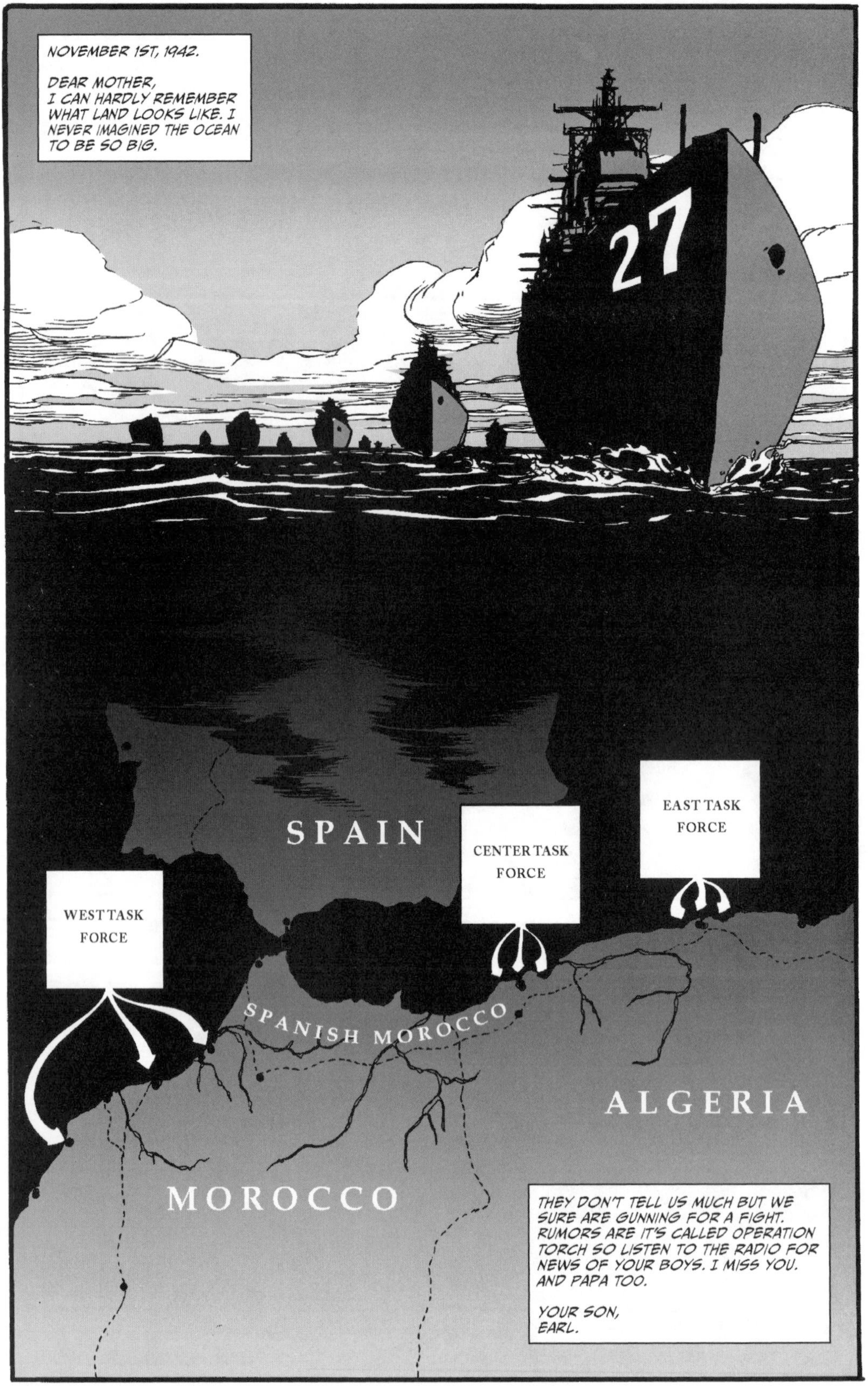
NOVEMBER 1ST, 1942.
DEAR MOTHER,
I CAN HARDLY REMEMBER WHAT LAND LOOKS LIKE. I NEVER IMAGINED THE OCEAN TO BE SO BIG.
27
SPAIN
WEST TASK FORCE
CENTER TASK FORCE
EAST TASK FORCE
SPANISH MOROCCO
ALGERIA
MOROCCO
THEY DON'T TELL US MUCH BUT WE SURE ARE GUNNING FOR A FIGHT. RUMORS ARE IT'S CALLED OPERATION TORCH SO LISTEN TO THE RADIO FOR NEWS OF YOUR BOYS. I MISS YOU. AND PAPA TOO.
YOUR SON,
EARL.

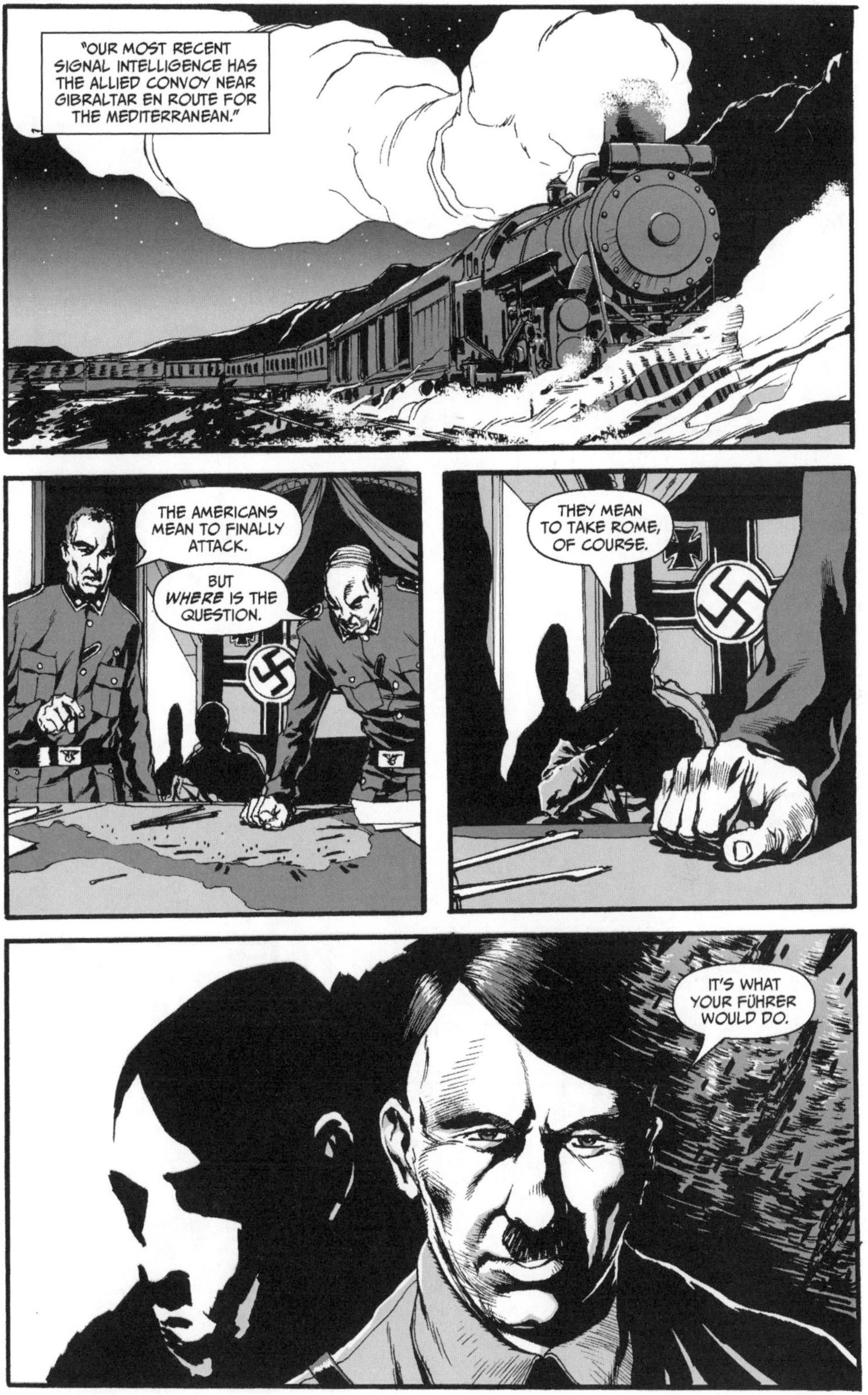
"OUR MOST RECENT SIGNAL INTELLIGENCE HAS THE ALLIED CONVOY NEAR GIBRALTAR EN ROUTE FOR THE MEDITERRANEAN."
THE AMERICANS MEAN TO FINALLY ATTACK.
BUT *WHERE* IS THE QUESTION.
THEY MEAN TO TAKE ROME, OF COURSE.
IT'S WHAT YOUR FÜHRER WOULD DO.

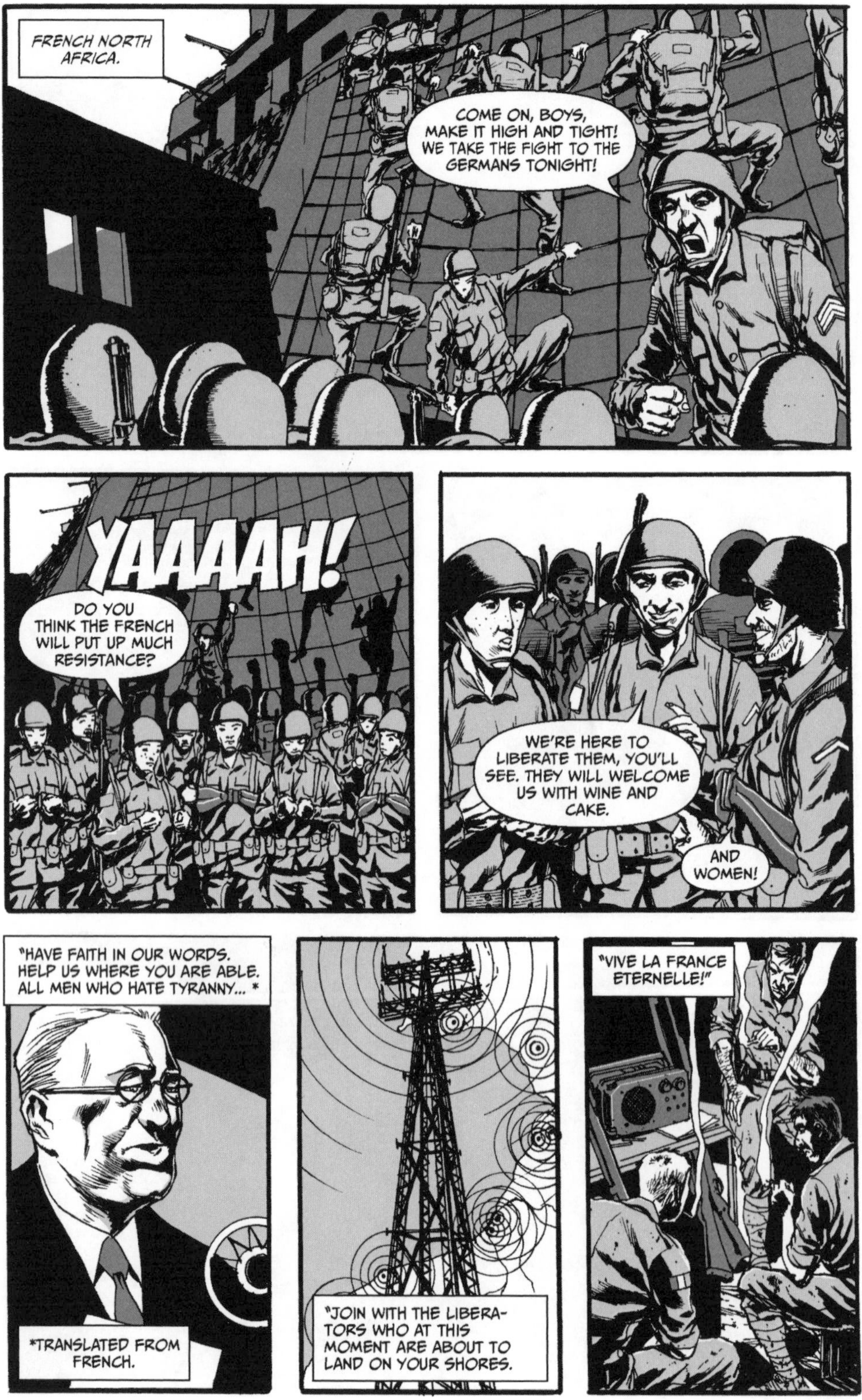
FRENCH NORTH AFRICA.
COME ON, BOYS, MAKE IT HIGH AND TIGHT! WE TAKE THE FIGHT TO THE GERMANS TONIGHT!
YAAAAH!
DO YOU THINK THE FRENCH WILL PUT UP MUCH RESISTANCE?
WE'RE HERE TO LIBERATE THEM, YOU'LL SEE. THEY WILL WELCOME US WITH WINE AND CAKE.
AND WOMEN!
"HAVE FAITH IN OUR WORDS. HELP US WHERE YOU ARE ABLE. ALL MEN WHO HATE TYRANNY... *
*TRANSLATED FROM FRENCH.
"JOIN WITH THE LIBERATORS WHO AT THIS MOMENT ARE ABOUT TO LAND ON YOUR SHORES.
"VIVE LA FRANCE ETERNELLE!"

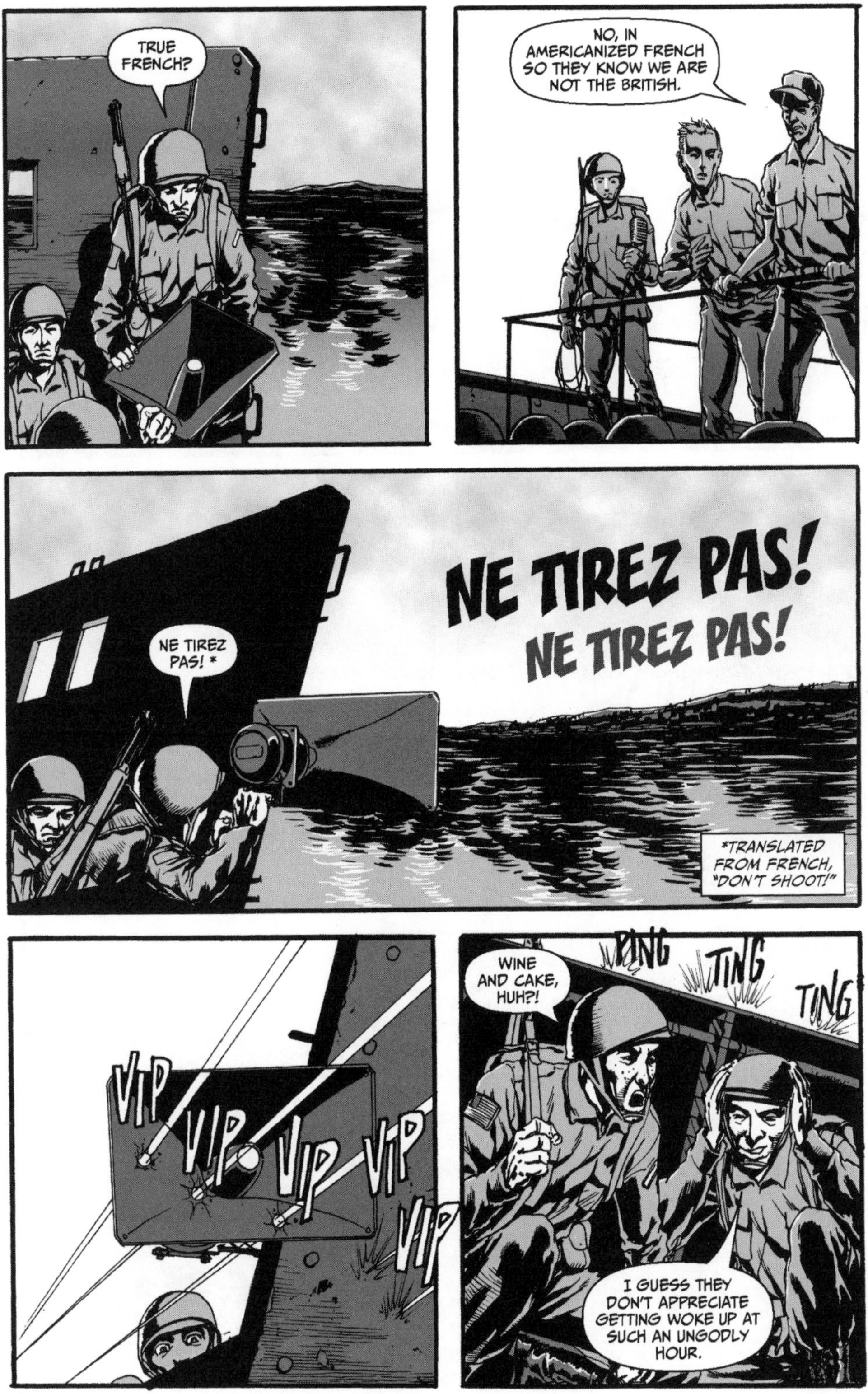
TRUE FRENCH?
NO, IN AMERICANIZED FRENCH SO THEY KNOW WE ARE NOT THE BRITISH.
NE TIREZ PAS! *
NE TIREZ PAS!
NE TIREZ PAS!
*TRANSLATED FROM FRENCH, "DON'T SHOOT!"
VIP
VIP
VIP
VIP
VIP
WINE AND CAKE, HUH?!
PING
TING
TING
I GUESS THEY DON'T APPRECIATE GETTING WOKE UP AT SUCH AN UNGODLY HOUR.

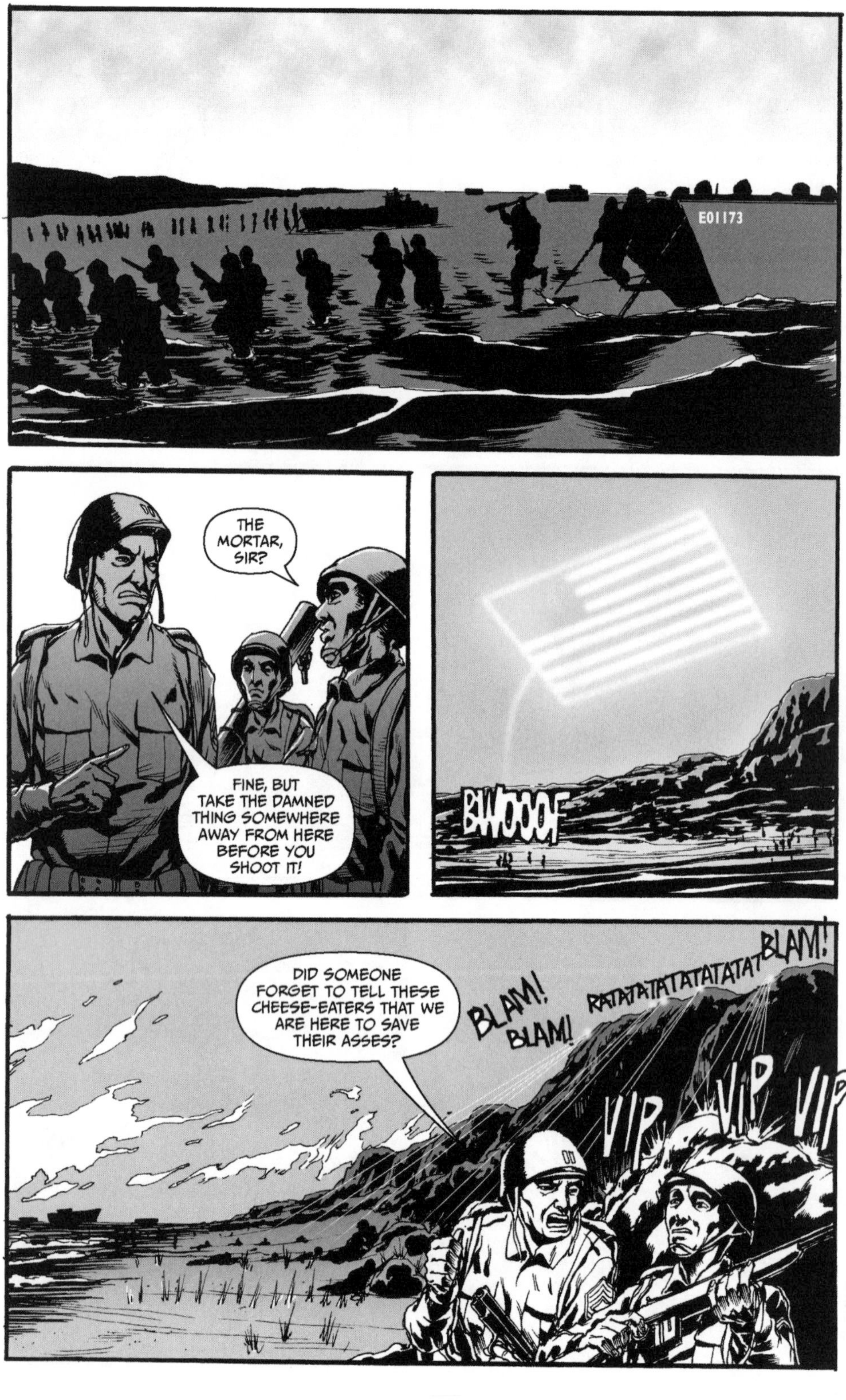
E01173
THE MORTAR, SIR?
FINE, BUT TAKE THE DAMNED THING SOMEWHERE AWAY FROM HERE BEFORE YOU SHOOT IT!
BWOOOOF
DID SOMEONE FORGET TO TELL THESE CHEESE-EATERS THAT WE ARE HERE TO SAVE THEIR ASSES?
BLAM!
BLAM!
RATATATATATATATAT
BLAM!
VIP
VIP
VIP

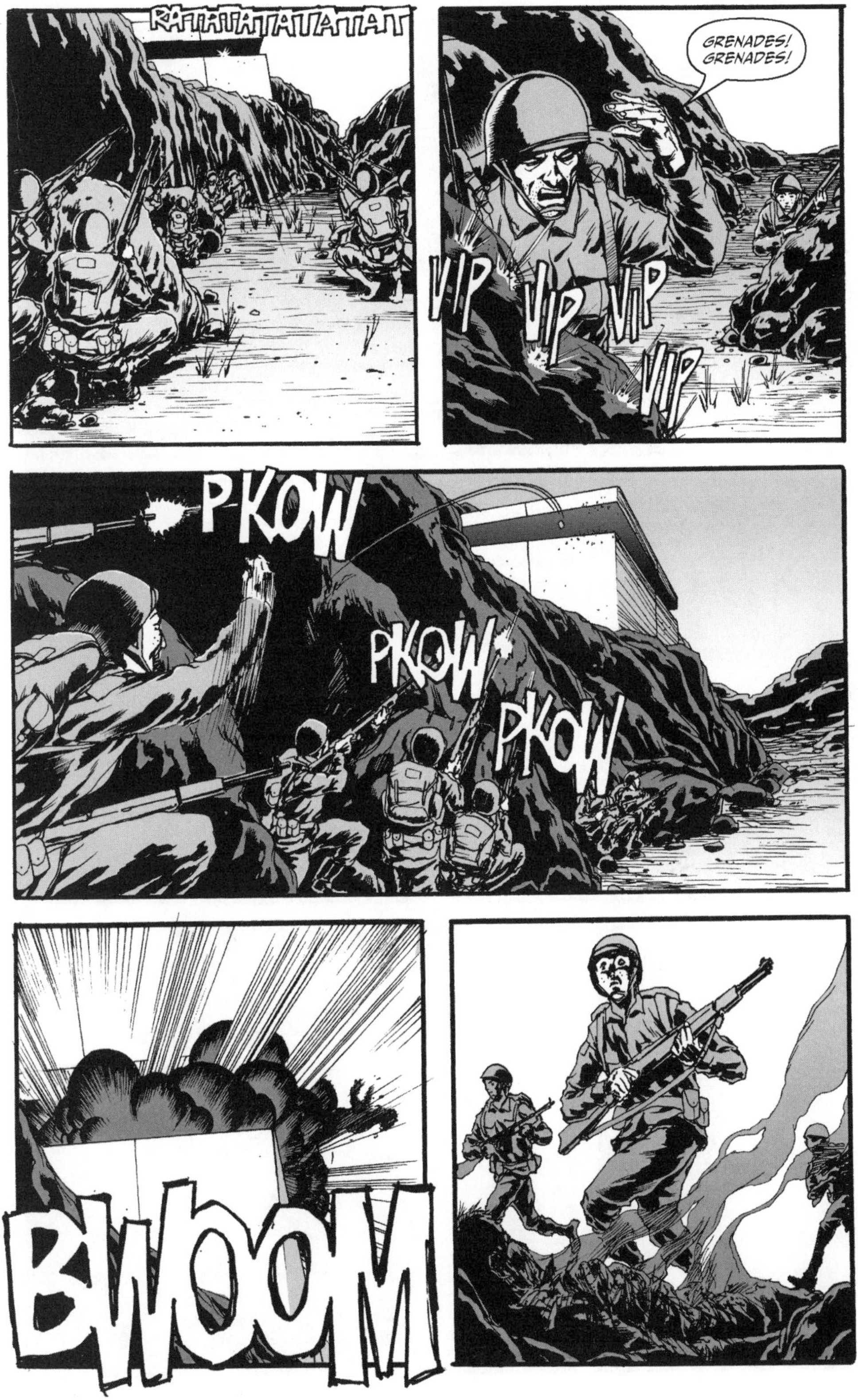
RATTATATATATAT
GRENADES! GRENADES!
VIP VIP VIP VIP
PKOW
PKOW
PKOW
BWOOM

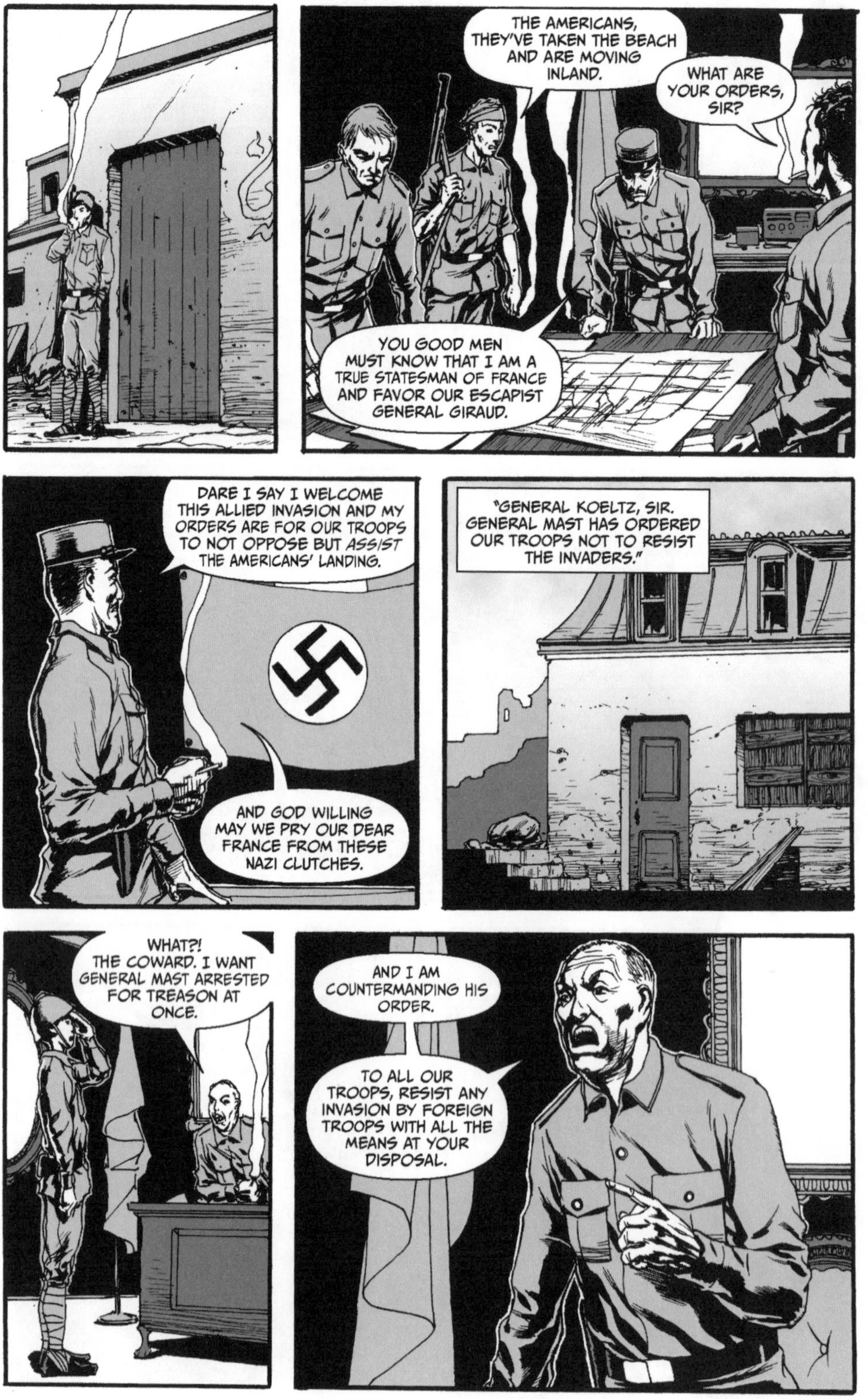
THE AMERICANS, THEY'VE TAKEN THE BEACH AND ARE MOVING INLAND.
WHAT ARE YOUR ORDERS, SIR?
YOU GOOD MEN MUST KNOW THAT I AM A TRUE STATESMAN OF FRANCE AND FAVOR OUR ESCAPIST GENERAL GIRAUD.
DARE I SAY I WELCOME THIS ALLIED INVASION AND MY ORDERS ARE FOR OUR TROOPS TO NOT OPPOSE BUT *ASSIST* THE AMERICANS' LANDING.
AND GOD WILLING MAY WE PRY OUR DEAR FRANCE FROM THESE NAZI CLUTCHES.
"GENERAL KOELTZ, SIR. GENERAL MAST HAS ORDERED OUR TROOPS NOT TO RESIST THE INVADERS."
WHAT?! THE COWARD. I WANT GENERAL MAST ARRESTED FOR TREASON AT ONCE.
AND I AM COUNTERMANDING HIS ORDER.
TO ALL OUR TROOPS, RESIST ANY INVASION BY FOREIGN TROOPS WITH ALL THE MEANS AT YOUR DISPOSAL.

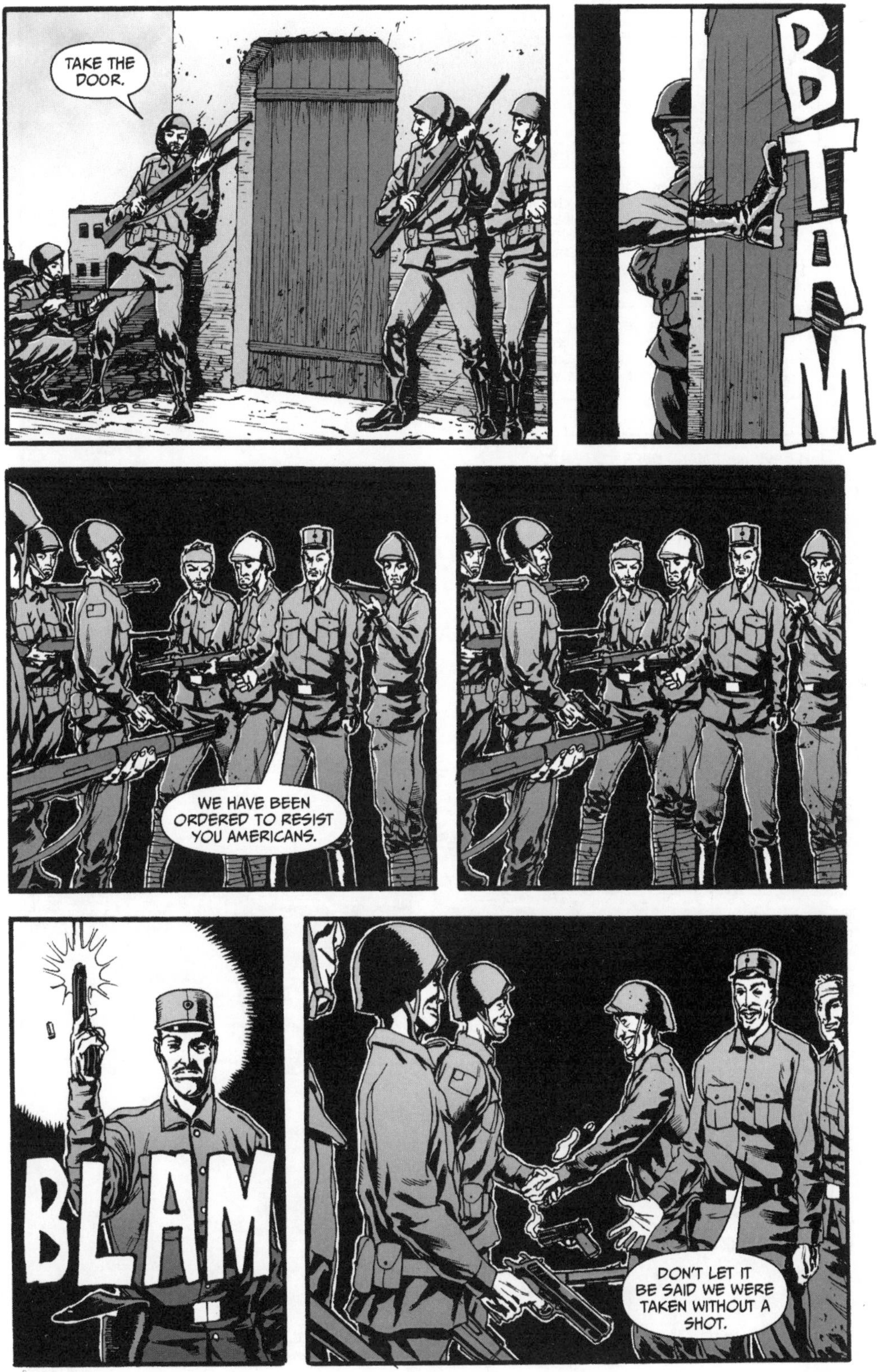
TAKE THE DOOR.
BTAM
WE HAVE BEEN ORDERED TO RESIST YOU AMERICANS.
BLAM
DON'T LET IT BE SAID WE WERE TAKEN WITHOUT A SHOT.

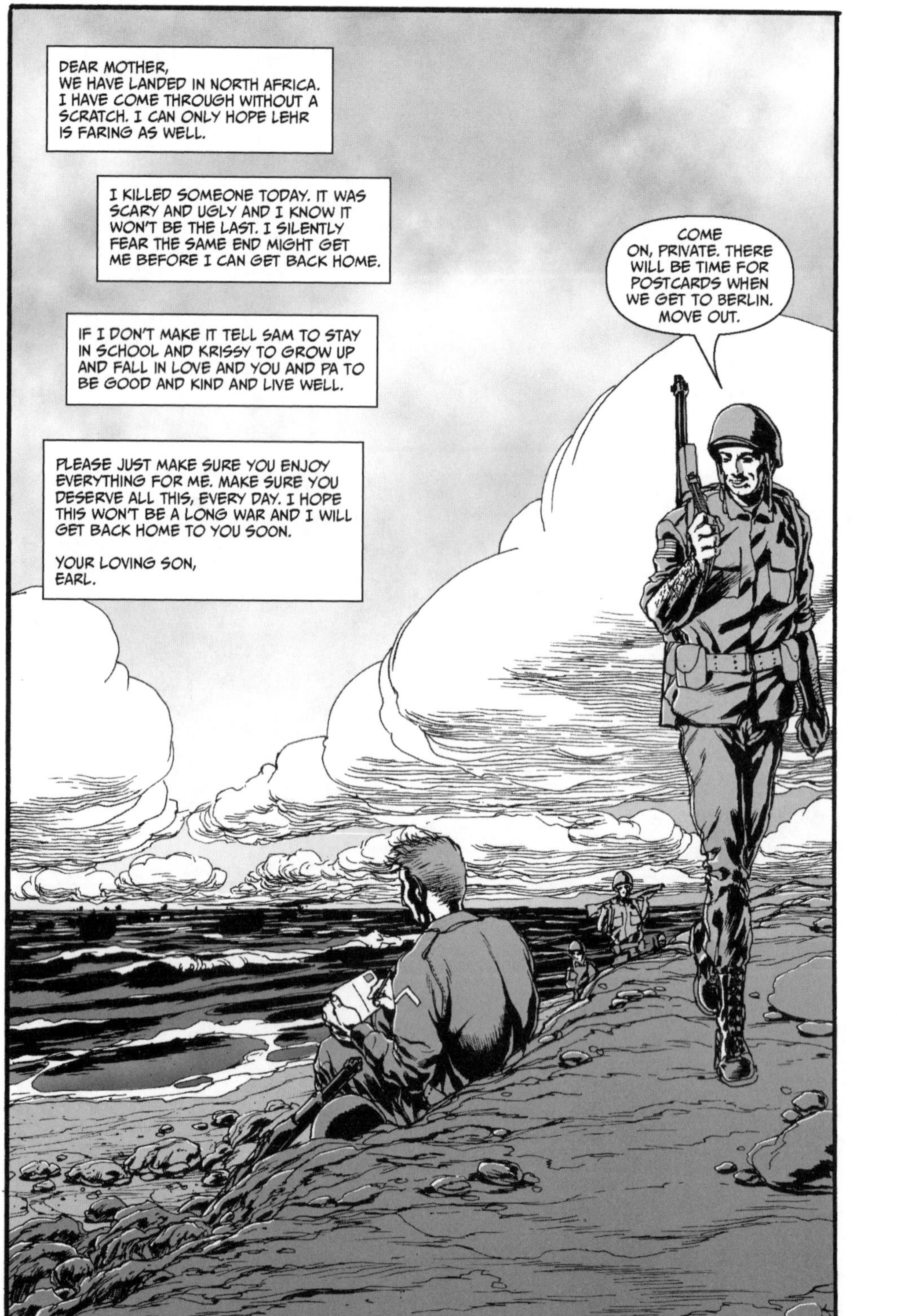
DEAR MOTHER,
WE HAVE LANDED IN NORTH AFRICA. I HAVE COME THROUGH WITHOUT A SCRATCH. I CAN ONLY HOPE LEHR IS FARING AS WELL.
I KILLED SOMEONE TODAY. IT WAS SCARY AND UGLY AND I KNOW IT WON'T BE THE LAST. I SILENTLY FEAR THE SAME END MIGHT GET ME BEFORE I CAN GET BACK HOME.
IF I DON'T MAKE IT TELL SAM TO STAY IN SCHOOL AND KRISSY TO GROW UP AND FALL IN LOVE AND YOU AND PA TO BE GOOD AND KIND AND LIVE WELL.
PLEASE JUST MAKE SURE YOU ENJOY EVERYTHING FOR ME. MAKE SURE YOU DESERVE ALL THIS, EVERY DAY. I HOPE THIS WON'T BE A LONG WAR AND I WILL GET BACK HOME TO YOU SOON.
YOUR LOVING SON,
EARL.
COME ON, PRIVATE. THERE WILL BE TIME FOR POSTCARDS WHEN WE GET TO BERLIN. MOVE OUT.

THE END.

Harvey met his wife, Joyce, when she sent him a postcard asking if he had any copies of American Splendor for sale. It's such a little thing. So little, in fact, that if I found that postcard at an antique shop, I'd probably skip over it. I wouldn't see how it'd make for an interesting story, especially when compared to postcards that talk about secret marriages, quarantine zones, and World Wars.

But that postcard helped define a story that would go on to become an award-winning graphic novel and the plotline of an Academy Award–nominated motion picture.

Harvey and Joyce's story is a retelling of their life together through postcards they've sent or received over the years. It is an excellent way to end this book. We began with a story that explored how the front of a postcard can cause someone to remember a detail; now we'll explore how the backs of multiple postcards can be used to reconstruct a life, one filled with moments that parallel the other stories in this anthology.

Beautifully illustrated by Matt Kindt, "The History of a Marriage" is a true story, one sparked by a simple, everyday postcard.

Dear Mr. Pekar
Do you have any
American Splendor
Illustration by Matt Kindt

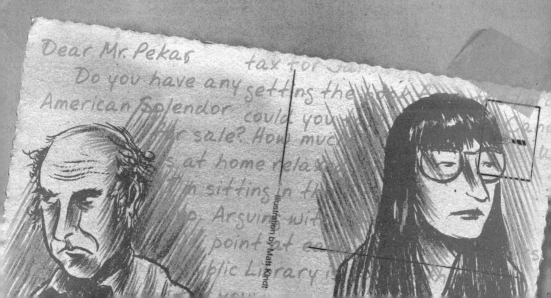

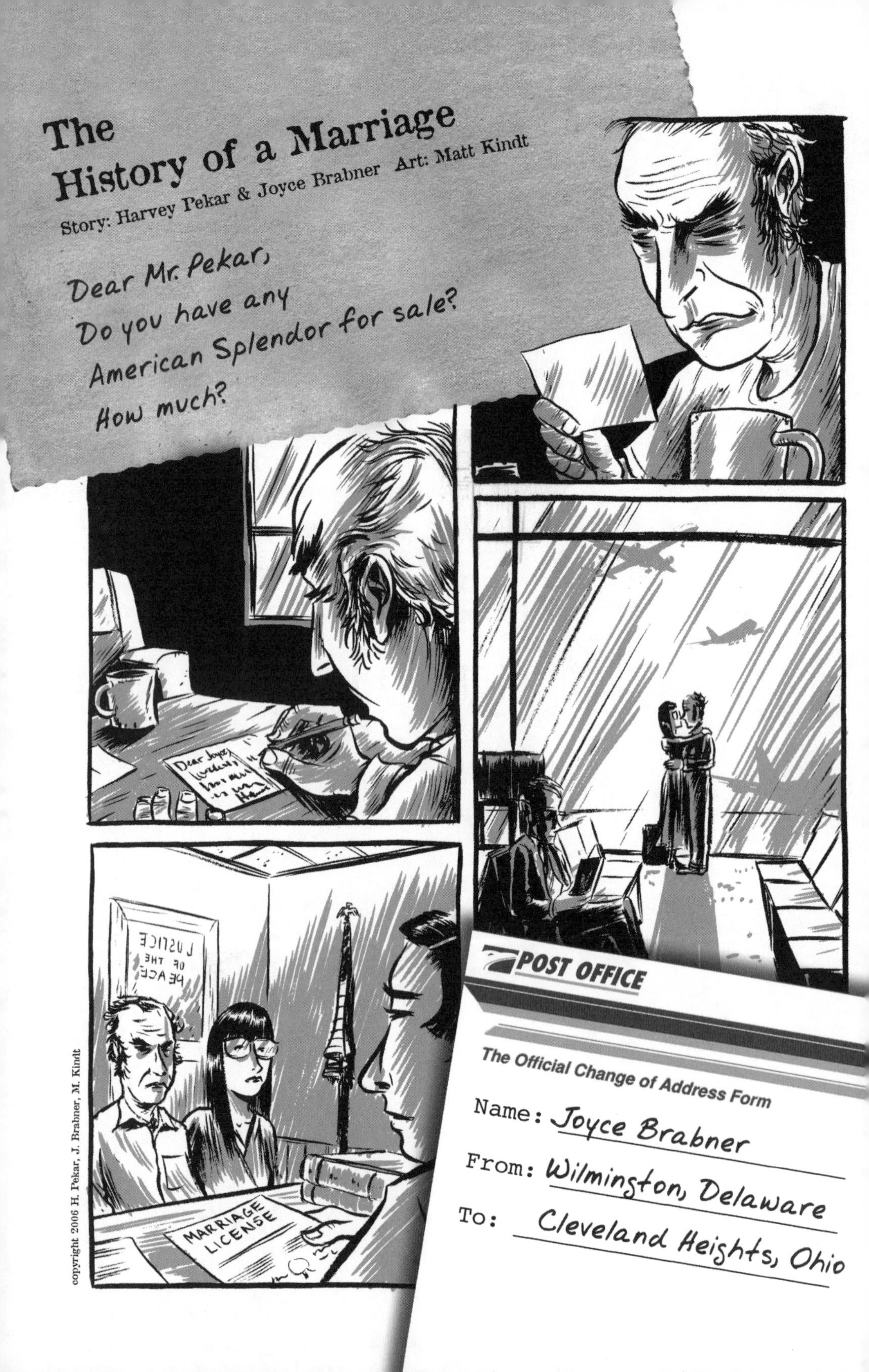
The History of a Marriage
Story: Harvey Pekar & Joyce Brabner Art: Matt Kindt
Dear Mr. Pekar,
Do you have any
American Splendor for sale?
How much?
MARRIAGE LICENSE
POST OFFICE
The Official Change of Address Form
Name: Joyce Brabner
From: Wilmingston, Delaware
To: Cleveland Heights, Ohio

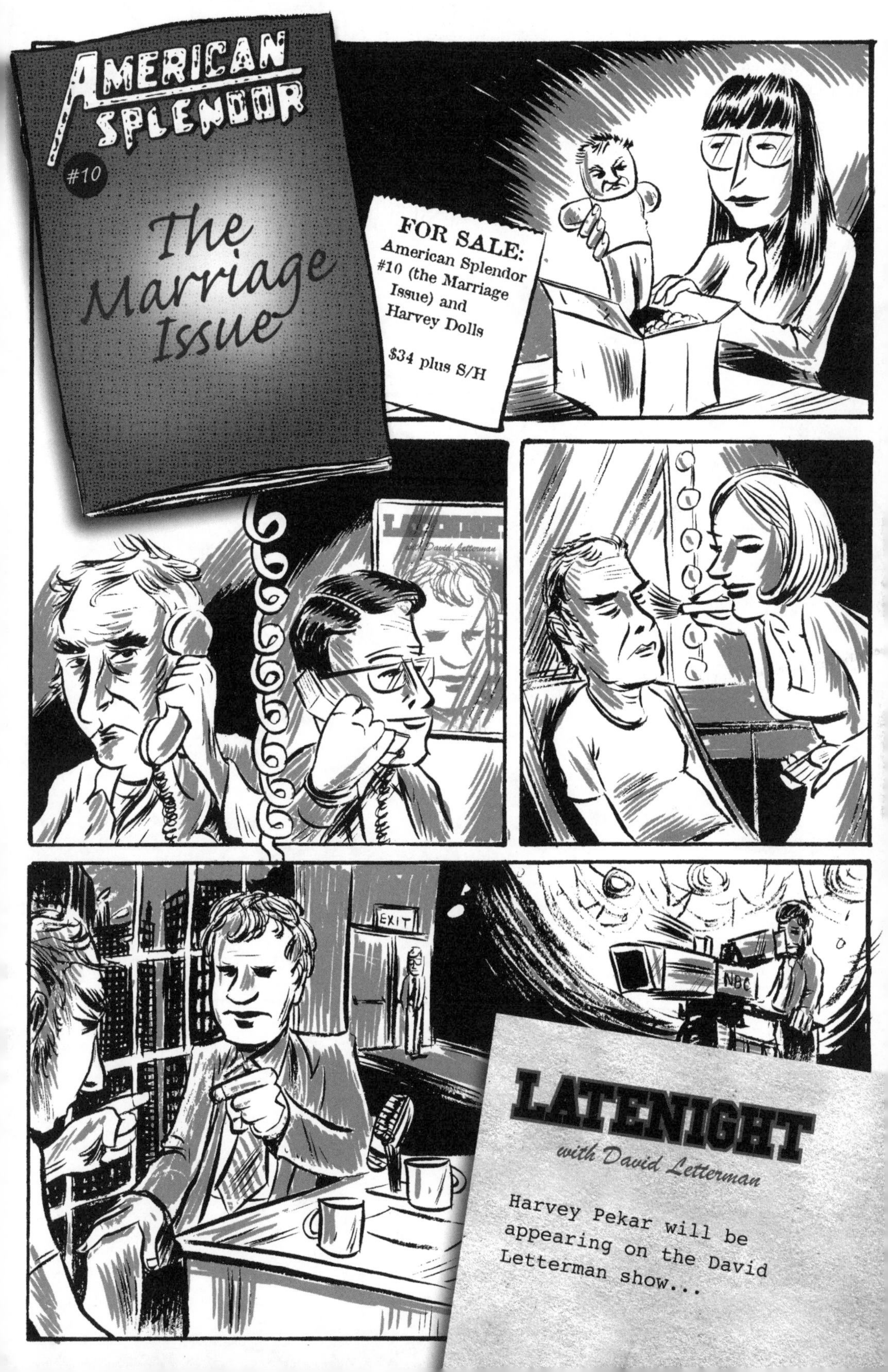
AMERICAN SPLENDOR
#10
The Marriage Issue
FOR SALE: American Splendor #10 (the Marriage Issue) and Harvey Dolls
$34 plus S/H
LATENIGHT with David Letterman
EXIT
NBC
LATENIGHT
with David Letterman
Harvey Pekar will be appearing on the David Letterman show...

The Cleveland Library
has the following book
for you:

_____

_____

Title: The Financier
Author: Theodore Dreiser

JUNE

WITHDRAW   22.00
Bank   105.0
Grocery   62.00
Electric   17.00
Coal
BALANCE ?

USBANK

Congratulations, new
homeowner. Your
property tax for
January through June
will be ___$2100___

Please send payment
early. If received
later than June 30
a late fee and
penalties will
be assessed.

Harvey
P.O. Bo
Clevela

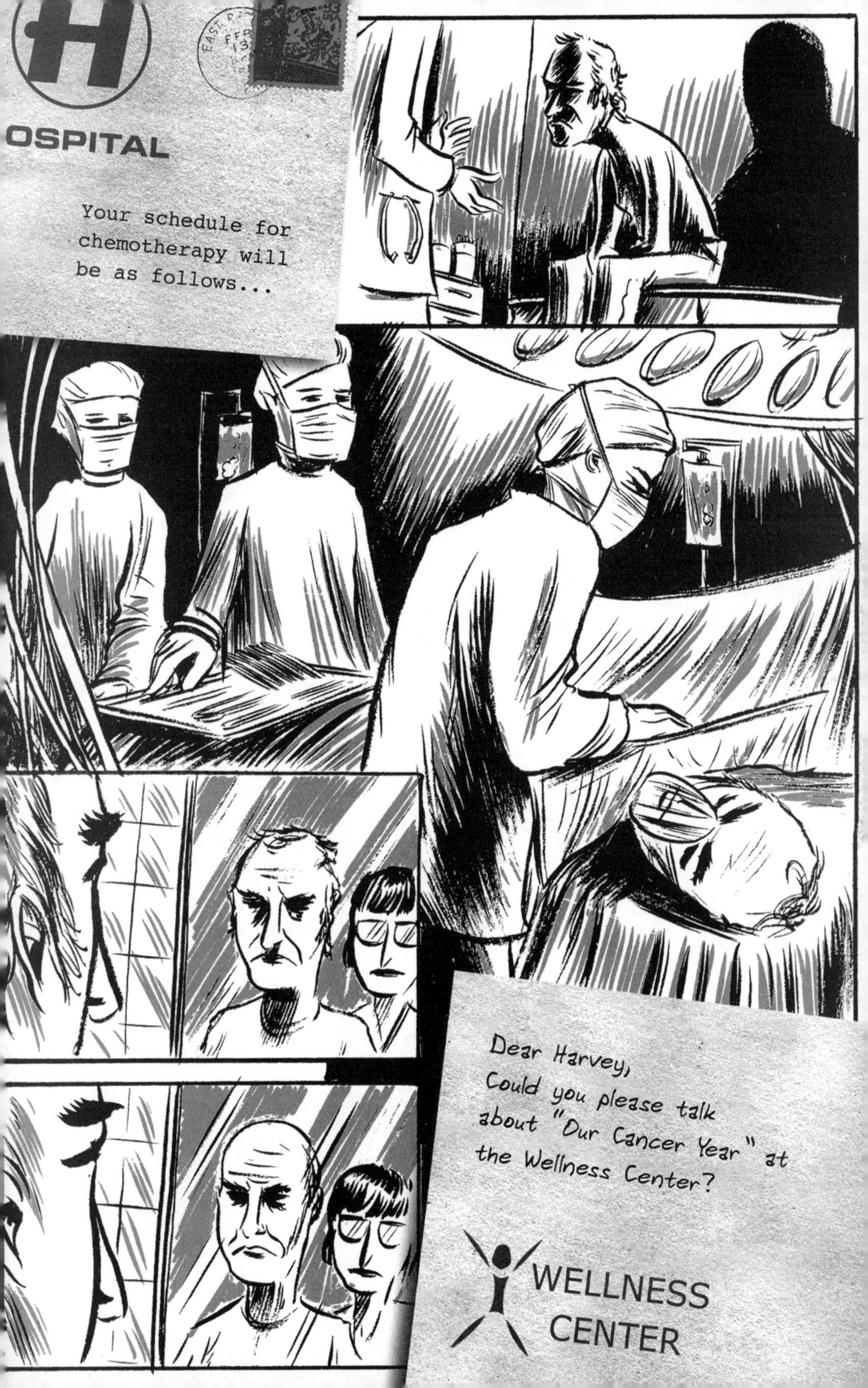

OSPITAL
Your schedule for chemotherapy will be as follows...
Dear Harvey,
Could you please talk about "Our Cancer Year" at the Wellness Center?
WELLNESS CENTER

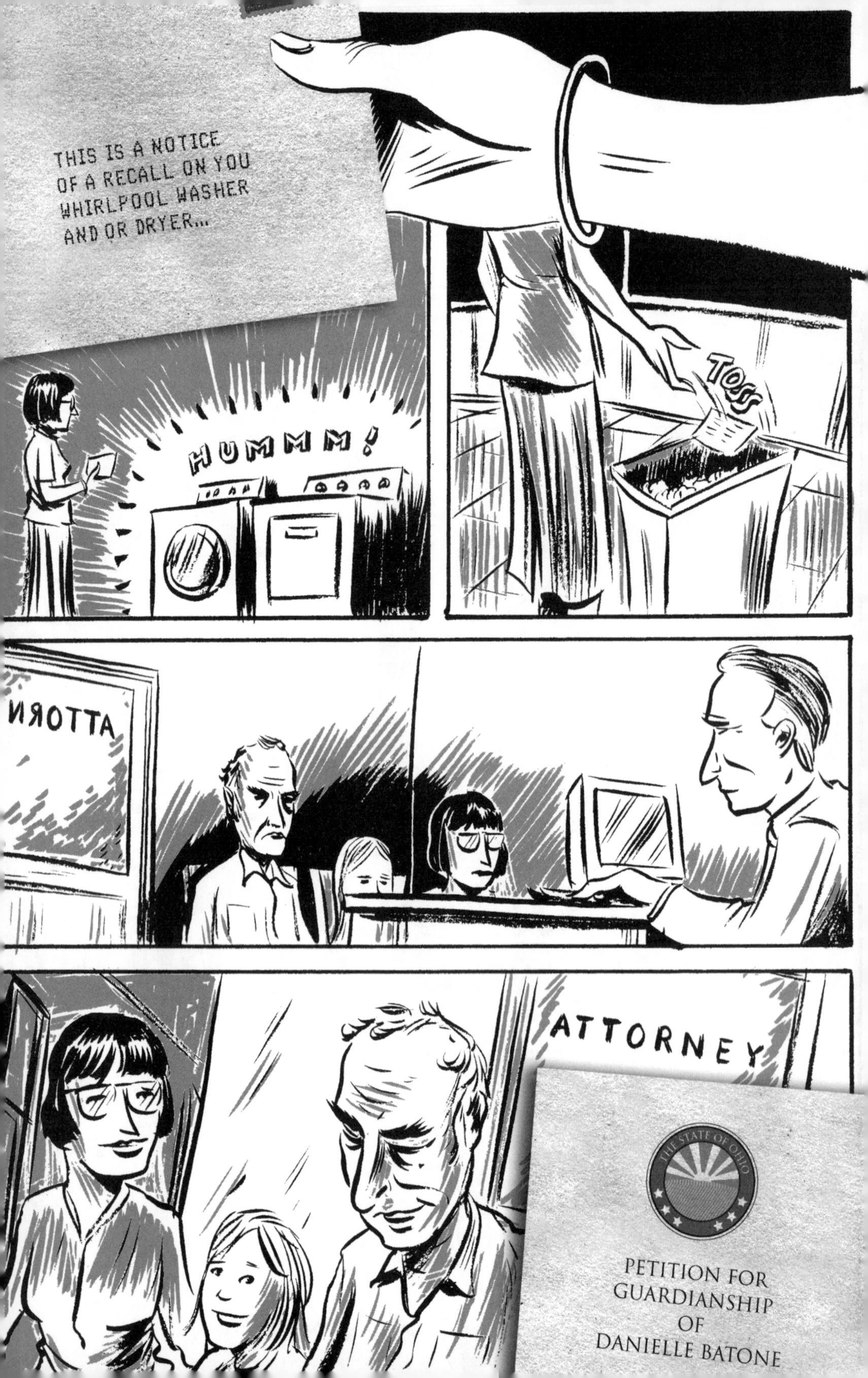

THIS IS A NOTICE OF A RECALL ON YOU WHIRLPOOL WASHER AND OR DRYER...
HUMMMM!
TOSS
ATTORN
ATTORNEY
THE STATE OF OHIO
PETITION FOR GUARDIANSHIP OF DANIELLE BATONE

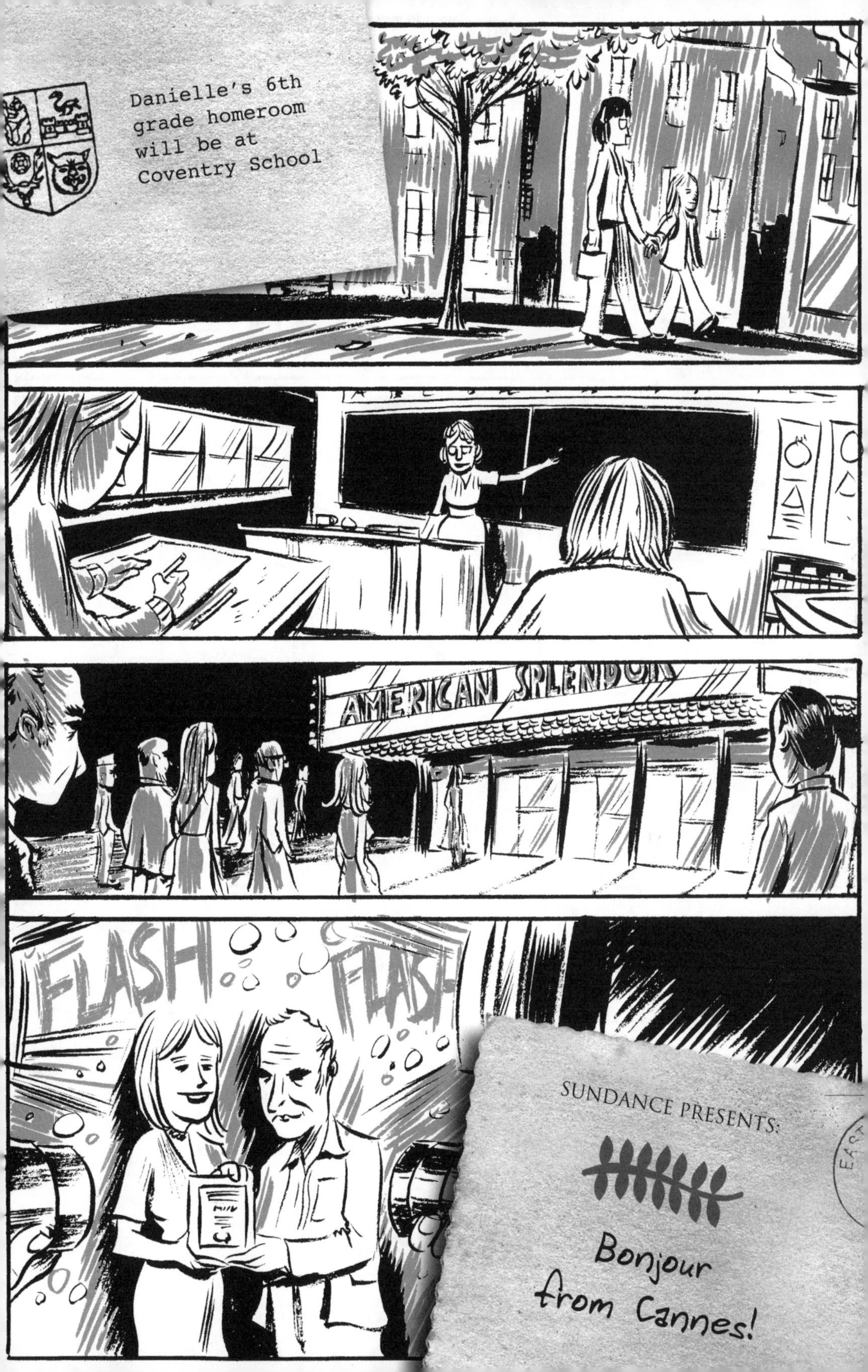
Danielle's 6th grade homeroom will be at Coventry School
AMERICAN SPLENDOR
FLASH
FLASH
SUNDANCE PRESENTS:
Bonjour from Cannes!

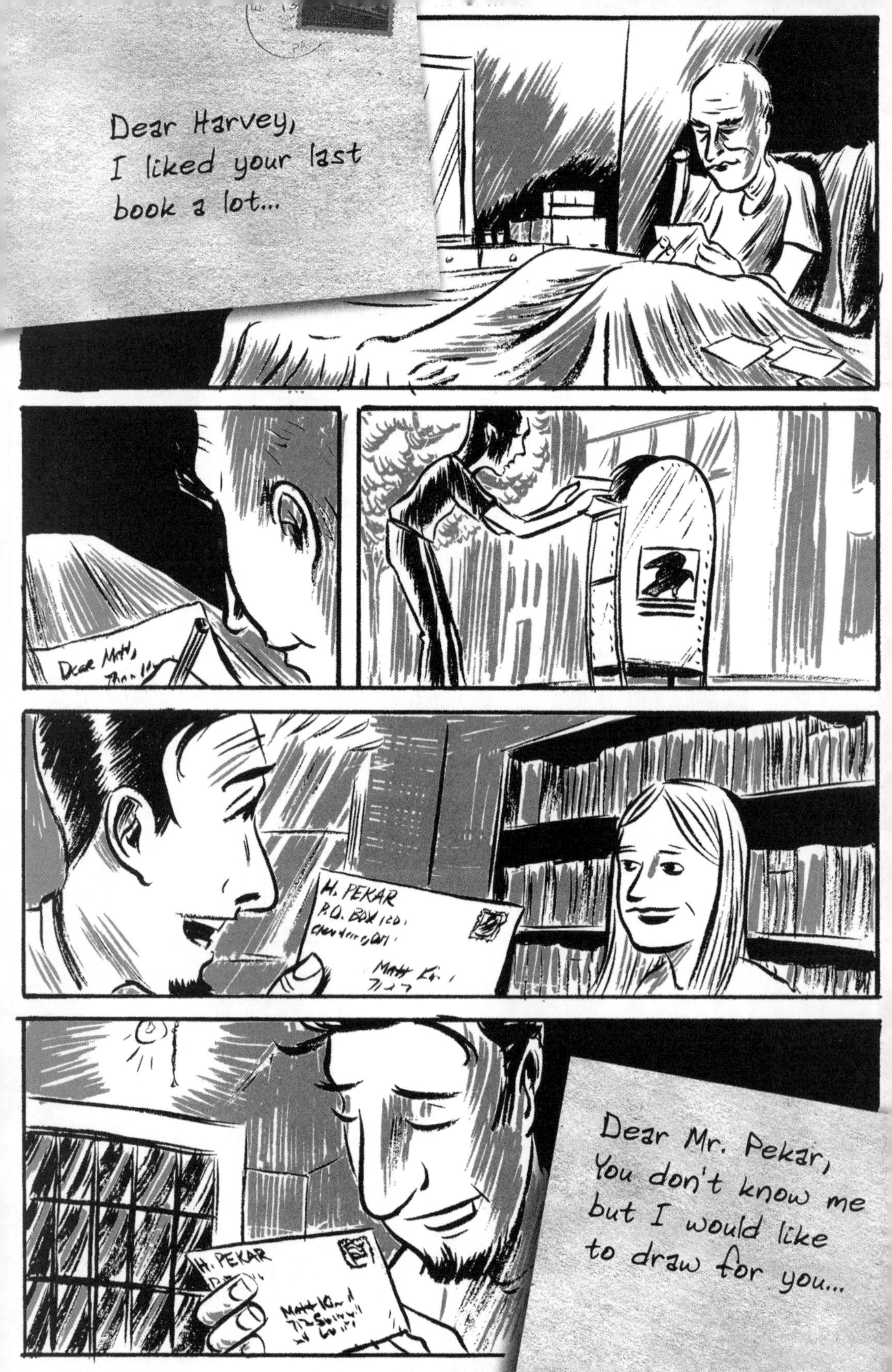

Dear Harvey,
I liked your last book a lot...
H. PEKAR
H. PEKAR
Dear Mr. Pekar,
You don't know me but I would like to draw for you...

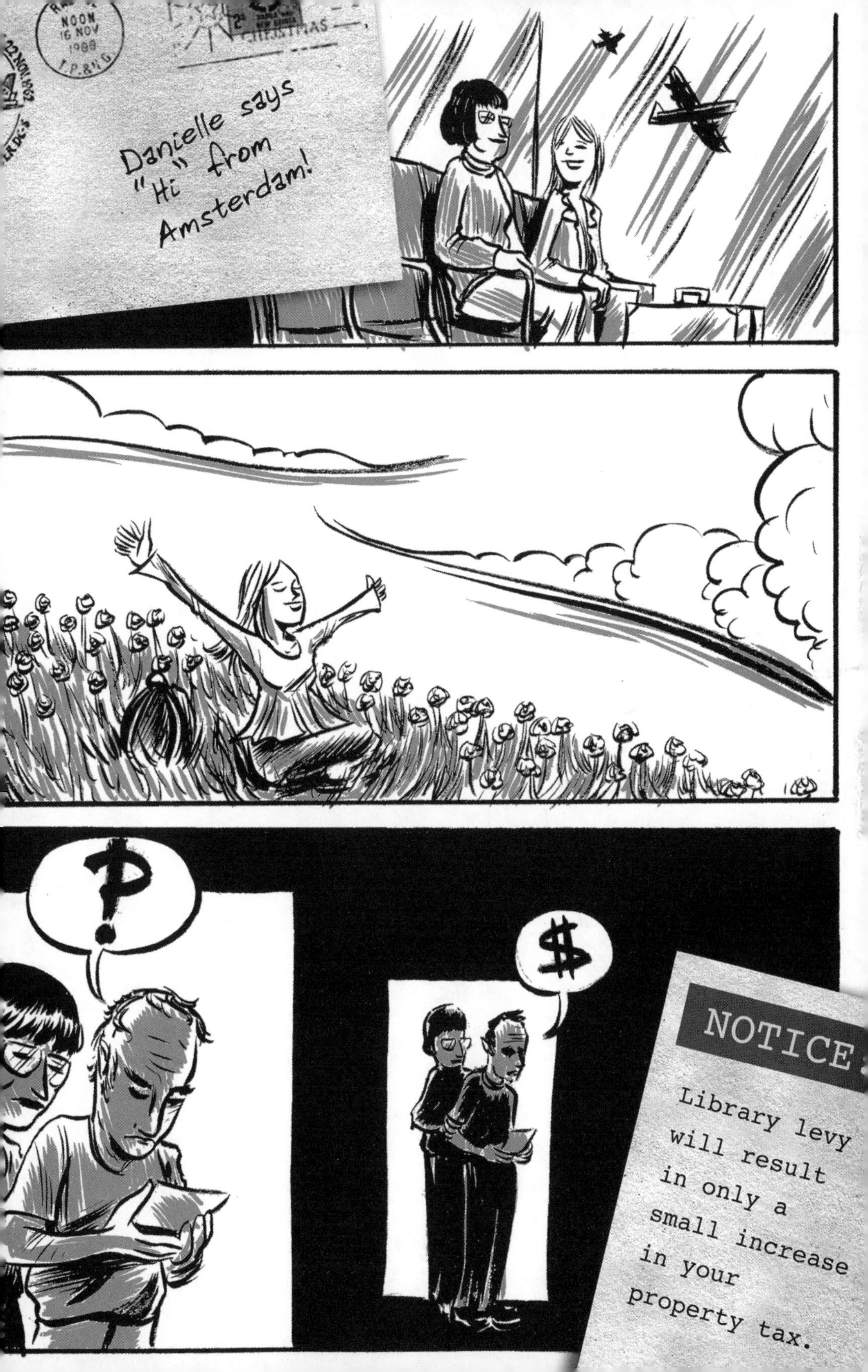
NOON
16 NOV
1988
CHRISTMAS
Danielle says "Hi" from Amsterdam!
?
$
NOTICE
Library levy will result in only a small increase in your property tax.

Epilogue

When I first began developing the idea behind this anthology, I joked that I'd end up with sixteen stories that featured various family members dying of typhoid. Maybe it was my own bias — all I saw in these old cards was death. The people involved have all passed away; that's the one constant in all of their lives. But, thankfully, the creators I invited to reconstruct these lives didn't see these postcards the way I saw them. Maybe it was because they were detached from the collecting process a bit; they weren't the ones rifling through three-sentence fragments of thousands of people's lives. Or maybe it's simply because not everyone is as morbid as I am.

My original subtitle for this book was "All you leave is a paragraph." It's such a depressing thought, looking back on it, and it took all of the wonderful creators gathered in these pages to show me what this book truly represents. True stories that never happened. They can be remorseful or uplifting, or they can play with the notions of faith. But, at the end of the day, the stories are about life, not death, as all good stories are.

I'd like to thank all of the creators involved, for without them none of this would have been possible. I'd also like to thank their friends and family who support them so they can continue to create fantastic comics. I'd like to thank James W. Powell for keeping everyone in line and working to the best of their abilities, including myself. And Jason Hanley and Matt Kindt, who worked behind the scenes to help make this anthology greater than the sum of its parts. Joshua Hale Fialkov, who has done so much for me over the past couple of years. Also Dallas Middaugh at Random House for keeping the faith. Of course, I can't forget the three women in my life who keep me strong and determined: my mom; my sister, Elizabeth; and my love, Robin. And my dad, who sacrificed so much to provide me with the opportunities I needed.

And, of course, I want to thank you. For buying the book, for taking a chance. For living your lives and leaving your artifacts that are, in some way, the inspirations behind this book.

— Jason Rodriguez
Arlington, VA

PS — Wish you were here...

Contributors

Jake Allen attended the Joe Kubert School of Cartoon and Graphic Arts for two years and took classes at Montserrat College of Art in Beverley, Massachusetts. He illustrated *Brownsville* with Neil Kleid for NBM Publishing and contributed illustrations for two shorts in Andrew Dabb's *Slices*. Currently, Allen does graphics for 5-Star Surfboards and the rock band Firewalk in New Hampshire.

Tom Beland has been writing and drawing comics for ten years. His series, *True Story, Swear to God*, has been nominated for six Eisner Awards and is currently published by Image Comics. His writing gigs include Marvel's *Web of Romance* and *Spider-Man Unlimited #12*. His anthology work includes *9/11 Emergency Relief* and *Sparks Generators*. He lives with his wife, Lily Garcia, who made all the above work possible with her love and support.

You never know what to expect from **Joseph Bergin III**. He has incredible range and can adapt his style to any project that comes his way. His first published work was in the pages of *Western Tales of Terror*, where he did a four-page short for the anthology, as well as webstrips with Joshua Fialkov. For more than a year he's been an entrant in the Daily Grind competition, posting brand-new webcomics five days a week without taking a break.

Joyce Brabner edited Eclipse's *Real War Stories*, an anthology featuring some of independent comics' highest-profile writers and creators. Brabner is also the writer of *Activists!*, PETA's *Animal Rights Comics*, and "Flashpoint: The LA Penca Bombing" for Eclipse's political graphic novel *Brought to Light*. She coauthored the Harvey Award–nominated *American Splendor: Our Cancer Year* with her husband, Harvey Pekar.

Jay Busbee is the author of the novel *The Face of the River* and the upcoming *Bluff City*. He's written several comics series, including *Sundown: Arizona*, *The Network*, and *Ripped*. He is a contributing editor of *Atlanta Magazine* and regularly writes for ESPN.com, *Slam*, *The Chicago Sports Review*, and many other publications. He's living the suburban dream in Atlanta with his wife and two kids.

Jason Copland graduated from the Emily Carr Institute of Art and Design. He drew and cocreated the miniseries *Empty Chamber* and also provided the art for Stuart Moore's "Other Folks' Troubles" from *Western Tales of Terror #4* and two *Mortal Coils* stories for A. David Lewis. Jason lives in Vancouver, Canada, with his wife, Jackie, and their son, Stewart. When he's not drawing, you can find him guarding the net for a local recreational hockey team.

Danielle Corsetto is the artist and writer behind the webcomic *Girls with Slingshots* (www.gwscomic.com). She lives in a little town in West Virginia where she enjoys photography, traveling, and indie music. You can buy her a Red-Headed Slut next time you see her at the bar.

Matt Dembicki writes and draws the nature mini-comic *Mr. Big* and publishes the two-time Howard E. Day Memorial Award finalist *Attic Wit*. In addition to contributing to numerous anthologies, Matt also writes and coillustrates the weekly webcomic *Spadefoot*, which features the adventures of an intergalactic anthropomorphic space frog on the quest for righteousness and glory.

Micah Farritor is an illustrator whose previous titles include *The Living and the Dead* and *Night Trippers*. Admittedly a traveler who rarely gets his postcards mailed out while on vacation, he returns home where he writes anything he can remember about the images on each card. That said, he wishes you were here.

Harvey Award Nominee for Best New Talent and Best Writer, **Joshua Hale Fialkov** is the creator of the Random House/Villard graphic novel *Elk's Run*, hit indie anthology *Western Tales of Terror*, and the Internet cult hit *Poorly Drawn Animals*. His comics work has appeared in books for Boom Studios, IDW Publishing, and all across the Internet. He was raised in Pittsburgh and currently enjoys a writer's life in Los Angeles.

Tony Fleecs is the cartoonist behind *In My Lifetime*, an autobiographical series of graphic novellas published by Silent Devil Productions. He came to *Postcards* by way of Josh Fialkov, who collaborated with Fleecs on a five-page comedy short entitled "Pancakes for Jimmy."

Brendon and Brian Fraim are best known for *Knights of the Dinner Table: Illustrated* and the comic book sections in the Random House novel *Wolf Boy* by Evan Kuhlman. They are currently illustrating a webcomic, *America, Jr.*, at www.americajr.net, and the weekly serial *Antiques: The Comic Strip*, for *Antique Trader*. Visit them at www.brosfraim.com.

Rob G has worked for DC Comics, Humanoids Publishing, AiT/PlanetLar, and Gigantic Graphic Novels, with *Teenagers from Mars* and *The Couriers* being particular fan favorites. He is currently working on a series from Image Comics called *Repo*. He lives in Brooklyn, New York, with his wife and bunny.

Michael Gaydos is a painter and illustrator whose sequential art for Marvel's *Alias* set the bar high for the publisher's line of mature titles. In Marvel's *Daredevil: Redemption* and *The Pulse*, Gaydos again focuses on realism and uses darkness and a balance of black and white to create a noir tone for the story. Gaydos is also illustrating Virgin Comic's flagship title, *Snakewoman*.

Born in Vermont and currently residing outside Dallas, Texas, **Drew Gilbert** is a commercial artist and animator who lives with his wife and two Labrador retrievers. His previous comic work is the graphic novel *Rosemary's Backpack* with writer Antony Johnston. His work can be seen online at www.drewgilbert.com.

Jason Hanley lives in Lincoln, New Brunswick, Canada. Deciding that he no longer wanted to work for "the man," Jason quit his day job to create and letter comics full-time. Jason has worked on such acclaimed titles as *Hatter M*, *The Cryptics*, and *Elk's Run*. He was nominated for a Harvey Award for Best Lettering in 2006.

Seamus Heffernan is trying harder than anyone to cripple his left hand. He has found Portland, Oregon, to be the perfect place to do just this and will continue his quest there, through the medium of comics. You may reap the rewards of his efforts at www.seaheff.com.

Phillip Hester began his career while a student at the University of Iowa. Over the past two decades his work has been featured in both mainstream and alternative comics, including long runs on *Swamp Thing* and *Green Arrow* for DC. He lives in rural Iowa with his wife and two children.

Antony Johnston is an award-winning writer with fourteen graphic novels and books, plus numerous series, to his credit. His range includes horror, romantic comedy, espionage, children's books and more. He currently writes the science fiction epic *Wasteland* and the children's Western *Texas Strangers*, and he continues to adapt the best-selling Alex Rider novels to comics. Antony lives in rural England with his fiancée, Marcia. Visit him at www.mostlyblack.com.

Matt Kindt is a graphic designer who never lost his love for comics, spies, or bygone eras. He displayed a unique visual storytelling style with action, mystery, and intrigue as cocreator of the critically acclaimed debut graphic novels *Pistolwhip* and *Pistolwhip: The Yellow Menace*. Kindt delivered his most complex and ambitious work in 2005 when Top Shelf Productions released *2 Sisters*, a three-hundred-page spy thriller filled with crime noir, swashbuckling pirates, and romance. The multiple Eisner and Harvey Award nominee is currently working on his fifty-two-week run of *Super Spy* comics. It's a free online weekly comic that can be found at www.supersecretspy.com.

Neil Kleid is the Xeric Award–winning cartoonist of *Ninety Candles*, a graphic novella about life, death, legacy, and comics. He wrote the graphic novel *Brownsville* with artist Jake Allen for NBM Publishing and has written for Slave Labor Graphics, Puffin Graphics, Marvel Comics, Image Comics, and Alternative Comics. He is currently working on his second cartoon book, *Migdal David*, for Seraphic Press. In his day job as art director, Neil has worked on campaigns for Comedy Central and Miramax Films. For more, visit www.rantcomics.com.

A. David Lewis is the creator of *Mortal Coils* as well as the writer of *Empty Chamber* and the Harvey Award–nominated graphic novel *Lone and Level Sands*. An academic lecturer on comics, he also serves as an editorial board member for *The International Journal of Comic Art* and is currently a Ph.D. student at Boston University. Visit him at http://www.captionbox.net.

Stuart Moore has been a writer, a book editor, and an award-winning comics editor. His recent writing includes *Firestorm* (DC Comics), *The Punisher Xmas Special* (Marvel), *Earthlight* (Tokyopop), *Stargate Atlantis* (Avatar Press), and the prose novel *Reality Bites* (Games Workshop). Stuart lives in Brooklyn, New York.

Ande Parks has been inking comics for well over a decade, his bold style earning him praise on such titles as *Green Arrow* and *Nightwing*. In recent years, he has launched a new career as a writer, penning two historical fiction graphic novels, *Union Station* and *Capote in Kansas*, both for Oni Press. Ande lives in Kansas with his lovely wife and two children.

Harvey Pekar, a native of Cleveland, is best known for his autobiographical slice-of-life comic book series, *American Splendor*, a first-person account of his downtrodden life, which was made into a movie starring Paul Giamatti. He is also the author of *Best of American Splendor* and *American Splendor: Our Movie Year*. He is an omnivorous reader, an obsessive-compulsive collector, and a jazz critic whose reviews have been published in *The Boston Herald*, *The Austin Chronicle*, and *Jazz Times*. He has done freelance work for the critically acclaimed radio station WKSU and has appeared eight times on *Late Night with David Letterman* and twice on *The Late Show with David Letterman*.

Not much is known about the enigmatic **James W. Powell**. He is believed to have written reviews and interviews for several websites such as DVDtalk.com and BrokenFrontier.com before deciding he'd rather create stories than write about them. He recently coedited *The Wicked West II: Abomination and Other Stories* with Robert Tinnell, but many consider his *Postcards* story, "Cora's Dress," to be his first published comics story. He was last seen living in Denver with his beautiful wife, Stephanie.

Jason Rodriguez is the editor of the Harvey Award–nominated Random House/Villard graphic novel *Elk's Run* and the hit indie anthology *Western Tales of Terror*. He has spent entire afternoons in antique shops across America, purchasing one paragraph glimpses into people's lives for inclusion in *Postcards*, his most ambitious project to date.

RJ Rodriguez dedicates his *Postcards* story, "Quarantined," to his daughter, Akemi, whom he'd walk into a quarantined area for without thinking twice.

Rick Spears has been writing for comics since 2001. In 2004 he started his own publishing company, Gigantic Graphic Novels. His credits include the critically acclaimed *Teenagers from Mars*, the genre-smashing zombie/western *Dead West*, and the hard-hitting noir *Filler*. Spears has also partnered with Image Comics to publish his latest works, *The Pirates of Coney Island* with artist Vasilis Lolos and *Repo* with Rob G.

Chris Stevens dedicates his story to his grandmother Natalie. This is his first published work. His forthcoming book, *Dream Compass*, a collection of stories illustrated by Arthur Adams, Nick Bradshaw, Farel Dalrymple, James Jean, Jae Lee, and Nate Powell, arrives in 2008.

As a boy, writer/director **Robert Tinnell** camped out in front of his television watching horror films. His debut graphic novel, *The Black Forest*, perfectly captured the feel of those B movies, as did follow-ups *The Wicked West*, *The Living and the Dead*, and *Sight Unseen*. Ironically, it was Tinnell's romantic comedy comic strip, *Feast of the Seven Fishes*, that netted him his first Will Eisner Award nomination.

Gia-Bao Tran (aka GB) self-publishes the Xeric Award–winning comic series *Content*. He thanks Jason Rodriguez for finding him in the small press trenches and including him in such fine comics company. Check out what he's up to at www.gbtran.com.

Noel Tuazon was born in Manila, Philippines, but has lived most of his life in Toronto, Ontario, Canada. He studied fine arts at the University of Toronto and took some storyboard and more life drawing courses at Max the Mutt Animation School (also in Toronto). His current illustration output includes anthologies (*Drawing the Line 1 and 2*), miniseries (*Elk's Run* with Josh Fialkov, *Redchapel* with Caleb Monroe), and children's books (*Sunny Bear's Rainy Day* with Caryn A. Tate).